THE PERILS OF
PEARL BRYAN

Betrayal and Murder in the Midwest in 1896

Cast not your pearls before swine,
for they will trample them underfoot.

Matthew 7:6

Mike – We've sure put a lot of miles together on the Moe Trail !
Jim

James McDonald and Joan Christen

Jim McDonald
Joan Christen

authorHOUSE®

AuthorHouse™
1663 Liberty Drive
Bloomington, IN 47403
www.authorhouse.com
Phone: 1-800-839-8640

© *2012 James McDonald and Joan Christen. All rights reserved.*

No part of this book may be reproduced, stored in a retrieval system, or transmitted by any means without the written permission of the author.

Published by AuthorHouse 7/5/2012

ISBN: 978-1-4634-4443-3 (sc)
ISBN: 978-1-4634-4444-0 (hc)
ISBN: 978-1-4634-4442-6 (e)

Library of Congress Control Number: 2011914163

Any people depicted in stock imagery provided by Thinkstock are models, and such images are being used for illustrative purposes only. Certain stock imagery © Thinkstock.

This book is printed on acid-free paper.

Because of the dynamic nature of the Internet, any web addresses or links contained in this book may have changed since publication and may no longer be valid. The views expressed in this work are solely those of the author and do not necessarily reflect the views of the publisher, and the publisher hereby disclaims any responsibility for them.

When Lovely Woman Stoops to Folly

When lovely woman stoops to folly,
And finds too late that men betray.
What charm can soothe her melancholy?
What art can wash her guilt away?
The only art her guilt to cover,
To hide her shame from every eye,
To give repentance to her lover,
And wring his bosom, is ------ to die.

Oliver Goldsmith (1730-1774)

FORWARD

I retired as Professor and Dean of Education at the Indiana University School of Dentistry in 2004. Shortly after my retirement, I was browsing through a 14-page life journal that my grandfather had written shortly before his death in 1968. As I focused carefully on the words he had laboriously typed with arthritic fingers at the age of 85, I was struck by his following description:

> "During 1895-1897, I sold *The Kentucky Post* in South Carrollton, Kentucky. My sales boomed during the time of the Pearl Bryan murder case, and the subsequent trials of the two accused dental students. After the guilty verdicts were reached and the executions completed, my newspaper sales declined considerably."

As I read this brief account, my mind was quickly deluged with questions: "Who was Pearl Bryan? How had she been murdered? Who were the two indicted dental students and where had they attended school? Had they actually confessed to the crime? Why had my grandfather's newspaper sales grown so much during this event?"

I immediately conducted a brief internet search to learn more about the crime, and soon discovered that the murder victim was from Greencastle, Indiana and that she had not only been murdered, but also decapitated while still alive. I was astounded to learn that the two dental students charged with the crime had attended the Indiana Dental College in Indianapolis, the precursor to the dental school where I had taught for 36 years.

The next day, I mentioned my findings to my friend, colleague, and dental historian, Dr. Arden Christen. We immediately agreed that this topic would make a fascinating subject for publication, and that because of her editorial and writing skills, Joan Christen would be an ideal addition to our team which would write the Pearl Bryan story.

My grandfather, the newsboy, grew to become an Optometrist in Somerset Kentucky. He wrote extensively as a avocation, and founded and published The Kentucky Optometrist magazine. He also served as its Editor for many years. I believe he would have been extremely proud and excited to see this publication of the story that he was responsible for bringing to my attention.

James L McDonald, PhD
Professor Emeritus of Oral Biology
Indiana University School of Dentistry

PREFACE

In the early spring of 2004, Jim McDonald approached Joan and me with an enticing and challenging offer. He asked both of us if we would join him in an effort to investigate and record a most compelling historical event: the murder of an Indiana citizen, Miss Pearl Bryan, and its convoluted, 13 month aftermath, which incriminated two dental students, also from Indiana. While the complex account and cast of characters were to be based on actual fact, the "fleshing out" of certain involved individuals and some circumstances would be fictional, although as true to life as possible.

At that time, Joan and I had already gained previous experience in researching and recording unusual tales involving dental history, for we had coauthored 25 articles relating to that topic, all published by the American Academy of the History of Dentistry in the <u>Journal of the History of Dentistry</u>.

This gruesome event, which occurred late on the evening of January 31, 1896, involved the murder of a 22 year old, pregnant woman who was found beheaded on a hillside, at Fort Thomas, Kentucky, the following morning. Specific events in this complicated case chiefly took place in three geographical areas: Greencastle (Putnam County) and Indianapolis (Marion County), in central Indiana; Fort Thomas and Newport (Campbell County), in northern Kentucky; and Cincinnati (Hamilton County), in Ohio. The suspected murderers were two dental students, Scott Jackson and Alonzo Walling, who had both attended the Indiana Dental College, in Indianapolis, and later, the Ohio College of Dental Surgery in Cincinnati.

During our initial investigation, which continued for over a year, Jim and I located and studied all the written materials that we could uncover concerning Pearl Bryan's murder. Many of the booklets, articles and pamphlets which we reviewed were found to be anecdotal, only partially factual, and/or full of discrepancies, blank spaces and other questionable inclusions. At this point, it became painfully clear – we simply had to obtain more extensive, detailed information about this tragedy. As the search continued, I soon realized that my contribution to this project would not be in co-authorship, but rather, in intense data collection and analysis, in providing technical support and in continually locating more reliable information.

One night in a dream – I received the breakthrough that I needed to help me pinpoint and utilize these yet to be uncovered sources. In my somnolent state, I recalled that for 13 months (from February 1, 1896 until March 20, 1897), the Pearl Bryan Case was termed by the local and national press as being "The Crime of the 19th Century!" The point of my dream was clear! To discover more viable and accurate information on this grizzly event, we could access the regional and national newspaper accounts of that day, now available through current microfilm records.

When I excitedly informed Jim, almost immediately, he and I began a tedious, year-long task of locating, reviewing and copying the microfilm newspaper records which covered those 13 months. We utilized two sources in downtown Indianapolis; The Indiana State Library and Historical Bureau, and University Library IUPUI (Indiana University-Purdue University Indianapolis). Through this data, we obtained about 350 germaine newspaper articles which had reported that crime. Interestingly, during this period, the New York Times explored virtually every aspect of the murder, sending reporters to Kentucky and Cincinnati for that purpose. The March 21, 1897 issue of the New York Times covered the final outcome of the two murder trials in great detail. In reviewing these newspaper accounts, we were able to use many drawings, photographs, editorials and factually-based insights. However, we put aside others, because they were excessively charged with emotion, controversy, hearsay and judgment.

During the seven years of this book's preparation, Jim and I have taken numerous investigative excursions to all of the tri-state locations involved in this story. Visits to the Putnam County Public Library and to the Forest Lawn Cemetery (where Pearl is buried), both in Greencastle, have been especially helpful. Also, trips to Fort Thomas and Newport, Kentucky and to the Campbell County Historical and Genealogical

Society in Alexandria, Kentucky, have provided substantive help. The information gleaned at the Public Library of Cincinnati and Hamilton County was also extremely valuable in preparing this manuscript. Finally, the continuing guidance which we have received from Archivist Mike Delporte, at the Indiana University School of Dentistry, has been invaluable to our cause.

I congratulate Jim McDonald and Joan Christen for their superb job of creating an entirely readable and believable book on an extremely difficult and complex subject! These two master authors have expertly edited and revised each chapter, draft after painful draft. We can all be proud of the result!

Arden G Christen, DDS
Professor Emeritus of Oral Biology
Indiana University School of Dentistry

PROLOGUE

Early on the damp, foggy morning of February 1, 1896, 17 year-old Jack Hewling trudged along an abandoned lane running through an apple orchard adjacent to the Alexandria Pike near Ft. Thomas, Kentucky. The teenager often took this shortcut on his way to work at the nearby Locke farm. Squinting ahead into the dim light, he noticed what appeared to be a bundle of clothing located between several bushes on a nearby hillside. Drawing closer, he was riveted, for the disheveled pile began to resemble the silhouette of a person. Then, in absolute horror, he recognized it as a woman's body, dressed in light clothing, and lying on her stomach at a downward incline. Her arms were extended outward and upward, as though in abject surrender. Below her shoulders, he discerned only a bloody stump. Her head was missing! Shivering in revulsion and panic, he sprinted toward John Locke's farmhouse to summon aid.

Thus began the unfolding of one of the most heinous murders, gripping investigations, and bizarre trials and outcomes in United States history.

CHAPTER ONE

When the headless body of a woman was discovered on the Locke farm, America was in the midst of an extremely turbulent time in its history. The so-called "Gilded Age" was concluding. This phrase had been coined by American author and humorist, Mark Twain, and described the time span falling between the end of the Civil War in 1865 and the beginning of the 20ᵗʰ century. The United States had recently emerged as the most highly industrialized nation in the world. Twain's cynical reference had been directed at the marked contrast existing between the outwardly successful world of wealthy America, and the frequently corrupt political system and deplorable working conditions with which many within the same society had to deal. The term Gilded Age was derived from the golden peaked structures that so often were positioned on the tops of the fences and walls surrounding the huge, lavish mansions of the rich and which reflected their opulent self-indulgence.

Both an abundant supply of natural resources and a rapidly advancing technology had fueled the commercial advancement of the era. The swift expansion of the U.S. rail system and the development of the telegraph, telephone, and ultimately, of electricity, all contributed to the shift from a largely agrarian society to one in which manufacturing was the cornerstone. To gain employment in factories, farm laborers and immigrants alike flocked to the cities. To accommodate the massive influx of newcomers from abroad, the federal government constructed Ellis Island in 1892 at the mouth of the Hudson River, and adjacent to the Statue of Liberty. During the next 5 years, some 1.5 million immigrants were processed. However, the inexorable march of urbanization inevitably produced contradictory outcomes. New employment opportunities, technology and culture flourished in the big cities, but were at odds with the slums, tenements, disease, sanitation problems, child labor issues, graft, and corruption, which thrived as well.

1887 sketch of an ocean steamer passing the Statue of Liberty. Immigrants stand on the steerage deck. Harry T. Peters Collection. Library of Congress Prints and Photographs Division, Washington, D.C.

In contrast to the big cities, rural life in the Midwest had not changed significantly since the end of the Civil War. Although everyday existence continued to be a fairly grim task for many, small rural towns afforded their inhabitants one major advantage: a strong sense of community and security. Families were typically well acquainted with one another, and generally provided assistance and aid to relatives, friends, and colleagues in need. Although worries about personal safety appeared to be minimal, acts of extreme violence, including murder, were not unusual across America. In fact, grisly homicides, scandalous trials, and shocking executions transpired during these times and often captured the imagination of many Americans.

The most notorious murderer of this era emerged without warning in England in the Whitechapel area of east London between August and November of 1888. There, the brutal murders of five prostitutes occurred in the course of a three-month time span. The perpetrator, who slashed and disfigured his victims horribly, soon came to be widely known as "Jack, the Ripper." Although the killer was never caught nor even identified, after the passage of that November, the alarming homicides ended mysteriously, as quickly as they had begun.

The American Midwest experienced its own share of vicious murders during the relatively brief time period of the 1880's and 1890's. On Christmas Eve, 1885, Nathaniel S. Bates left Council Bluffs, Iowa, and traveled to Hagerstown, Indiana, where he hoped to make peace with his estranged wife Kitty, and their two daughters, Stella and Mary. For three months, he undertook every conceivable plan to reconcile with Kitty, but to no avail. On the morning of March 23, 1886, angered by the continuing futility of his efforts, he entered the house where his wife and children lived. Finding Kitty alone and bathing in the kitchen, he once again pressed her to take him back. She dismissed his appeal scornfully, and told him she would rather die than accept his plea. In a fit of rage and frustration, he grabbed an ax handle standing in a corner of the room, and used it to crack her on the head. As Kitty slumped to the kitchen floor, he pulled a razor-sharp pocketknife from his pants pocket, bent over, and slit her throat. Quickly, she bled to death.

Several hours later, Nathaniel nonchalantly walked down the main street of Hagerstown, and shortly encountered Town Marshall Thomas Murray, who was perched on a wooden box in front of the local hardware store. Bates immediately confessed his crime to the disbelieving law enforcement officer, who then handcuffed him and led him back down the street to the local fire engine house. A large iron cage stood within this edifice, and served as the town jail. It was here that Bates was confined. As word of the brutal murder spread throughout the town, the authorities feared that an irate citizenry might organize a lynch party. Nationally, lynching had grown each year from 1866 through the 1880s, and had peaked in 1892. It was later estimated that from 1889 through 1918, mobs lynched 129 persons in the Midwest, as opposed to 2915 such victims in the South and the states bordering the South. By 1900, this punishment was reserved almost exclusively for African-Americans, a fact which bore testimony to the abysmal state of race relations at the time.

In response to growing concern over his safety, Nathaniel was quickly transported 20 miles east to the Richmond, Indiana jail where he was incarcerated, and subsequently charged with first-degree murder. Testimony at the trial characterized Bates as a mean-tempered, physically abusive husband with a chronic drinking problem who had previously threatened to take Kitty's life. On May 7, 1886, Nathaniel Bates was found guilty of murder, and his punishment was set at death by hanging. Approximately three months later, the sentence was carried out on the gallows located next to the jail. Some 100 witnesses attended, each of whom had been issued a pass in order to observe the event. During the procedure, several thousand additional spectators, including many residents from Hagerstown, celebrated in the streets of Richmond. This official public execution was the last one to be conducted in Indiana outside of prison walls.

While Kitty's murder and Nathaniel's subsequent execution were occurring in central Indiana, one of the nation's first female serial killers was about to begin her murderous onslaughts in Chicago, although she eventually found her way to a small farm located in rural, northern Indiana. Belle Gunness, a Scandanavian immigrant, had married fellow countryman, Max Sorensen, in Chicago in 1883. Max died mysteriously in 1890, and although Belle was widely suspected as having poisoned him, no formal charges were ever filed. In fact, Belle managed to collect $8500 from her husband's life insurance policy. Two years later, she married a man named Gunness and the two moved to a farm near La Porte, Indiana. Within a few years, her second husband was found dead on the premises, with the back of his head crushed. Belle's explanation to the investigating officers was that a sausage grinder had fallen from a shelf and killed him. No one was able to disprove her spurious account, and again she managed to claim her husband's life insurance money amounting to a sum of $3000.

Shortly thereafter, Belle began to methodically advertise for replacement husbands in various newspapers. Her strategy was frequently successful, and periodically she would be observed meeting a newly arrived stranger at the La Porte railroad depot, and then departing with her unsuspecting victim for her farm. In due course, these men would always disappear without a trace. Belle and her assorted male partners typically experienced life as rural recluses, and during this period, she bore several children, all of whom lived with the family on the farm. The mysterious goings-on at the farm generated a profusion of gossip among Belle's neighbors, and though suspicions ran rampant, no criminal investigation was ever initiated.

In April 1908, a fire of mysterious origin swept through the Gunness farmhouse, destroying it and apparently leaving no survivors. During the subsequent investigation of the blaze, numerous "soft spots" were noted in the ground adjacent to the house. Authorities began digging immediately, and the dismembered body of her most recent husband was soon discovered. More digging unearthed additional corpses, until a total of nine was found. Three were female. Belle's corpse was not identified among the ashes, and she was not to be seen again. Citizens of La Porte resolutely hypothesized that on the night of the fire, Belle Gunness had murdered her children and buried them next to the house in close proximity to her deceased husbands as well as an unidentified female corpse that she hoped would be identified as her own. She had then set fire to the house, and fled with all her ill-gotten money. Her legacy endures, and remains an intriguing mystery that is still unsolved 100 years later.

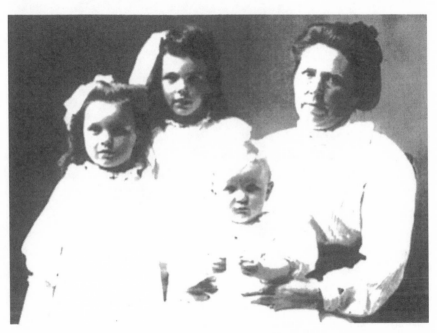

Belle Gunness pictured with her children Lucy, Myrtle and Philip. Courtesy of the La Porte County Historical Society, La Porte, IN.

*A shed on the Gunness farm used as a makeshift morgue for the nine unearthed bodies.
Also pictured are a number of the curious onlookers who swarmed the property following
the gruesome discovery. Courtesy of the La Porte County Historical Society, La Porte, IN.*

Honora Kelly was born in Massachusetts in 1854 and as a toddler
was raised in a poverty-stricken family which had a history of physical
abuse, alcoholism and mental illness. After her mother's death, Honora's
father raised her by himself, but when she was six years old, he abandoned
her at a Boston orphanage. The little girl was soon assigned to a wealthy
local family as an indentured servant. Her foster mother was Ann
Toppan, who changed Honora's name to Jane Toppan. Jane came to
despise her violent and abusive foster mother as well as her foster sister,
Elizabeth. Nevertheless, she continued to live with the Toppans for the
next 25 years.

In 1885, Jane left home to begin nurses' training at Cambridge
Hospital. While a student there, she excelled in all her classes, but
several of her professors were alarmed to see her unusual fascination
with human autopsies. During her residency, she surreptitiously began
to change her patients' prescribed dosages of morphine and atropine,
and was enthralled to see major changes in their nervous system
responses. Although a number of her patients died as a result of her
drug manipulations, neither her teachers nor coworkers was aware of
her clandestine activities..

Paradoxically, Jane was well-liked by her patients and her associates, and they nicknamed her "Jolly Jane." She passed her nursing exam in 1887, and became adept at currying favor with several influential physicians, eventually securing a recommendation from them for a position at the prestigious Massachusetts General Hospital. Shortly after assuming that vacancy, Jane began to walk the corridors of the hospital, secretly injecting patients with lethal drug doses. She was literally committing murder in the wards while functioning "under the radar." However, in 1889, she was abruptly fired because of an unrelated issue and had to quickly find new employment. As a result, she briefly returned to the Cambridge Hospital, but it wasn't long before she lost her position there for "prescribing opiates carelessly."

Jane next embarked upon a career as a private nurse, during which time she was later discovered to have poisoned her two landlords while also killing her foster sister, Elizabeth, with a dose of strychnine. Although death by poisoning was difficult to detect (much less to prove) during this era, a pattern had begun to emerge and authorities were becoming suspicious of Jane's connections with people who were dying suddenly of no obvious cause.

In 1901, Toppan moved in with the family of Alden Davis, an elderly man whose wife had recently died. She was assigned to provide care for Alden, but within a few weeks, Davis and two of his daughters had died mysteriously. Jane was obliged to move back to her hometown of Lowell where she began courting her late foster sister's husband. Her plan was to administer poison to him, and then nurse him back to health thus demonstrating her competence and love for him. However, he grew increasingly wary of her intentions and dismissed her from his home. Meanwhile, the surviving members of the Davis family ordered a toxicology exam of Alden's youngest daughter. Results verified their suspicions that she had been poisoned, and the authorities immediately put out an arrest warrant for Jane Toppan.

She was taken into custody on October 26, 1901, and within a few months had confessed to eleven murders. At her trial on June 23, 1902, Jane was found not guilty of murder by reason of insanity and was committed for life to the Taunton Massachusetts Insane Hospital, where she died in 1938. Following her trial, she was said to have confessed to her attorney that she had killed more than 31 people in all. She was also quoted as boasting that her ambition was, "to have killed more people --- helpless people --- than any other man or woman who had ever lived ...."

One of the most imaginative, yet unconscionable and devious serial killers of the Gay Nineties was Dr. Herman Webster Mudgett, aka H. H. Holmes. His homicidal escapades have been well chronicled in Erik Larson's novel, Devil in the White City. Mudgett was born in Gilmantown, New Hampshire on May 16, 1860. As a child, he was beaten and abused on a regular basis by his alcoholic father. During his formative years, he had an intense fascination with dead bodies, and animal sacrifices. Early in life, he decided to target his preoccupation with anatomy and death toward the study of medicine.

Mudgett graduated from high school in 1876, married Clara Laveringat two years later, and in 1884 earned his medical degree from the University of Michigan. He taught part-time at the university, but abruptly ceased the ethical pursuit of his profession. Instead, he devised a clever scheme to fraudulently collect money from life insurance companies. He began to steal corpses at the medical school, made them unrecognizable by the judicious use of acid, provided the bodies with fictitious names, and cited himself as their life insurance beneficiary. This scam was successful for a few months, but was dealt a severe blow when a night watchman discovered him stealing a female corpse. Mudgett was immediately dismissed for what the school authorities called 'unusual activities."

By 1886, he had abandoned his wife, moved to the Chicago suburb of Englewood, and assumed the alias of Dr. Henry Howard Holmes. In 1888, he was hired to work in a local Englewood pharmacy as a chemist. The proprietress of the drugstore was an elderly widow, and within two years, she had "mysteriously disappeared." Dr. Holmes promptly took possession of her business, and began inventing his own patent medicines and selling them by mail order. The sale of patent medicines was a flourishing concern in the United States during the latter portion of the 19th century. These medicaments were of questionable efficacy and their ingredients were generally kept secret. They were sold under very colorful names, and gave rise to even more colorful claims. Three of the most popular included Widow Read's (Benjamin Franklin was her son-in-law) ointment for the Itch; Kickapoo Cough Syrup; and Dr. Kilmer's Swamp Root. Although the liquid concoctions that Holmes created had no therapeutic value, he highly touted several of them as cures for alcoholism and they became big sellers.

Without divorcing his first wife, he soon married a second woman, but she left him within the year. Holmes used the newly earned money from medicament sales and assorted other fraudulent schemes to begin the construction of a large wooden hotel located within a few blocks of what would become the site of the Great Chicago World Fair of 1893. His modus operandi was to hire contractors and workmen for short time periods and then fire them. Sometimes the laborers simply quit their jobs when he failed to pay them their rightful wages. Holmes had an insidious purpose for the building's ultimate use, but because of their short-term employment, workers shuffled in and out of the construction site, and remained unaware of what was to become an extremely bizarre and lethal floor plan.

The building came to be called "the Castle," and was completed shortly before the Fair began. What had emerged was a three-story edifice that contained shops on the first floor, and an odd maze of windowless apartments, rooms, shafts and a vault on the two upper floors. Many of the rooms were soundproof and could not be unlocked from the inside. A few others were lined with asbestos and had doors which opened to reveal only blank, brick walls. Most of the bedrooms had outside peepholes and were equipped with gas pipes connected to a control panel located in Holmes' closet. What the doctor had constructed was a literal gateway to death for the unsuspecting inhabitants of the hotel, who felt blessed to have found a convenient place to stay during the heavily attended World's Fair.

Holmes would routinely rent rooms to young women new to the city. The renters found their landlord to be a very attractive, charming, charismatic and sophisticated man. Holmes would often initially approach many of the lonely and isolated young ladies with an understanding and caring demeanor. After a brief get-acquainted period, he would attempt to seduce them, often utilizing drugs to control them. When those whom he had successfully drugged regained their senses, they would find themselves locked in the maze of empty shafts running through the building. The doomed young women would eventually enter one of the airtight chambers into which Holmes pumped a lethal gas. After they died, he would send their bodies sliding down a chute, which lead directly to the basement. There, he kept a dissecting table,

9

vats of acid and lime, and a kiln that could be ignited to a temperature of 3000 degrees Fahrenheit. Only Holmes had access to this powerful crematorium, and how frequently he utilized the apparatus for disposing of his victims' bodies is not known.

By the fall of 1893, many of the Castle's inhabitants, neighbors and the police were growing suspicious of his activities, and Holmes quickly fled Chicago. During the next 18 months, he committed fraud in Texas and Missouri, and claimed even more murder victims, including several children, in the cities of Philadelphia, Indianapolis, and Toronto. Holmes evaded authorities for several more months, but his luck ran out in June 1895 and he was arrested in Philadelphia and jailed awaiting trial.

Extensive searches of the Castle premises turned up many human remains. During his trial, Holmes provided very inconsistent testimonies, claiming to have killed anywhere from 2 to 27 people, depending upon his mood at the time of his declarations. His infamous Castle burned down on August 19, 1895, with the source of the fire never determined. In what was sometimes called the 'trial of the century,' Homes was convicted of first-degree murder on November 4, 1895. Six months later, he was executed by hanging at Philadelphia's Moyamensing Prison. In an interview conducted shortly before the sentence was carried out, Holmes was quoted as saying:

> "Like the man-eating tigers of the tropical jungle, whose appetites for blood have once been aroused, I roamed about this world seeking whom I could destroy."

Perhaps the most notorious homicidal episode in the U.S. during the Gay Nineties occurred in Fall River, Massachusetts on the stifling morning of August 4, 1892. The headline in the local paper screamed, "Shocking Crime: A Venerable Citizen and his Aged Wife Hacked to Pieces in their Home." The victims were a prominent Fall City businessman, Andrew Borden, and his second wife, Abby. Their skulls had literally been torn apart by countless blows to the head with an ax. Suspicion quickly turned to Lizzie, the Borden's 33 year-old spinster daughter. During her initial interrogation by the police, her testimony appeared confused and contradictory. It was later claimed that she hated her stepmother and other than her parents, she was the only person in the home at the time of the murders. Ultimately, Lizzie was indicted and charged with both murders. After a raucous and tempestuous trial starting on June 5, 1893, and lasting a little over a week, she was found innocent. Many believed that this decision was a major miscarriage of justice, although newspapers in the area generally praised the jury's verdict. No other suspect was ever identified nor charged with the crime, which remains unsolved to this day. Even today, what American child has not been intrigued by this sing-song playground verse?

> "Lizzie Borden took an ax, and gave her mother forty whacks. And when she saw what she had done, she gave her father forty-one."

Needless to say, when John Hewling discovered the headless body in northern Kentucky on February 1, 1896, Americans were not astonished to read the news, for they had previously experienced hearing of brutal murders and the sensational newspaper coverage that accompanied them. Nevertheless, in the three-state area of Indiana, Kentucky and Ohio, the murder and decapitation of this female victim was to become the focus of an unprecedented level of fascination that would continue with deep intensity for a year and a half, and then sustain a general appeal for the public, which remains to this day. For this Midwestern population, an abominable act and the manner in which it played out made it truly their "Crime of the Century."

CHAPTER TWO

During the last quarter of the 18th century, legendary pioneer and hunter Daniel Boone extensively explored a region west of the continental U.S. and south of the Ohio River, which would ultimately become the Commonwealth of Kentucky. Some three decades later, in Bourbon County, Kentucky, Alexander S Bryan was born, named for his frontier-farming father. His mother was Elizabeth Parker Bryan.

When Alex was 10 years old, his family moved 100 miles north to Hendricks County, Indiana, where rich farmland was more easily purchased. At the time, there were few other settlers in west central Indiana, and most roads even moderately fit for travel were simply wagon wheel ruts, which crisscrossed much of the landscape. The Bryans quickly discovered that during periods of heavy rain, these rudimentary carriageways were often impassable with mud. In spite of this major travel limitation, the elder Alexander purchased land in the area, cleared it of trees, built a cabin for his family and gradually converted his property into a productive farm. Bears and other wild animals still roamed the area, and contributed to the many burdens of eking out an existence in the untamed wilderness.

During this time period, Colonel Alexander S. Farrow and his wife, Elizabeth, had also settled in central Indiana in nearby Putnam County. It was the same year that 21 year-old Abe Lincoln had moved from Indiana to Macon County, Illinois, where he would ultimately become a country lawyer, an Illinois state representative, and, in 1860, the President of the United States. Colonel Farrow was a veteran of the War of 1812, and had been captured by the British, and subsequently held prisoner for several months before being released at war's end. This experience granted him instant celebrity in his Indiana community, where he could easily be persuaded to tell stories concerning his wartime exploits.

Many young men from Kentucky and Indiana had served in this war, with scores of them seeing action at the Battle of Thames, in Canada, where the Americans were victorious, and during which skirmish, the famous Shawnee Indian Chief, Tecumseh, was killed while supporting the British cause. Later, some of these same men also fought in the famed Battle of New Orleans, where Andrew Jackson had gained his reputation as a brilliant military commander and leader. Jackson had managed to repulse two major assaults on his positions outside the city, and then driven the invaders from the field of battle. As dusk fell, the British were estimated to have suffered some 2000 casualties and were in full retreat, while the American experienced only 71 dead and injured. With this stunning triumph in New Orleans, Jackson and his men had reveled in one of the most lopsided victories in military history.

At the conclusion of this war, the Farrow family had temporarily lived in several eastern states before eventually settling in Indiana. On March 18, 1833, their daughter Susan Jane, familiarly known simply as "Jane," was born. As leading citizens in their two adjacent Indiana counties, the Bryan and Farrow families soon became acquainted and formed a close friendship. Both families were financially successful and highly respected in their local communities. Ironically, the two couples also shared the same first names: Alexander and Elizabeth. Initially, their respective children, Alex and Jane, showed little interest in one another, largely because Alex was 9 years older than she. The young lad spent most of his days working in his father's fields planting and harvesting crops, tending to the livestock, and, whenever possible, acquiring what little formal education was available to him at the time.

Meanwhile, Jane played with her friends, and, over time and under her mother's tutelage, developed into a proper young lady. By the time she was a fifteen, she was vivacious, attractive and a subject of great interest among the single men in her locale. In the rural mid-west in the 1840's, a woman of this age was considered marriageable. Alex was not immune to her allure, and soon became captivated with young Miss Farrow. As the couple began to court, both families expressed great delight and pleasure in the potential match.

At the time, the "dating" ritual in America was in a transition period, and the old colonial custom of bundling, in which a courting couple shared a common bed while remaining fully clothed and wearing underclothes, was no longer widely in favor. It had been used as a means to promote intimacy between a romantic twosome, without fostering sexual intercourse. However, other physical forms of affection were gradually becoming a more common and acceptable component of a courtship. Nevertheless, such intimacies were limited and could only occur in private, since purity of the bride-to-be was considered absolutely essential. Thus, Alex and Jane conducted the major part of their courtship in a highly chaperoned environment. In spite of this limitation, their romance blossomed and on April 10, 1849, Minister Cyrus Nutt wed the two in Putnam County. The marriage was the beginning of a long, and fruitful union.

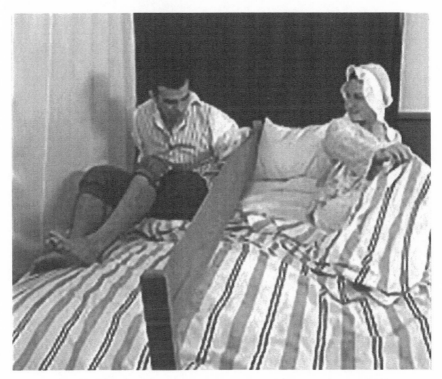

Simulation of the practice of "bundling." Often, a bundling board was strategically placed between the couple to further discourage any suggestion of intimacy.
CW Journal: Holiday 2007, Courtship, Sex, and the Single Colonist.

Sixteen months later, Alex and Jane were blessed with their first child, a daughter who they named Belle. Their first son, James, was born two years after that. Meanwhile young Alex, who was extremely industrious and hard working, was investing shrewdly in land and cattle. Gradually he became one of the most successful farmers and livestock breeders in the region. With their expanding family, the Bryans needed larger living quarters, as well as additional land to cultivate and to raise cattle and pigs. Opportunity beckoned in the rich outlying farmlands of Putnam County where ample acreage was available. Moreover, by moving the family from town to the country, Jane would be even closer to her parents, the Farrows.

By 1853, Alex and Jane owned their own home and a large tract of prime farmland just south of Greencastle, Indiana. This small community, the county seat, was the largest in Putnam County, having a population approaching 5,000. Founded in 1821, it lay approximately 45 miles west of Indianapolis. The town was considered culturally advanced for the time, a reputation enhanced by the presence of Indiana Asbury College. Founded by frontier Methodists in 1837, the school was located in the rolling hills around Greencastle. The college had originally adopted the name of the first American Bishop of the Methodist Episcopal Church, and was then renamed DePauw University in the 1870s. This name change was in no small part prompted by a donation of $600,000 made to the institution by Mr. Washington C. DePauw. This philanthropist had amassed his fortune by investing heavily in farms, flourmills, steel, railroads, and plate glass, and for a time was considered to be the wealthiest man in Indiana.

Although Alex and Jane began their married life in harmony and serenity, their future together would prove to hold daunting challenges. Over the next decade, their family increased to nine members, with Elvira (Ella) and Flora born between 1854 and 1858, and Marion, Mary, and Elizabeth subsequently arriving during the American Civil War (1861-1865) era.

Family life and tranquility throughout much of the nation was severely disrupted during these extremely difficult times. Even though Indiana was spared any major battles on its soil during this bloody conflict, in early July 1863 as the Battle of Gettysburg was raging in Pennsylvania, Confederate Brigadier General John Hunt Morgan and 2,500 cavalrymen crossed the Ohio River downstream from Louisville and invaded Indiana. For 5 days, Morgan and his men roamed several southern counties and were responsible for looting, pillaging and producing a significant amount of destruction to the countryside. This invasion was short-lived, and Morgan's marauders never advanced into central or northern Indiana. Soon, General Edward Hobson and his Union forces drove Morgan into Ohio, where he was promptly captured, while Indiana communities such as Greencastle breathed collective sighs of relief.

When the war began, there were virtually no trained soldiers in the state of Indiana. However, within a week of the South's attack upon Fort Sumter in South Carolina, thousands of young men assembled in Indianapolis to volunteer for the army of the North. In all, Indiana provided almost 200,000 soldiers for the conflict, and lost almost 25,000 to combat, as well as to disease, and accidents. Hoosiers fought some 7,300 engagements in all theaters of the War. Although some of its citizens were sympathetic to the South's cause, most were not. Oliver P. Morton, the wartime Governor of Indiana, was strongly pledged to the Union cause: he raised more than twice the number of Indiana troops that President Lincoln had mandated.

These units were frequently recruited on the basis of nationality. For example, the Thirty-Fifth Regiment "First Irish" was composed of Irish immigrants, who wore dazzling green caps to distinguish themselves from the other troops. The Thirty-Second, also called the "First German" Regiment, recruited men of German descent from all over the state. The 28th United States Colored Troops, though not technically an Indiana Regiment, consisted primarily of Indianapolis men of color. All of these units saw extensive and bloody action throughout the war.

Eli Lilly had been a pharmacology student at Indiana Asbury College prior to the war and had graduated in two years. Within a year, he and his wife met in Indianapolis and subsequently returned to Greencastle where Lilly opened his own drugstore in 1861. However, he enlisted in the Union Army at the war's outbreak, and formed his own unit known as the 18th Battery, Indiana Light Artillery consisting of six 10-pound guns and 150 men. The unit saw action in the Second Battle of Chattanooga and the Battle of Chickamauga. He reenlisted in 1864, was promoted to Major, and given command of 9th Indiana Cavalry. During a mission in Alabama, he was captured by Confederate Major Nathan B Forest and held in a prisoner-of-war camp for the duration of hostilities.

Pictured are Col George W Jackson (Union County) on the left, and Lt Col Eli Lilly (Putnam County) on the right, 9ᵗʰ Cavalry, 121ˢᵗ Regiment, Indiana Volunteers. Digital image © 2005 Indiana Historical Society.

At the Civil War's conclusion, Lilly became a pharmaceutical chemist and opened his own business. In 1876, he founded Eli Lilly and Company in Indianapolis and soon became wealthy after developing numerous significant advances in pharmaceutical drug manufacturing.

In Indiana, initial hopes were high for a quick victory over the South, but following several unexpected and dramatic losses in early battles, it was apparent that the nation was in store for a long, bloody, costly conflict. As momentum for a quick resolution of the conflict stalled in 1861 and 1862, and setbacks on the battlefields mounted, there were insufficient numbers of volunteers to meet military needs. Governmental officials were plagued with manpower shortages, and compulsory service was seen as the only realistic means to sustain an effective fighting force. Thus, in March 1863, Congress passed legislation, known as the Enrollment Act, which theoretically imposed liability for service on virtually every able-bodied American male between the ages of 20 and 45. There was a loophole, however. A provision existed that enabled draftees to become exempt from service by either supplying a substitute willing to serve in one's place, or by submitting a three hundred dollar payment. Thus, for anyone with sufficient resources, the draft was a moot point.

The military draft elicited outrage from many private citizens who recognized the inequity of the system, and insisted it represented a total infringement of their rights. As a consequence, in July of 1863, residents of New York City, who were upset over the federal government's new Conscription Act, rioted and looted for three days. Indiana harbored its own resentment over the military draft. Peace Democrats, called Copperheads by their opposition, were generally more conciliatory toward the South than were Republicans. The Copperheads' major strength lay in the Midwest, where mistrust of the northeast was widespread and where there were more economic and cultural ties with the south. Additionally, anti-abolitionist Midwesterners feared that emancipation would result in a large migration of freed slaves entering into their states. Blackford County in east central Indiana was a haven for Peace Democrats, and violence in response to the draft broke out there in 1863. Rioters destroyed the draft enrollment lists and the draft ballot box there, and 300 infantry had to be called in to quell the disturbance.

Putnam County residents also had growing reservations about the military draft process. The announcement shown on the following page describes an urgent call for a meeting to be held for the citizens of Greencastle Township. Its purpose was to devise ways for the "township, hitherto foremost in answering the call of the authorities" to "be relieved from the draft." Such "broadsides" were posted all over town to announce the meeting. A.S. Bryan's name can be seen on the second line, bottom left of the announcement.

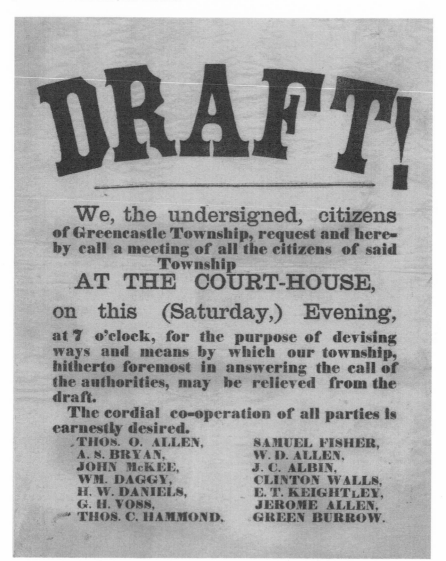

Copy of Greencastle Township anti-draft handbill. Such broadsides were not typically preserved, but were usually discarded after serving their purpose. Digital image © 2005 Indiana Historical Society.

Because of their efficient production of critical food supplies, which served the need of Federal forces, farmers in the Midwest were vital contributors to the northern war cause. However, their task had been made especially difficult by the prolonged shortage of available farm laborers, many of whom had been called to the military service of their county.

As the Civil War entered its fourth year, momentum began to shift in favor of the North, but the residents living in and around Greencastle faced a new crisis: an epidemic of diphtheria. For many, this threat was far more real and frightening than was any danger from the distant war being fought hundreds of miles away.

Diphtheria epidemics were usually caused by consumption of bacterially contaminated drinking water. The often fatal disease had swept through Europe in the 17th century causing devastating effects. Diphtheria had crossed the ocean to America in the 18th century, and had reached epidemic proportions in the New England colonies in 1735. In a matter of weeks, entire families could be lost to the disease. Contracting an upper respiratory tract infection during times of a diphtheria outbreak had terrifying implications. Typically, the first signs of infection were a sore throat and fever. In its worst form, the lymph nodes in the neck as well as the tonsils swelled dramatically, and a leathery, whitish-gray membrane appeared in the throat. These circumstances often lead to airway obstruction, which made victims feel as though they were choking to death. Thus, this highly contagious infection acquired the nickname "the strangler."

Although a few neighbors fell victim to the disease, the Bryan family was thankful to have survived the diphtheria scare unscathed. Research finally identified the specific bacterium which produced diphtheria some twenty years later, but it took many more years to develop a vaccine to prevent it.

With Robert E. Lee's surrender to Ulysses S Grant at Appomattox Court House, Virginia, on April 9, 1865, the uncertainty associated with the War gradually dissipated and life returned to a certain normalcy. In 1866, the Bryans had another daughter, Auta, whose birth was quickly followed by that of Fred in 1867 and Jennie in 1869.

In the immediate post-Civil War era, in addition to potentially fatal diseases, Greencastle residents feared fire more than any other potential natural disaster. Fires were constant threats in colonial America, and continued to be a hazard throughout the Midwest during the last half of the 19th century. Barn fires occurred most frequently, and the flames often engulfed the tall, wooden structures before any aid could arrive. In a small town such as Greencastle, when a blaze was detected, observers quickly shouted "FIRE!" As quickly as possible, the townspeople would arm themselves with buckets, dishpans, or any large, manageable object capable of holding water and race to the nearest water source. With their filled containers undertow, they then would dash to the fire, hurriedly dump their water on it, and repeat the process as long as it took to achieve success.

Communities with superior resources owned hand- or often horse-drawn fire engines: they contained a large water reservoir or tub from which water could be sprayed onto the fire with some degree of force and accuracy. The power behind the stream of water came from a simple hand-operated, piston pump or in some instances, a steam-pumper. In using this system, bucket brigades of volunteers continually supplied the reservoir with additional water from any available source.

This relatively inefficient system was improved considerably when a method was devised to quickly suck water from a town's public cistern into the fire wagon. There tended to be a morbid fascination by the population when large fires broke out in a town. Whenever a water-laden fire wagon headed toward a fire and careened past the onlookers, many were mesmerized by the action, and typically halted whatever they were doing to watch. Invariably, young boys would run after the galloping horses, hoping to participate in the action in some way.

Horse-drawn fire wagon with boys running alongside in Newport, Kentucky, 1907, during a Decoration Day parade. Courtesy of the Kenton County Public Library, Covington, KY.

Unfortunately, to passively stand around and watch either of the horrific fires that occurred in Chicago and Peshtigo, Wisconsin in the fall of 1871 would have been a fatal choice. Ironically, these two fires broke out almost simultaneously.

The Great Chicago Fire began around 9 pm on Sunday, October 8, 1871. It originated somewhere on the outskirts of the city in the vicinity of the infamous O'Leary barn. Driven by a strong wind from the southwest, the rapidly expanding flames soon headed straight for the center of the city. Relentlessly, they leaped across the South Branch of the Chicago River around midnight and by 1:30 am, the business district was in flames. From here, the colossal blaze raced northward across the main branch of the river. Chicago's fire department was helpless before the onslaught. When the great conflagration finally burned itself out, 300 Chicagoans were dead, 90,000 were homeless, and property loss had exceeded $200 million.

In an almost unbelievable coincidence, on the same evening while Chicago burned, the worst recorded forest fire in North American history raged through Peshtigo, Wisconsin and the town's one and a half million surrounding acres of farmland and timber. Before it was over, between 1,200 and 2,400 lives were lost, as were millions of dollars in property and timber. This fire had been preceded by a prolonged and widespread drought as well as unseasonably hot weather. Additionally, the devastation was compounded by the negligence of the logging and railroad industries: they had widely scattered vast quantities of highly flammable downed trees, brush, grass, bark and sawdust, creating an immense reservoir of dry tinder which served as an almost inexhaustible fuel source for the inferno.

Three years later, the Greencastle community suffered a major fire of their own, which resulted in massive destruction to the city. The fire department had been formed in 1849 and still existed as a volunteer department on October 28, 1874. That day saw what was perhaps the worst fire in Greencastle history. Driven by high winds, a small fire in a downtown business spread quickly, and in a short time, much of the downtown area was ablaze. The fire department was quickly overwhelmed, and they frantically dispatched telegrams to Indianapolis and Terre Haute asking for additional men and equipment. Before the fire was contained, more than 40 businesses, 12 homes, two livery stables, and the Post Office were destroyed. In proportion to relative size, population and wealth of the two communities, the damage was said to exceed that of the Chicago conflagration. The Bryan's holdings were located on the southern outskirts of town, and thus the massive downtown Greencastle fire spared them property damage nor any other personal losses. Life continued to be good for Alex and Jane as they raised their ten children in a peaceful, agrarian setting.

CHAPTER THREE

An eleventh child was born to Jane and Alex Bryan on October 25, 1872, and they named her, "Pearl," which to them symbolized something having great value and preciousness. The family considered her name to be an emblem of modesty, chastity, and purity, and the proud parents were confident that this name would faithfully reflect the future characteristics of their new baby girl. Two weeks after the birth, President Ulysses S Grant handily defeated the leader of the Liberal Republican Party, Horace Greeley in the presidential election of 1872, winning his 2nd term in office. Alex Bryan was elated. Greeley was a newspaper editor, and a liberal social reformer, and Alex was a staunch Republican on most issues. Thus, he viewed Greeley's political views as eccentric and generally out of touch with reality.

During the election, Susan B Anthony had been arrested and brought to trial in Rochester, New York, for attempting to cast a vote for President Grant. Since women did not have the legal right to vote at the time, this case was followed nationally with great interest. Ultimately, Anthony was fined $100 and released from jail. She scornfully refused to pay the charge, but the government made no serious effort to collect it.

Two years later, the Woman's Christian Temperance Union was founded to lead the drive for prohibition. The organization also became a major force in the fight for women's suffrage, and in Greencastle, Indiana, a local WCTU chapter was soon organized in response to a perceived wide scale abuse of alcohol in that town. Not surprisingly, the most vehement opponent to women's enfranchisement during this period was the liquor lobby, which feared that women might use their votes to prohibit the sale of alcohol. In addition to promoting both women's suffrage and alcohol prohibition, as time passed, the WCTU also became extremely active in prison reform.

The Bryan family continued to prosper economically during the 1870s. Alex was not only a prominent farmer and stockbreeder in the county, but also had established a dairy business. His success was often attributed to his astute ability to quickly recognize and seize business opportunities as they arose. By all accounts, he was a reliable, public-spirited citizen; a man of great integrity and community influence. All the Bryan family members were very well respected in and around Greencastle. When Pearl reached two years of age, Jane and Alex gave birth to their last child, a boy named Alexander III. The parents were 50, and 41 years old, respectively.

In the fall of 1873, a major economic downturn, which had begun in Europe, reached the United States. The financial failure of Jay Cooke and Company, which was the nation's premier investment bank, initiated a series of events that ultimately produced the "Panic of 1873." When the New York Stock Exchange was forced to close for a 10-day period, credit dried up across America. Mortgage foreclosures became common. Banks failed, factories closed, and thousands of workers lost their jobs. Economic conditions were very difficult in much of the country. Widespread economic recovery did not occur until five years had passed. However, farmers in Greencastle, and in the Midwest in general, were less vulnerable to the financial crises than many, since the country's demand for food continued unabated, in spite of Wall Street's problems. It is estimated that the population in America grew during the decade of the 1870s from 39 to 50 million.

Historic events were also unfolding across the entire nation. In South Dakota on June 25, 1876, George Armstrong Custer and 265 men under his command in the 7th Cavalry were surprised by the Sioux Indian forces of Sitting Bull and Crazy Horse at the Battle of Little Big Horn. Custer's entire party was killed, and the infamous encounter has forever been noted as "Custer's Last Stand." With this stunning victory, native Americans reached the zenith of their military power, but outraged American citizens demanded harsh retribution, and within a year the Sioux nation was defeated and broken.

Meanwhile, 29 year-old Alexander Graham Bell invented the telephone at Boston University. This innovation would soon revolutionize communication capabilities across the continent. November of 1876 also saw the most disputed presidential election in American history. Samuel J. Tilden, the Democratic candidate, received a clear majority of the popular vote. However, he lacked one electoral vote needed to carry a clear majority in the Electoral College. This problem had emerged because there were 22 disputed electoral votes in the states of Florida, Louisiana, South Carolina, and Oregon. The issue quickly became mired in political partisanship, and threatened to tear the country apart. Facing an unprecedented constitutional crisis, in January 1877, the U.S. Congress passed a law forming a 15-member Electoral Commission to settle the outcome. Ultimately, in the Compromise of 1877, the Republican candidate, Rutherford B. Hayes, was elected president in exchange for the removal of federal troops from the South, whose presence there was a carryover from the Civil War. This political settlement effectively ended Reconstruction in the region, and proponents of black suffrage suffered a major blow.

While the Bryan family was flourishing in Greencastle, working classes in the midst of the nation's economic doldrums were demonstrating increasing dissatisfaction and unrest at many factories and construction sites throughout the country. When Pearl was 5 years old, the Great Railroad Strike of 1877 erupted in West Virginia during an unusually hot summer. Workers had received two reductions in wages over the past year, and were in an ugly mood. Participation in the work stoppage soon spread to other states and involved additional occupations. In many cities, violent clashes occurred between the police and striking workers. In Chicago, such bloody encounters left 30 people dead and countless injured. Troops under General Philip Sheridan of Civil War fame were brought in to quell the Chicago riots. Six weeks passed before passions cooled and the strikes ceased.

In contrast, events in Greencastle were relatively peaceful. James Bryan was married that summer. Newspaper accounts of weddings at that time typically reported, "At the home of the bride's parents, Miss Fanny Clark of Hendricks County and Mr. James Bryan of Greencastle were united in holy matrimony in the presence of a number of friends. Immediately after the ceremony, the guests were invited to the dining room where a bountiful repast was laid, and it is hardly necessary to say that it was enjoyed by all present. The presents were numerous and handsome, showing the esteem in which Miss Clark was held by her many friends"

To provide entertainment and culture for its citizens, Greencastle built an "Opera House" in 1875. While community and civic events invariably took place in these structures, they did not typically host actual operatic performances. Rather, they held dances, community meetings, political gatherings, musical performances, plays, vaudeville acts, minstrels, lectures, roller-skating, and sometimes even boxing.

The presence of an opera house in any community was a major boon to social interactions, cultural growth, and personal enjoyment. Plays were particularly popular viewing events. A Greencastle Daily Banner story of that epoch states, "Manager Blake has succeeded in booking Perkins D. Fisher's well-known farce comedy, 'A Cold Day,' for one night only, February 11 at the Opera House. This will be an opportunity for those who like good singing, first class dancing, and clean wholesome fun to enjoy themselves. 'A Cold Day' requires no further endorsement than the fact that it has for the last eight years played most everywhere in the United States and has therefore well earned the saying, 'Once a success, always a success.'"

In 1877, the Greencastle Women's Reading Club was also established. Culture was expanding in the small community. These clubs were particularly popular with wealthier female citizens, who had the time and opportunity to invest in such endeavors. Works by Louisa May Alcott and Harriet Beecher Stowe were particularly admired, as were the essays of Ralph Waldo Emerson. Other social interactions in Greencastle were also evolving. The male-only Freemason fraternal organization was organized, as was the Order of Eastern Star, open to women age 18 and older. A newly established baseball team, the Greencastle Red Stockings, provided summertime action for sports enthusiasts. The team primarily competed against other nearby community squads and the well-attended games served as a major source of local pride.

The U.S. Census of 1880 showed that eight offspring were living at home with Alexander and Jane Bryan at the time. Ella, 25, and Marion, 19, worked as a store clerk and farmer, respectively. Mary, Auta, Fred and Jennie were attending school locally. Pearl, 7, and Alexander III, 5, had not yet reached school age, and remained at home. Flora, Elvira, James and Belle had married and moved into their own homes.

In her early years, Pearl lived a wholesome and happy life. By necessity, her parents divided their attention among many children, but Pearl felt secure and loved. Her care was often delegated to her older siblings, and the four of them agreed that she was sometimes willful and stubborn, while demonstrating a strong determination in getting what she wanted. Nevertheless, Pearl was usually amusing to be around and her brothers and sisters generally took great pleasure in her company, basking in her bright and sunny disposition. The tow-headed Pearl could often be found playing outside, and was fascinated by the diversity of animal and plant life that existed there. She spent hours contemplating everything that nature had to offer: the flute-like song of the wood thrush perched high in the trees; the repeated call of the whip-poor-will, sounding its own name; and the acrobatic flight patterns of the swallows and nighthawks, as they swooped down on their insect prey. Pearl giggled at the songs of the mockingbirds, which mimicked the call of many other birds including the Carolina wren and the song sparrow. Classmates recounted stories of Pearl trying to nurse injured baby birds back to life, even though she was rarely successful.

In early spring, Pearl explored the nearby woods with its carpet of vibrant wild flower blooms. She was astonished by the blend of colors, including the yellow blossoms of the wood poppy; the intense blue-violet hues of violets and Virginia bluebells; and the delicate pink-white flowers of the spring beauties. Every May, she was eager to see the hordes of May apples with their solitary flowers peeking out from beneath the large, flat leaves down low to the ground. She was intrigued by the Dutchman's breeches, which closely resembled the legs of tiny pantaloons. Whenever she saw a jack in the pulpit it made her smile and think of her minister preaching a boring sermon.

In the autumn, Pearl eagerly collected chestnuts, black walnuts, and hickory nuts that had fallen from the trees near her house. The Bryan children collected chestnuts in voluminous amounts, and the family saved some of them to roast during the winter holidays. For Pearl, eating warm chestnuts on a cold day was one of life's real pleasures. During the summer evenings, Pearl enjoyed catching lightning bugs in a canning jar, and taking them into the house: she naively hoped that their luminescence would enhance the feeble inside light provided by candles, lanterns, and later, gas chandeliers.

Pearl began attending public school in the fall of 1880 at the age of seven. The quality of public education in Indiana at that time was generally acknowledged to be mediocre and in need of improvement. Mandatory attendance was non-existent, and it was not until the 1890s that laws were passed requiring children between the ages of seven and fourteen to attend school for a period of twelve weeks each year. Because the Bryans viewed education as important, Pearl attended school in Greencastle regularly until she graduated from high school.

Her classmates described her as likeable, but sometimes shy and self-effacing. Occasionally after school she would invite schoolmates to her home on the outskirts of the main town. The youngsters played various children's games, including hide-and-seek, jacks, and hopscotch. They picked wild flowers, captured insects, and gathered acorns. Young boys would take the largest acorns, remove the top and scrape out the inner contents. They would then poke a small hole at the base of the shell, push a small twig into the hole, and take great pride in having produced their own version of a pipe. In contrast, little girls opted to make figures and dolls with their acorns. From time to time, small disputes and quarrels arose among the children, Pearl was said to take charge and serve as an effective peacemaker. She developed a reputation as a fair and just mediator.

On February 28, 1881, Pearl's comfortable and predictable life abruptly changed. Her 23-year old-sister Flora died suddenly, leaving two small children for the family to look after. It was the usual custom of the time that prior to burying the deceased, family members and neighbors would gather for a series of all-night vigils held in the parlor with the body. This was the case with Flora, whose body rested in an open coffin with kin and friends present. This practice made a lasting impression on Pearl, who despaired over her sister's permanent departure. Soon, "Aunt Pearl" was called upon to help care for the two little ones after school, a task which she accepted with few complaints, although inwardly, she missed playing with her classmates. Eighteen months after Flora's death, Pearl's 21-year old brother, Marion, died from chronic scarlet fever-related heart disease.

Sadly, death during early adulthood was not a rare event in the late 1800s. The leading causes of death were pneumonia, influenza, tuberculosis, gastrointestinal enteritis, and accidents. Occasionally, there were also outbreaks of diphtheria, smallpox, and cholera, which claimed lives suddenly and without warning. Pearl was only nine years old, but already recognized the uncertainty and fragility of life.

One muggy day late in July, Pearl observed her brother, Fred, showing Alex III how to play a game with a pocketknife called mumbly-peg. The purpose of this diversion was to attempt to stick the knife blade in the ground as it was flipped downward by an index finger from different sites on the body. After silently watching for a while, Pearl asked to take a turn, but Fred reminded her that this game was for boys only.

As she grew older, Pearl began to recognize numerous circumstances in which women's opportunities were unfairly restricted by society. It gradually dawned on her that it was likely that she would have many limited choices regarding how her future life might unfold. Though these thoughts were discouraging, she derived a great deal of pleasure in life from her family and community-related activities. She attended both church and Sunday School regularly, and had many friends who did likewise.

Pearl with her female Sunday School classmates, circa 1886. She can be identified in the second row where she is wearing a dark dress, and sitting immediately above the "Z" in the sign below her. Courtesy Putnam County Public Library, Greencastle, IN.

By 1889, 16-year-old Pearl regularly read the local newspapers and checked out books from the Greencastle library. She enjoyed reading, and perhaps her favorite author was Sarah Orne Jewett, particularly her collection of short stories, "The Country of the Pointed Firs." These tales were set in Maine, and were narrated by the main character in the book, a woman author spending her summers in a small seaside town. The stories were woven around the countryside and village life in the 1890s, and Pearl would sometimes imagine herself living with her husband in that distant state. What a distinct irony this would turn out to be!

As she grew older, Pearl grew increasingly aware of the historical extraordinary events unfolding in the nation, and extending far beyond central Indiana. In 1889, she read of a devastating flood in Johnstown, Pennsylvania that had claimed 5000 lives. She learned about a remarkable woman named Jane Addams, who had established a world famous social settlement called Hull House on Chicago's Westside. In December of 1890, she read that at Wounded Knee, South Dakota, two hundred members of the Sioux Nation had been massacred by U.S. soldiers; while in September of 1893, she learned that nearly 2 million acres of Native American land had been claimed by 50,000 American settlers racing one another across the Oklahoma Territory.

In the local news, a particular article published in the Greencastle newspaper in 1890 seized Pearl's attention. She was fascinated by Jennie Allen, who was born in Greencastle in 1854, and was one of the first female students admitted to Asbury College before its name was changed to DePauw University in 1884. While studying for her degree in History and English, Miss Allen had met the man who was to become her future husband, Marion McKinley Bovard. Marion, a practicing physician who had decided to enter the ministry, was enrolled in both a bachelor's and a master's degree program at Asbury. Jennie and Marion received their degrees in 1873, and were subsequently married. They moved to the Arizona Territory and worked there as missionaries for two years.

A few years later, the newly established University of Southern California (USC) opened its doors to 53 students and 10 faculty members. In 1880, Marion and Jennie were offered positions there. Marion ultimately became the first President of USC, and Jennie, one of the first faculty members and the school's first lady. After reading the article describing the life of Jennie Allen Bovard, Pearl became interested in attending DePauw University. She reasoned that a college education would improve her opportunity to learn more about many things and perhaps even to travel. Pearl began to reflect on how she might grow intellectually, and pursue a career not typically available to women. She was especially motivated because her older brother, Fred, was currently a student at DePauw, although circumstances would later change for him, preventing the completion of his final year of studies.

Pearl's high school principal was Martha Jane Ridpath, the younger sister of John Clark Ridpath, a noted educator, historian, and writer. Martha Ridpath had earned her A.B. from Asbury College in 1879 and her M.A. in 1882. Miss Ridpath also served as a role model for Pearl's aspirations to attend DePauw University. However, when Pearl graduated from high school, her parents suggested that she postpone plans for attending college temporarily, and to perhaps simply attend a few classes to begin. With marriage and eventual motherhood a more realistic goal, the Bryans encouraged Pearl to fully develop her domestic skills, and to enhance certain personal traits, such as modesty and virtuosity. They further implied that she would be well served not to outperform any potential male suitors who might be interested in her.

The Greencastle High School building was erected in 1877 at the cost of $26,000 and was located on Elm Street. Pearl graduated from high school in 1892. Historical post card published by the Indiana News Company, Indianapolis, Indiana.

In the 1890's, farm life for both men and women was burdensome. The men typically worked over 14 hours a day, dealing with the physical demands of successful, productive farming. Women, whose responsibilities took even longer, labored both inside and outdoors.

Housekeeping chores included cleaning, washing, ironing, sewing, canning, cooking, caring for children, and so forth. Outside, women planted and harvested extensive vegetable gardens, milked cows, gathered chicken eggs, and might even decapitate a hen or two and pluck their feathers before preparing Sunday dinner. The latter was an assignment that Pearl deplored.

In spite of these grueling workdays on farms, there were some opportunities for leisure. Families went to church on Sundays, and often during the week. They visited nearby neighbors and friends, made regular trips to town for groceries and supplies, and were eager to attend circuses, carnivals, or other traveling entertainment events that passed through their area. Among young people, courting activities typically revolved around church events, and evening conversations at home in the parlor. Occasionally other social interactions occurred: buggy rides, hay rides, sleigh rides, ice skating on ponds, ice cream socials and school programs.

Pearl spent much of her spare time tending to the orphaned children living in her home, and she enjoyed playing the piano. She especially delighted in playing the latest popular sheet music, and was intrigued by the song, "After the Ball." She would often rhythmically sway on the piano stool, while playing the instrument and softly sing the lyrics. At the song's conclusion, Pearl would shake her head sorrowfully and say, "This song is so sad to me. The two sweethearts in the ballad wasted their lives! Why didn't they just communicate better? They could have lived happily ever after!"

After Pearl graduated from high school in 1892, she had no shortage of beaus competing for her attentions. She was a bright, personable, pretty and trim young woman who came from a highly respected family. She treated everyone around her in a kind and respectful manner, and was friendly to them. Unfortunately, as time went by, none of these young men who would come calling caused Pearl's heart to beat any faster.

The fact was, Pearl had grown up with these potential suitors and their familiarity bored her. In addition, the Bryan's social status was considerably higher than that of many other families in town. Thus, most of the local boys did not feel that they met Pearl's dating standards. At this point in her life, she was a highly recognized entity in the social circles of Greencastle, and an active member of the Methodist church. In spite of her secure position in local society, Pearl felt that her environment was too familiar and predictable, and her possible options, too limited. She wanted a future where opportunities for travel, excitement and stimulation awaited her.

When Pearl was 20, tragedy entered the lives of the Bryan family yet again. After a brief illness, twenty-six year old Auta died of influenza, which had progressed into pneumonia. In addition to deeply mourning the loss of another sister, Pearl once again envisioned what her future seemed to hold. She sensed that she was doomed to replicate the fate of her sisters: getting married, bearing children, and dying young. She felt a distinct pointlessness to it all, and she vowed to begin living each day fully, for she embraced the concept that the future was promised to no one. This had been made clear by her own life experiences.

And then, Pearl met a young man named Scott Jackson, and her life changed forever.

Photograph of Pearl Bryan's graduating high school class in 1892. The fair-skinned Pearl may be identified in the second row on the far right. A larger replica of Pearl is placed in the upper right section. DePauw University Photos, Dr. Andrew Wallace Crandall (Picture file, Nell Crouch). See: Kurtz, Wilber G, 1882-1967. DC554, Folers #2, 12, 13. Coffman Family pg 80, Putnam County General vf.

CHAPTER FOUR

The year 1869 saw the birth of five men who significantly impacted human culture and history worldwide in very diverse, dramatic and lasting ways. Ten days into the year, Grigori Rasputin, a Russian mystic and healer, was born in a small Siberian village. The "Mad Monk" and his charismatic personality became a noteworthy factor in the downfall of the Romanov Dynasty. Rasputin's influence upon Czar Nicholas and his wife, Alexandra, as well as the Czar's ill advised political decisions, ultimately led to the family's execution by Russian revolutionaries in July,1918. The vacuum created in the Russian political system was quickly filled by Vladimir Ilyich Lenin and the Bolsheviks. From their foundational efforts, the Soviet Union was established and ultimately, the history of the 20th century was affected immensely.

Neville Chamberlain was born on the 18th of March 1869, in Birmingham, England. He served as Prime Minister of the United Kingdom between 1937 and 1940, and is best known for his policy of appeasement with Adolph Hitler and Nazi Germany during this era. In 1938, Chamberlain met with the Fuhrer in Munich, Germany, and returned to England with a mutual agreement, which he confidently claimed would lead to "peace in our time." This policy came to be severely criticized by both Clement Atlee and Winston Churchill. In March 1939, Hitler's troops seized Prague, Czechoslovakia and invaded Poland on September 1. These events plunged Europe into World War II, Chamberlain was forced to resign in disgrace, and the world lost more than 70 million people in the deadliest conflict in human history.

Three days after Chamberlain's birth, Florenz Ziegfeld, Jr. was born in Chicago, and within a few decades had become the major theatrical producer of his time. He first produced his famous Ziegfeld Follies in 1907. These annual revues were famous for their elaborate staging, and choruses composed of beautiful women. Over the next quarter century, these ongoing stage performances were wildly successful among the American public, but were eventually discontinued during the Great Depression. Among the theatrical stars developed by Ziegfeld were Will Rogers, W. C. Fields, Fanny Brice, Eddie Cantor and Marilyn Miller. Perhaps Ziegfeld's greatest artistic achievement was his production in 1927 of the original Broadway musical "Show Boat," based on Edna Ferber's novel and featuring music by Jerome Kern.

Mahatma Gandhi was born to Hindu parents on October 2 1869, in a small town located near Bombay, India. Gandhi led India's long struggle for independence from Britain, which was finally achieved in 1947. He never wavered from his strong belief in nonviolent protest and religious tolerance. Such notable world figures as Nelson Mandela of South Africa and Dr. Martin Luther King Jr. of the United States, subsequently used Gandhi's philosophy of peaceful means to help achieve remarkable success in their own political struggles.

Henri Matisse was born on New Year's Eve in north-central France in 1869. He became known for the striking use of color in his paintings. Although his art form was ridiculed early in his career, he later came to be considered by many experts as the most important French painter of the 20th century. He and Spain's Pablo Picasso have often been identified as "the indisputable giants of modern art."

The year 1869 also saw the birth of Scott Jackson, on March 1, in Wiscasset, Maine. His father, John Ebenezer Jackson, was a well-known Naval Commodore, and his mother, Sarah, was a leading literary and social figure in the community. Commodore Jackson was Sarah's second husband. John was 10 years the senior of Sarah, and had not been previously married. Sarah admired and respected him greatly, and knew that a marriage to the Commodore would bring her security, wealth, prestige, and certainly wouldn't diminish her own high social standing. Two years after the death of her first husband, Sarah and Commodore Jackson were married.

The term "Commodore" has a complicated history in the nomenclature of the United States Navy. Initially, it indicated a temporary ranking, falling between that of a Naval Captain and a Rear Admiral. During the Civil War, there was such an acute need for officers, that "Commodore" became a permanent commissioned rank.

Eighteen Commodores were authorized on July 16, 1862, in the midst of the Civil War, and Scott Jackson's father was likely one of them.

Following his service in the Navy of the North during the Civil War, and prior to the birth of his son, Commodore Jackson served as a Captain on several commercial vessels. He may have selected the name "Scott" for their baby in honor of General Winfield Scott, who was an American hero for half a century. Scott had seen action in the War of 1812, the Indian Wars of the 1830s, and the Mexican War (1846-1848). He was often called "Old Fuss and Feathers" because of his attention to detail and his love of gaudy uniforms. When the Civil War began, the General pressed Abraham Lincoln to adopt his specific plan for defeating the Confederacy. This strategy included instituting a vigorous naval blockade of all major southern ports. Commodore Jackson heartily endorsed the plan. However, many among the northern press derisively called it "Scott's Anaconda Plan" and they jested that its ultimate aim was "to squeeze the South to military death" much in the manner of an anaconda snake. These journalists felt that the war was going to end imminently with an overwhelming Union victory, and that any long-term strategies for conducting it would be unnecessary. Although Lincoln rejected Scott's plan, it had merit. Four years later, General Grant adopted a similar strategy, which proved to be a critical factor in defeating the South.

Wiscasset is a small town located on the Sheepscot River in southeastern Maine. In 1869, Wiscasset Bay, an enlargement of this river, bordered much of the eastern side of the town. During the 18th century, it was one of the most utilized harbors on the eastern seaboard. Between the end of the Revolutionary War and the beginning of the War of 1812, an extensive nautical business developed between Wiscasset and a number of foreign ports. Ships from her docks sailed on every sea. However, the Embargo Act of 1807 dealt a serious blow to the town's prosperity, and the War of 1812 contributed to a further decline in its fortunes. When Scott Jackson was born, Wiscasset, with a population of about 2000, was in economic decline. Nevertheless, writers of the time described the small town as being lovely and charming. Its esthetic appeal resulted from the beauty of the coastline on its eastern border, the magnificence of old growth forests dispersed all along its periphery, and the presence of countless brooks and inlets extending from the sea into the town.

Following the Civil War, Scott's father was appointed as a Captain on a passenger vessel traveling from the east coast of the United States, across the Atlantic Ocean to Europe. During his first six years of life, Scott was to a large extent raised by his mother, who benefited from the help of a nanny. His father was often absent from the home while on his ocean journeys; as a result, Scott lacked paternal discipline during his formative years. When Commodore Jackson did find time to spend with Scott, they sometimes strolled along the riverside, the bay, and the docks located in the Wiscasset area. Scott enjoyed the smell of salt water, and liked to imitate the raucous calls of the gulls frequently flying overhead. Although the introverted Commodore Jackson was often stiff in his interactions with his son, Scott admired him greatly and dreamed of someday traveling on the open seas, as his father had. Eventually, he would realize this dream many times over.

The earliest American ocean-going vessels carried cargo, but seldom had passengers aboard. The first shipping company to actually focus on transporting people across the Atlantic Ocean was the Black Ball Line out of New York City. As early as 1818, this company offered passenger service to England on sailing ships. The advent of actual pleasure cruises, though, dates back to 1844. Although personal comfort and quality service on these voyages was minimal, drastic improvements in the provision of such amenities were being made in the 1850's and 1860's. Electric lights, additional deck space, and live entertainment were among these new luxuries. At the same time, steamships were introduced, and began to dominate the market over their sailing counterparts. The transition from sail to steam on the oceans, which was completed by 1876, also had an enormous impact on U.S. immigration. Steamships were significantly larger and faster, and this improvement shortened the length of a transatlantic voyage from a minimum of 5-6 weeks to 10 days or less. Thus, the newer mode of sea travel contributed in great measure to the horde of newcomers pouring into the east coast region in search of a better life in America.

Between the ages of 7 and 14, Scott accompanied his father on more than a dozen sea voyages. Sarah had urged Captain Jackson to spend more time with the boy, and he had somewhat reluctantly agreed. Thus, at an early age, Scott was able to visit England, Ireland, and a number of Mediterranean seaports. Many of his experiences were similar to those described by Mark Twain in *The Innocents Abroad*. Two years before Scott's birth, a San Francisco newspaper had sponsored Mr. Twain's 6-month trip aboard the "Quaker City" to Europe and the Holy Land. The journal, which the famous author wrote during the trip, documented his adventures, and served as the major resource for writing and publishing the book in 1869.

Scott was grateful for his apparent immunity to the ravages of seasickness, which plagued many of the other passengers on his voyages. This allowed him to spend much of his time on deck, looking out at the sea and its ever-changing panoramas. Scott was fascinated by the rhythmic propulsions of porpoises in and out of the water next to the ship, as well as the views of humpback whales, which kept the passengers entertained with their antics and acrobatics in the water. He tried to imitate their eerie, yet enchanting, songs consisting of squeaks, grunts, and whistles. But Scott's father was focused on the demands of his command. As a result, the young boy spent much of his time wandering the ship, and being entertained by members of the ship's crew and staff. With good intentions, they met Scott's every desire.

On his final trip across the Atlantic, it is likely that the unsupervised teenager experienced some less innocent activities on board. He was introduced to the taste of alcohol, which was to entice him for the remainder of his life. He also enjoyed the company of some of the young chambermaids working on the ship. By the age of 14, Scott already had attained a level of sophistication and pleasure-seeking behavior that would normally have been experienced only by someone much older. As a result, his expectations were that life was always going to be exciting and stimulating for him. Perhaps this marked the beginning of Scott's slavery to pleasure-seeking behaviors and self-centered passions. From this point on, he was at their mercy.

During this period, the Jackson family moved first to Portland, Maine, and later to Jersey City, New Jersey. John Ebenezer Jackson had become a very successful man. He was described as somewhat aloof and reserved, but among his peers, he was an extremely bright and articulate conversationalist. As Captain of a large passenger ship, he received a handsome salary. His family lacked neither money, nor social prestige. The Captain worried at times about his son's diversions and leisure activities, as well as his own reticence in communicating with the boy at a personal level. Ebenezer was a private man, and struggled to get close to Scott. Meanwhile, Sarah Jackson had become increasingly active in the literary field, and had even published a book on proper child-rearing techniques, an ironic endeavor that would become evident when tragedy struck a decade later. As a woman of letters, Sarah Jackson held membership in the prestigious Sorosis Club of New York City, and was rapidly ascending into the higher echelons of "Society" in the New York City area.

In essence, Scott grew up as an only child. Although he had a half-sister, Minnie, who was his mother's daughter from a previous marriage, he seldom interacted with her, largely because she was much older than he. In 1879, Minnie married Dr. Edwin Post, a well-known Professor of Latin at DePauw University. The couple made their home in Greencastle, Indiana and had one child.

Scott Jackson's life changed abruptly in 1883. His father died suddenly of an apparent heart attack. Almost immediately, fourteen-year old Scott was faced with multiple critical life decisions. In retrospect, it is obvious that these choices were thrust upon him before he was mature enough to make good choices. As events unfolded, his father's premature death helped initiate a progressive downward spiral for Scott, both ethically and spiritually.

At 14, Scott was short and slight, but seemingly an outwardly confident teen-ager. His sandy-colored hair and pale complexion earned him the nickname, "Dusty." His intense blue-violet eyes held an almost hypnotic quality, and his dimples were accompanied by a winsome smile. He was said to have effeminate characteristics and mannerisms, and displayed a certain vulnerability that many young ladies found appealing. In contrast, his male peers typically saw him as sissified and soft. Some young bullies who were common in the rough and tumble area of New York where Scott grew up took sadistic delight in tormenting him.

During his high school years, Dusty worked as a messenger and errand boy in and around Jersey City, where he rode one of the wildly popular new fangled bicycles which had pneumatic tires, and provided a much more comfortable ride than any of their predecessors. Men were not alone in their fascination with the two-wheelers. Young women also frequently rode these mechanical contraptions about town. In the interest of comfort, long skirts, bustles, and corsets had to be discarded by many of the female riders. At the time, Susan B. Anthony quipped, "the bicycle has done more for the emancipation of women than anything else in the world."

In 1895, Theodore Roosevelt would be appointed President of the Board of the New York City Police Commissioners. With his typical passion and vigor, he radically reformed the police department, attacking its reputation as one of the most corrupt in the United States. Among the significant changes he instituted was the creation of a 29-member "bicycle squad," whose major function was to apprehend speeding horse-drawn carriages, which was a substantial problem in the crowded city streets. Over the next six years, Roosevelt's career would skyrocket. He would serve as Assistant Secretary of the Navy; resign to lead a small regiment known as the "Rough Riders" in Cuba during the Spanish-American War; be elected as the 33rd Governor of New York; be elected as the 25th Vice-President of the United States; and assume the Presidency in 1901 following the assassination of President William McKinley.

Vintage photograph of Theodore Roosevelt's bike-squad, also known as the "Scorcher Squad." Courtesy, New York City Police Department. From www.nyc.gov/html/nyc100/html/classroom/hist_info/nycfacts.html.

Scott's deliveries frequently took him into New York City. With his new mobility and rapidly escalating "street smarts", he soon became acquainted with Five Points, a lower Manhattan district where gambling, prostitution, and alcoholism flourished. Scott became intimately familiar with all these vices. In this region, the garment industry had grown dramatically in the late 1800s, providing jobs for the flood of newcomers to the U.S. Skilled American seamstresses had been largely replaced by immigrant girls, who were doing piecework for a pittance in the terrible sweatshops of the trade.

Clothing manufacturing absorbed the influx of immigrants housed in the tenement buildings which were as stuffed with humanity, in the same manner a small boy's trousers might appear if they contained a 300 pound man. In this borough and surrounding areas crime was rampant, and a corrupt city government kept the police at bay. Typically, recent immigrants from Ireland, Italy, and Russia, as well as African-Americans from the southern states settled there. Over time, as many of these hard-working residents were able to move to less odious surroundings, they would be quickly replaced by new waves of immigrants, and the cycle would again repeat itself.

Atlantic Gardens, located on the Bowery (Fifth Avenue on the East Side), was a popular hangout for German immigrants and many others in the neighborhood. It was a great hall lined with bars and lunch counters where people went to eat and drink beer. Scott was a regular patron of the bars there. The establishment often presented polka music, accordion playing, and vaudeville acts in the evening. In this permissive environment, Scott developed many delinquent behaviors: he squandered most of his earnings and some of his mother's money on shooting craps in the back alleys, where he also had ready access to his growing fondness for alcohol. It was in Five Points where he also developed a strong appetite for having sex with prostitutes.

By his late-teens, Scott had grown to his adult size of 5'7" and 135 pounds. As a young man, he experimented with various designs of facial hair including mustaches, full beards, and goatees. He emulated the latest hirsute fashions exemplified in the Presidential election of 1888, where Grover Cleveland sported an elegant mustache, and managed to defeat his opponent, the fully bearded Benjamin Harrison. Sarah Jackson was financially comfortable by virtue of money from her family and a substantial inheritance from her deceased husband, but she did not closely monitor Scott's fiscal activities. Although she provided him with a generous allowance and occasional monetary supplements from time to time to maintain his lifestyle and penchant for fashionable clothes, she noticed that he still made frequent pleas for additional funds.

To deal with the grief associated with the loss of her husband, Sarah kept a very busy social schedule. Every Sunday, she attended a Universalist Church, located at the corner of Ivy and Summit Avenues in Jersey City. Sarah was an avid supporter of the preaching message of the Reverend Phebe A. Hanaford, a pioneer in women's rights and the first New England female to be ordained to the ministry. Although Rev. Hanaford was a highly respected speaker, male members of both the church and local community often challenged her because of her gender and

The only known picture of Scott Jackson, taken during his early adult years.

strong allegiance to the social and political causes of women. Others simply boycotted her sermons. One particular point of dispute was her membership in the Sorosis Club of New York. Many men believed that it was offensive to have their pastor associated with an organization having this type of political agenda for social reform.

Sorosis was a women's literary club, founded by Journalist Jane Cunningham Croly shortly after the Civil War had ended. Jane wrote for the New York Times under the pseudonym "Jennie June." Her columns appeared in several newspapers and other national publications, and she traveled in the company of the New York City's leading journalists. In 1868, the New York City Press Club hosted a reception for the famed British author Charles Dickens, who was in the United States completing his 2nd reading tour. Jennie June applied for a ticket to the affair, but was refused admittance because of her gender. She and other female journalists vehemently challenged the policy, and as a result, were provided with assigned seats for the reception. The only condition was that they sit behind a curtain, separated from the main audience! Reluctantly, they accepted.

Acting on this connection, Jane and her female associates founded the aforementioned Sorosis club, by and for women. Out of this group eventually grew the Federation of Women's Clubs, established in 1899. Sarah Jackson was well acquainted with both Reverand Hanaford and Jane Cunningham Croly. As a published author, Sarah was respected in women's literary circles in the region, and was elected President of the Sorosis Club of New York in the mid-1880's.

Meanwhile, the railroads had become the country's largest industry of the 19th century. The completion of the transcontinental railroad in 1869 not only promoted travel across the uncharted areas of the U.S. territories, but also opened a gateway to the west. This new mode of transportation and communication provided a major boost to the entire American economy. At that time, the Pennsylvania Railroad was one of America's largest companies. As swampy areas around Jersey City were filled in, huge buildings were constructed, transforming the area into a massive freight yard. At the time, it was the largest railway passenger shed in the world. The immense rail yards of the New Jersey Central and the Lehigh Valley Railroads were also located in Jersey City. The Lorillard Tobacco Company was nearby, which was also the largest company in the world in its field. Jersey City's intense level of business activity in this location was impressively lucrative.

Scott dropped out of school at this time, declaring that his life experiences were teaching him far more than could any school curriculum. He decided to get a fulltime job, but vacillated between seeking employment with the railroad or the tobacco companies. He eventually applied for a railroad job in Jersey City. With the influence of his late father's sterling reputation, and his mother's respectable social standing, Scott had no difficulty in being hired by the Pennsylvania Railroad. His immediate supervisor, Alexander Letts, was only a few years older than he. Scott's first job assignment was to open and distribute mail directed to the central office. Many of these letters contained payment checks made out to the company.

After Scott had been employed for several months at the Railroad, he began courting Miss Elsie Ramsey, an attractive schoolteacher from Jersey City. By this time, he had learned the importance of determining what women wanted to hear, and then verbalizing those words to them.

This strategy generally resulted in Scott getting what he wanted from most of them. It was only at a later time that his lady friends would discover that they should judge him solely by his actions, not by his words and promises.

Scott and Elsie soon became engaged. In his work environment, Scott became very friendly with his supervisor, Alexander Letts, and the two men began sharing their mutual taste for alcohol, women, horse-racing, and fast living. Unknown to Miss Elsie, Scott began spending increasing amounts of time and money pursuing these shady activities with Letts. Soon, the two new friends became well known in sporting circles as high-flyers, and wagered recklessly at the Monmouth Park racetrack. Horse racing here on the shores of New Jersey had begun on Independence Day, 1870. The track became extremely successful, and at times offered the highest track distribution (return on bets) of any in North America. In 1890, it was completely rebuilt into one of the finest facilities in the country. In 1892 and 1893, Jackson and Letts were at the height of their gambling activities at the site. However, as a consequence of strong anti-gambling sentiments conveyed by the public and supported by their elected officials, legislation was enacted in 1894, which closed the track.

As their financial losses at the racetrack mounted, Letts and Scott began to look for ways to supplement their incomes. Periodically, Scott would concoct some sort of story that might convince his mother to advance him money. Often, the lie worked, but not frequently enough to support his lavish lifestyle. Sarah Jackson began to sense that her son was deceiving her, and falling under the influence of Letts, a man she didn't like or trust. Meanwhile, Miss Elsie, who now only saw Scott sporadically, was becoming suspicious of the "busy schedule" he claimed to have after normal working hours. She also confronted Scott about his frequent drinking, which she was convinced was a serious problem. Scott normally treated her with respect, but when he was intoxicated, he became extremely moody and verbally abusive. Within a year, Letts and Scott had managed to borrow money and open a gentleman's drinking club, located near both the ferries and the racetrack. It was an ideal location. Although their establishment quickly did a booming business, and became quite profitable, the two owners were guzzling and gambling away their profits faster than they could earn enough money to break even.

During this time period, Scott also became acquainted with the cast of an amateur acting company, which performed in the New York City-Jersey City region. He ultimately became the manager of the company, and spent many late evenings drinking with the actors following their performances. After a time, he began to perform in some of the plays himself. When queried about his sudden interest in becoming a thespian, he responded that one never knew when the ability to play-act might prove very beneficial in life. He found it extremely satisfying to convince people that he was someone other than whom he really was. His philosophy became, "I can reinvent myself to be whoever I need to be." It was a talent he would utilize to his advantage countless times in the future.

In July 1893, Jackson and Letts devised a scheme to get money illegally from the Pennsylvania Railroad in order to cover their mounting debts. Periodically, Scott would remove sizable checks from the mail he opened, and transfer them to Letts, who would convert them to cash, and split the tainted money with Scott. The simple scheme worked so well that within six months, the two had bilked the company out of $32,000. With their continued success, they removed and cashed checks ever more frequently. However, in the spring of 1894, the two were finally discovered, arrested, and charged with embezzlement. Their initial trials ended in hung juries. The prosecutor subsequently gathered additional incriminating evidence, called Scott to his office, and offered him a deal. If Scott would turn state's evidence against Letts, then Scott could go free. If not, the prosecutor would see that both of them would receive long prison sentences. Scott never hesitated. He quickly accepted the offer, and testified against Letts, who was found guilty and sentenced to serve a term behind bars. As promised, Scott went free.

Miss Elsie broke her engagement to Scott following his arrest, and Sarah Jackson was at her wit's end with her son. Devastated by these humiliating events, she decided that the two of them must leave Jersey City and get a fresh start far from the locale where everyone knew about the shameful scandal. On August 13, 1894, scorned yet pitied for the entire disgraceful episode, they moved to Greencastle, Indiana, where they initially settled in with Sarah's daughter, Minnie, and her husband, Dr. Edwin Post, a Latin scholar at DePauw University. Sarah hoped that in this conservative Midwestern town, Scott would not face the temptations of the big cities, and that he might still be redeemed. Miraculously, Scott's tainted reputation had not followed them. Encouraged by this stroke of luck, Sarah devised a plan: Scott would become a dentist!

The nearest dental school was in Indianapolis. On October 10, 1894, Sarah and Scott moved to Indianapolis, establishing residence at Mrs. Lotshar's boarding house located at the corner of New York and Delaware streets. To give credence to his promise to change, Scott agreed to sing in a choir for local revival meetings. These meetings were held in Tomlinson Hall, which had been constructed in the late 1880s at the northeast corner of Market and Delaware streets. The first floor of the building was reserved for a city market, while the second floor served as an auditorium and was frequently used for public meetings, conventions, and concerts. Although Scott was performing in the choir as he had promised his mother, following the performances, he would often go drinking with his new acquaintances in Indy.

Scott began his dental studies at the Indiana Dental College during the fall semester. The school was located at the southwest corner of Delaware and Ohio streets, and offered a 3-year curriculum, with a seven-month annual session. The dental class of '97 would eventually graduate 54 new dentists, but sadly, Scott would not be among them. As a new student, Scott fervently assured his mother that he had

W. W. Mitchel, D.D.S.: One of Scott's instructors during the 1894 fall semester at the Indiana Dental College.

Picture courtesy of the Indiana University School of Dentistry.

changed his ways, and that he really wanted to pursue dentistry as a career. Almost immediately, many of his classmates disliked him. He frequently drank, visited prostitutes, borrowed money from his peers without repaying it, and studied only periodically. He was not usually inclined to physically defend himself against his peers when they ridiculed him about his small stature and perceived effeminate mannerisms. As a result, some classmate regarded him as cowardly and weak. Many of the dental faculty believed that although his grades were more than adequate, he would never succeed in completing the term. And yet, one of his professors,

Dr. William Mitchel, later described Scott as a good student with a lot of potential whose only serious problem was drinking to excess.

One of Scott's favorite young ladies in Indianapolis was Miss Nellie Crane, a woman known for her loose morality. The two were often seen together during the fall and early winter of 1894. Soon after Scott began seeing Nellie on a regular basis, she discovered that he was quite worldly and often charming, but only when it suited him. He showered her with gifts from "the When," a downtown department store where he worked part time. Nellie became increasingly captivated by the violet-eyed charmer, and suggested to him that she would reform and change professions if he would seriously court her. Scott never gave her a direct response, which she interpreted, correctly, as an unambiguous rejection.

The "When" Building, seen here in a 1905 photograph. The curious name was derived from a promotional campaign by store owner John Brush, who wanted to get free publicity while his clothing store was closed for remodeling in 1875. He teased potential patrons by advertising heavily using the phrase, "WHEN is the store going to re-open?" This approach became so successful that the structure at 36 North Pennsylvania came to be known as the When Building and the emporium as the When Store. Scott worked here part-time during the fall months of 1894. Postcard courtesy of the Indiana Historical Society, Bass Photo Co. Collection, 6514

Regrettably, when Scott was drinking, she saw another side of him. He would turn into an angry, mean, demeaning, and abusive bully. During one such violent episode, Scott admitted to Nellie that all the gifts he had given her had been shoplifted from his employer. She became furious, and told him that stolen gifts meant nothing to her, and that she didn't want any of them. In response, he swore at her, grabbed a razor, held it at her throat, and threatened to slash her from ear to ear.

The last time that Nellie saw Scott was on New Year's Eve. The two had been out on the town drinking, and had gone back to her room. An argument ensued, and she called him an 'inebriated idiot.' Again, Scott erupted, threw her down on the bed and screamed threats at her. In response to all the commotion, the police were summoned, ending in Scott's arrest at 2 am for drunk and disorderly conduct and for associating with a prostitute. George W. Stubbs was the police judge, and since Scott didn't have enough money to pay the $10 fine, Mr. Stubbs jailed him overnight. When word of his perverse and illegal behavior circulated back to the Indiana Dental College, Scott was immediately dismissed from the program and told to clean out his locker and leave the premises. When Sarah Jackson discovered what her son had done, she was devastated, but paid his fine and the two made plans to move back to Greencastle in the spring. In the meantime, Sarah sent word to her family and friends there that Scott had contracted a serious illness and had been forced to drop out of dental school. She assured them that the two of them would return to Minnie's house in the spring after he was mended. Sarah Jackson had once again shielded her son from the consequences of his illicit and immoral behaviors. But these decisions would haunt Sarah Jackson later in her life, for insulating him from the repercussions of his poor choices would only lead to more outrageous deeds by the miscreant.

In early April, Sarah and Scott took the train back to Greencastle. With the exception of Minnie and her husband Edwin, Sarah was able to hide her son's delinquencies from everyone in the community. Through her influence, Scott soon acquired a part-time job in Dr. Gillespie's dental office. Sarah was tireless in her efforts to help Scott find a respected career, and plans were next made for Scott to attend the Ohio Dental College in Cincinnati in the fall of 1895. Meanwhile, Scott made a good friend in Greencastle. Will Wood, son of a local Methodist minister, possessed a well-deserved reputation for drinking and partying, and for being an immature mischief-maker in general. He was just the sort of company that the delinquent Scott wanted to keep. Wood was delighted to introduce him to the unattached young ladies from the town's upper social class. Meanwhile, Scott still maintained a wide written correspondence with a number of young ladies from his past, who were living outside the Greencastle community. As always, he was keeping his options open.

Photograph of the intersection of Illinois and Washington streets, Indianapolis, 1906. Scott's boarding house and the Indiana Dental College where he attended were located just a few blocks northeast of here. Postcard courtesy of the Indiana Historical Society, Bass Photo Co. Collection, 6487.

CHAPTER FIVE

It was a bleak, rainy April morning, when 22 year-old Pearl Bryan hitched her gray dappled pony to the family buggy, and drove a mile and a half north to 23½ Washington Street in downtown Greencastle. She had a 10 am appointment with Dr. Reverdy Gillespie to repair a cracked filling: the affected tooth had become painfully sensitive to both hot and cold food and liquids. Dr. Gillespie was a recent graduate of the Indiana Dental College in Indianapolis, and had joined the elderly Dr. H. H. Morrison in his practice only a week ago. As Pearl settled into the dental chair, she was nervous about her treatment procedure, but couldn't help notice a striking young man who was working in an adjacent laboratory room. Unexpectedly, he stopped what he was doing, caught her gaze and momentarily held it. Enthralled by the intensity of his violet-blue eyes, she gave him the slightest suggestion of a smile and looked away quickly,

After Dr. Gillespie had replaced the faulty filling, and Pearl had left the office, the young man casually approached the new graduate. "Well, Dr. Gillespie," he said in an exaggerated tone of reverence, smiling ironically, "I'd like to know more about your 10 am patient."

Preoccupied with a dental cast he was examining, Dr. Gillespie glanced up and smiled. "That's Pearl Bryan, Dusty. If you are thinking about stepping out with her, be forewarned that half the young men in Greencastle are already waiting in line to court her --- and the other half would like to be."

Nodding knowingly, Jackson answered, "Well, maybe I'll just move up to the front of that line. I've always had a hankering for pretty blondes."

Although Will Wood's extended family appreciated his outgoing personality, they were also well aware of his past improprieties and immature behaviors. Those dubious pursuits and assorted troubles, which seemed to beset him with discouraging regularity, had often brought disgrace to the family and to his father, Reverend D.M. Wood, a highly respected, local clergyman.

Blond, and standing almost 6 feet tall, Will commonly exhibited a smug, condescending air of self-importance. While his demeanor and ready smile stirred the pulses of many young ladies in Greencastle, his elders suspected that his "wild streak" would eventually be his undoing.

To date, Will's career path had been lackadaisical and uninspired. In the two years since graduating from high school, he had attended DePauw University for a few months, and then suddenly had withdrawn. Soon after, he embarked on a 12-month stint as an apprentice piano tuner, but soon grew bored and quit abruptly. He next worked in the home construction sector, but concluded that he lacked the aptitude for this endeavor. After this, he simply idled around town, but periodically traveled to the northern part of the state to visit friends in Michigan City and South Bend. Invariably, he stayed there for a couple of weeks until his money or his welcome had been depleted. More recently, under intense urging from his father, Will decided that he would next pursue medicine as his career objective, and planned to study with his uncle in his northern Indiana medical practice sometime in the near future.

In the meantime, he lolled around town, generally making a pest of himself. However, on this particular spring morning, Scott Jackson had sent Will on a mission. He had asked him to deliver a message to his friend and distant cousin, Pearl, who worked part time at her sister's millinery shop, selling hats and dresses. Entering the establishment, Will glanced around the premises for a moment, spotted Pearl and slowly strolled up to her, loudly proclaiming, "Well Cousin Pearlie, I have a new friend in town who can't wait to meet you."

Pearl frowned and quickly responded, "Will! First of all, you don't need to shout. I am not hard of hearing. And secondly, I don't need any 'new friends' who have been selected by you!"

Ignoring her sarcasm, Will continued, "Relax, Pearl. He's a high-caliber gentleman named Scott Jackson, who's studying dentistry with

Dr. Gillespie, an old classmate of his back at the Indiana Dental College. Scott told me he had seen this beautiful lady at the office the other day, and that Dr. Gillespie had divulged that it was you. Just this morning, Scott raved to me again how attractive you are!"

Pearl was flattered by Will's words, but also wary, since she was well aware of his glib tongue. Looking puzzled, she feigned disinterest, although she had taken the bait. "I didn't notice him when I was at the office last week" she said, lying accordingly. "How long will he be working with Dr. Gillespie?"

"He'll just be there temporarily. This fall he plans to resume his dental studies in Cincinnati. But I must tell you, my dear cousin, Scott certainly took notice of you. He's been in Greencastle less than a month and is from out east originally. He said that you looked quite charming sitting there in the dental chair, and he will leave no stone unturned until he makes your acquaintance. He's staying with relatives here until he enrolls in the Ohio Dental College. What do you say, Pearlie? Will you grant him his wish? The privilege of meeting you?"

Pearl hesitated, and then softened. "Well, I imagine he may be lonesome moving to town and not knowing many people. I suppose you could bring him over for lemonade and cookies next Sunday afternoon." Meanwhile, Pearl's mind was racing as she reflected on Will's words. "Is this fellow a big blow-hard like Will? Is he really going to become a dentist? Does he seriously think I'm attractive?" Unaware of Pearl's silent queries, Will grinned broadly. "Good. I'll do that very thing. We'll see you then."

Pearl awoke on Sunday with conflicted feelings. Will and Scott would be calling on her after dinner that afternoon. She knew that she would be decked out in her best clothes when she went to church. Oh, how she hated wearing all of her Sunday trappings. Being trussed up in a laced girdle for hours on end did not feel good. Neither did the hot thick stockings, cinched bodice, crinoline petty coats and flowing skirt. Her Sunday shoes hadn't been broken in yet and added to her discomfort. Collectively, all this finery was heavy enough to give one "the vapors.*" Nevertheless, she had to concede that her full length Victorian mirror reflected an attractive, well-dressed young woman.

---

* *During the Victorian era, women were usually considered as the 'weaker' sex. Under stress, they were said to be susceptible to "fainting spells, swooning, or 'the vapors'."*

Though she had some misgivings, Pearl still wanted to impress Scott –
and Will as well. Then she thought of Scott's piercing, violet eyes, and
her indecision was settled.

She would disregard the negatives. The dress would stay on. She was
determined to put aside her pessimistic preconceptions and give Scott
a chance to become her friend; but only if he behaved himself. Her
older brother, Fred, had met Scott previously, scornfully labeling him
"a dandy." Pearl smiled to herself and mused, "Scott is certain to be far
more interesting than any of the other single boys in town."

Will and Scott reached the Bryan farm in mid-afternoon. As Will
drove the horse and buggy into the driveway, Scott looked intently at
the rambling, white, wooden frame house punctuated by bright green
shutters. The home was situated back from the road, standing in the
midst of a clump of pines. "Not a bad place to live," he thought." As the
buggy pulled up to the front of the house, Pearl was demurely seated
on the front porch swing, sewing a quilt. She caught her breath as Scott
exited the carriage. Dressed in the very latest of fashion, a cape covered
his shoulders. He cut quite a dashing figure. The two men bounded
up the steps, and Will immediately introduced Pearl to Scott. Scott
surveyed her from head to toe, holding his gaze for a full 5 seconds.

"It's so nice to make your acquaintance, Miss Bryan. I've waited a
long time for this moment."

"How can that be, Mr. Jackson?' Pearl replied. "It's my understanding
that you've only been in town for a few weeks."

Quickly backtracking, Scott responded, "Oh, but I've heard all about
you from Will, and our friendship goes back a long way." Switching
to a more respectful approach, Scott proceeded cautiously, "May I
call you Pearl, Miss Bryan?" In a polite, but perfunctory tone, Pearl
assented. Now confident that he could break through her resistance,
Scott reverted to flattery. "Actually, though I like the name 'Pearl', I
don't think that it really fits you."

With tentative, but now piqued interest, Pearl inquired, "And what
name do you think fits me, Sir?"

"Amabel, a French endearment meaning 'my lovely.'"

Pearl ignored the contrived compliment, and steered their
conversation in a different direction. "Have you ever been to France?"

"Yes. Many times, Amabel."

Pearl countered: "My name is not Amabel, and I am not French!"

Will interjected, "Her friends often call her 'Bert'; she acquired the name when she was just a little girl. It was in honor of her Aunt Bertha."

Scott quickly reversed course. "My apologies. I didn't mean to be so forward and presumptuous. Please excuse my poor manners. I simply wanted to give you a sincere compliment. From the first moment I saw you, I was charmed, and it makes me very nervous now that I'm actually in your presence."

Pearl smiled forgivingly, even though his words could have come out of a cheap, romance novel. Scott returned to their prior conversation. "I meant to tell you, Pearl, that I have traveled extensively, ... from the Atlantic on the east coast to Liverpool and countless other ports. You see, my father was a sea Captain."

"WAS a sea Captain?" she queried

Soberly, Scott responded, "Yes. He died suddenly about 10 years ago."

Embarrassed by the answer to her somewhat brazen question, Pearl mumbled in a barely audible whisper, "Oh ..... I'm so sorry."

A moment earlier, Will had eased into the Bryan house, with the sole intention of making himself scarce, as he and Scott had previously planned. Scott then sat down on the swing, right next to Pearl. Her initial reaction was one of shock. "Has he no concept of the social graces?" she wondered. "A real gentleman would not take such liberties with a lady." However, since he made no further inappropriate advances, she began to relax. And thus they swung slowly back and forth, as the poorly lubricated hinges squeaked in protest. As they rocked, Scott said little, consistent with his plan to force Pearl to take the initiative in the conversation. To break the silence, Pearl did just that.

"I've always wondered what it would be like to spend time in a large city such as New York. How did you find it living there?"

Pleased that Pearl had not yet objected to his close proximity, Scott replied, "Wildly exciting, and full of many varied experiences. There are so many worthwhile undertakings to spend one's time: the theater, many museums, beautiful parks to stroll through, endless shops selling all kinds of goods ranging from ladies' fur coats down to the finest leather shoes. I really can't do justice to describing the city. I hope that someday you will see for yourself." Omitting the onerous details of the nefarious attractions that he had experienced in his life in New York,

Scott exchanged a knowing glance with Will, who had just returned to the porch from inside.

Considering what Scott had said, Pearl parried, "Then, you will probably not like it here. Nothing exciting ever seems to happen in Greencastle."

"I don't agree, Pearl," Will interrupted. "There's plenty of excitement around here. You just have to look for it, or create it." Deciding that it wasn't wise to gang up on Pearl, Scott remained silent.

Growing wary by the direction of the discussion, she wondered, "Why is Will arguing with me, and what does he mean when he says "create it?" Weary of her analysis, Pearl ended the topic, "Whatever you say, Will. Apparently, you have found it, and I haven't."

This time, Scott could not resist making a comment. Looking at her boldly, he said, "Don't be so sure, my dear young lady. You may have just found all of the excitement you could ever want."

Pearl considered the meaning of his vain comment, but made no response. Rather, she quickly changed the subject. "Why did you leave the east, Mr. Jackson?"

Scott lowered his head and sighed. "For my mother's sake. She wanted to get back to the Midwest where my sister lives. I didn't have the heart to disappoint her, even though it meant that I had to leave a lucrative job." Jokingly he added, "She may have even feared that the fast life on the east coast would eventually corrupt me!"

Will snickered, "No danger of that happening. Right, Dusty?"

Pearl knit her brow. "Dusty?"

"That's just an old nickname of mine," he explained. Scott suddenly frowned, leaned forward, very close to Pearl, and said, "But I wish you wouldn't call me Mr. Jackson."

Pearl looked baffled. "Why? Isn't that your name?"

Scott rolled his eyes and said, "Of course it's my name. But I'd like you to call me Scott …. or Dusty, for that matter. Those who are really close to me call me Dusty."

Looking away from him, Pearl responded, "I suppose I can call you Scott, but not Dusty. That name seems more appropriate for a pet dog than for a young man." She had made this cutting remark so spontaneously, that she even shocked herself, and wondered why she had blurted it out so readily.

Laughing off the remark, Scott suddenly stood, and looked into the parlor from the front porch. "Ah, I see a piano inside. Do you play, Pearl?"

Pearl had become a quite proficient pianist, but she demurred at the question. "I play from time to time, but my sisters are more talented than I," she answered. In truth, Pearl had taken lessons from her mother through her teen years just as her older sisters had.

Seizing the moment, Scott stood directly in front of her, gazed into her eyes, and said softly, "That may be so, but I'll bet there are some things you do much better than your sisters."

This ambiguous comment made Pearl uncomfortable. She thought, "It isn't so much what he just said, but how he said it."

A few moments later, Pearl's mother and her older sister, Jennie appeared from inside. Pearl introduced the two women to Scott and after exchanging pleasantries, Jane and Jennie made their way around the side of the house to the well, to pump water for cooking. Taking this gesture as a sign for them to depart, the two men bade their farewells.

"I hope to see you soon, Pearl," smiled Scott.

"Time will tell, Mr. Jackson, uh … I mean Scott," Pearl said from behind hopeful eyes.

Riding away in the buggy, the two young men were quiet. Finally, Will asked, "Well, what did you think of Pearl?"

"Your cousin is easy on the eyes, but a little feisty. I like that in a woman – hard to get. I'd like to get to know her better," ventured Scott.

"Come on old chum! Let's not kid one another. You'd love to bed her, wouldn't you? Especially if she is, like you said, hard to get. That would be quite a challenge for you," Will snickered.

"The truth? She's seems pretty naïve and inexperienced, so I'd likely have more fun in bed with the pillows, than with her," Scott laughed.

"Don't sell Pearl short, old buddy. If she weren't my cousin, I might go after her myself," Will responded.

The two friends were each lost in their own thoughts as the carriage swayed and the hooves clip-clopped rhythmically along the stone road. But Will's question remained with Scott as he contemplated his real intentions toward Pearl. In any case, he knew he would have to wait for just the right moment to make his next move with her.

As Pearl watched the buggy disappear over a hill, her emotions were equivocal. Although she found Scott to be quite brash and forward, he was also eloquent, exciting, and handsome. He seemed to have looked at her with unconcealed desire, and that felt disconcerting. But, she couldn't deny her attraction to him either. In his presence, her body became filled with a deep, yet unnamed longing. She had never before felt such a magnetic pull toward any young man. She was thrilled by his mysterious, probing eyes. But, she had just met him and she needed to slow down, and her common sense began to prevail. She had already observed irrefutable danger signs. Along with his brash and forward ways, he seemed arrogant and rather controlling, and he was just too sure of himself. She felt like she had to spar with him, just to "hold her own." But, he also seemed to be the kind of man who could bring some flavor to her mundane, predictable life. For the first time in a long while, Pearl dared to believe that she just might encounter some zest in her life through the efforts of this man, Mr. Scott Jackson.

Over the next several days, Pearl anticipated some contact from Scott, but none came. She wondered if she had offended him by expounding on his nickname, Dusty. Then, on Thursday, Will dropped by the dress shop once again.

"Pearlie," he grinned. "I've got a proposition for you. Dusty regularly attends church, and he'd like to meet you there this Sunday."

"But, how can I do that," protested Pearl.

"What do you mean?" chuckled Will. "Aren't people allowed to meet in church on Sunday?"

"Of course," said Pearl. "But my family always attends church together. You know that. And they hardly know that Scott exists."

"Pearl! You're twenty-two years old. Surely you can go to church just once without being surrounded by your entire family. Look. You all attend the Locust Street Methodist Church, so I'll pick you up on Sunday, and we'll go to the College Avenue Methodist Church and meet Scott there. That way, we'll avoid any complications. What do you say?" Pearl looked perplexed. "Just tell your family that you want to check out a different church with me for a change," said Will.

"I'll think about it, Will."

"I'll be by in my buggy to pick you up about 9:30 am on Sunday," beamed Will.

The next three days passed slowly for Pearl, and when she retired on Saturday night, it was with both hesitancy and anticipation regarding her next meeting with Scott. When morning arrived, it was unseasonably warm and sunny – a beautiful day. Will pulled up at the Bryan house sharply at 9:30 am.

As Pearl settled in the carriage, Will asked, "So, Pearl ... have you taken a shine to Dusty yet?"

"Why no, I've only spoken with him one time," she replied.

"Well, I think he's already stuck on you."

"Where did you get that idea? Did he say that? I doubt very much if he said so."

"Not in so many words, but he did say that he wants to get to know you much better."

Pearl reflected, "But is that what I want?" Pearl's conventional, safe side was confronting her raw emotions. The battle was wearing her out, so she simply concentrated on the passing scenery as the two of them rode toward Greencastle and the church.

They passed fields where countless cows, feeding on piles of golden hay, looked up at them dumbly as they rode by. As a cattle-raiser's daughter, she knew that these empty-headed animals had no idea of their future fate at the slaughterhouse, where they would be hammered on the skull and their throats slit. She hoped that they would be killed without ever knowing what hit them, and contemplated the thought of how awful it would be to witness your own violent death. That gruesome image jolted her back to reality.

Now they were passing the limestone quarries, which held slabs of piled up stone, waiting to be stacked on some wagon and delivered to their appointed destinations. As that scene faded from their view, they noticed the region's impressive stands of trees: maple, oak, beech, poplar, and hickory, not yet bursting into summer foliage. As Will and Pearl entered town, they saw 3-story limestone office buildings, including the Western Union headquarters located at 14 South Indiana Street. Pearl recalled that it had opened for business when she was ten years old. The twosome soon arrived at the College Avenue Methodist Episcopal Church, and secured their horse and buggy to a hitching post reserved for parishioners at the rear of the building. They had arrived just in time for the 10:30 am service. Sunday school was scheduled for 2 pm, and a 7 pm service was also traditionally held. Pearl often attended all three offerings at her own church. As they entered the building through a designated side door, Will made certain that Pearl was walking ahead of him. Thus, when they spotted Scott, who had spread his outer garments over the pew seats to save them, Pearl slid into the pew first, sitting next to him. She tried to leave a respectable distance between them, but Scott managed to edge toward her, imperceptibly.

Early into the service, Scott gradually slid his leg gently against Pearl's, and held it there. "This is no way to behave in God's house," Pearl thought critically, and shifted her leg away from the contact. However, her negative feelings were neutralized to a degree by the sense of excitement radiating from her pounding heart. From that moment on, she didn't hear a word that the pastor was saying. At the close of the sermon, the congregation sang several well-known hymns, including "The Sweet Bye and Bye," and "God Be With You Till We Meet Again." Pearl, a soprano who had sung in her high school choir and chorus, added her lyrical voice to the mix. She was surprised by Scott's dulcet tenor tones, and even Will joined in, singing vigorously, if not melodiously. The three of them harmonized with great enthusiasm, and to be heard, Pearl belted out her notes, as seldom before.

Will took Pearl directly home after the service, and departed. As the family ate fried chicken, gravy, green beans, biscuits and mashed potatoes for dinner, her father asked her what the sermon topic had been. She stammered, "Uh, it was mostly about sin, and the minister was against it."

Alexander Bryan smiled broadly. "I certainly hope so," he chuckled.

Late that afternoon, Will and Scott came calling on Pearl. As they drove up the long dirt road that lead to the farmhouse, they met Mr. Bryan, who was repairing a nearby fence. Even though the Sabbath was designated as a day of rest, the cattle must not escape and roam the countryside. And, of course, some barnyard chores could not be ignored, including feeding all the animals, and milking the cows. Will, who was driving, stopped the horse and buggy and walked over to his Uncle Alex. Scott followed, and introductions were made. Alex knew of the boys' previous visit, and Jane had told her husband privately of her concerns about Scott's apparent interest in Pearl. To Jane, he seemed worldly and a bit pushy - - a fast-mover. Yes, he was polite, and he said all the proper things. But sometimes his words came across as a well-rehearsed script. She felt they seemed too polished, and at times, insincere.

Nevertheless, for the moment, Alex laid aside any pre-conceived judgments he might have had, and gave Scott a hearty handshake. Then, in his characteristically deep, resonant voice, he said, "I'm pleased to meet you young man. And that's quite a fancy poncho you're wearin'!"

In turn, Scott replied with a deep grin, "I'm glad you like it, sir, and it's a great pleasure to make your acquaintance as well."

Hearing this faultlessly delivered response, Alex thought, "I can see what Jane means. He sounds and acts like a slick politician." However, feeling a little repentant about making such a hasty judgment, Alex continued, "And how do you feel about living in Greencastle Scott?"

"Well, for a small farm town, it's not too bad. I only had to set my watch back about 50 years when I got here." Scott laughed and was pleased with his witty response: he would need to remember this clever line and use it again. But contrary to Scott's expectation, Alex Bryan did not find the comment amusing, and couldn't help but take offense to such an obvious insult to his hometown.

Again taking the high road, he ignored the remark, commenting, "I understand that you are going to the Ohio Dental College in Cincinnati next fall."

With a look of complete confidence and with flawless enunciation, Scott declared: "Yes sir. That is indeed my plan. I am confident that I am sufficiently motivated and bright enough to be very successful in this endeavor, and in life in general." Scott was proud of his response, and felt that it contained elements of both self-assurance and humility.

Alex, however, believed otherwise. Having heard vague rumors about Scott's sudden departure from his Indianapolis school, he decided to verbally spar with him a little. "Folks around here have said that you were enrolled at the Indiana Dental College just a few months ago. I wonder why you are now in Greencastle?"

Not surprised by an inquiry such as this from "a local," Scott elaborated: "You know, that was a very unfortunate situation. I was doing quite well with my studies at Indianapolis, but I contracted some mysterious ailment in December. I was quite sick and the illness lasted so long, that I was forced to drop out of the Dental College."

Now fully into the verbal competition, Alex retorted, "That was a bad break for you. If you don't mind me asking, what was your ailment?" he queried.

"Well, based on my symptoms, my doctor had narrowed my infirmity down to three possibilities. But all these diseases had long, complicated names, which I couldn't even pronounce. Because he could never make a definitive diagnosis, he recommended that I take some vitamins, maintain a high fluid intake, and rest in bed. Unfortunately, I couldn't follow this regimen without leaving school. In any case, the physician's advice was beneficial. I'm better now than I ever was," said Scott with a grin.

"I'm pleased to hear of your miraculous recovery, Mr. Jackson, but I am curious about one more thing. I don't mean to pry into your affairs, but why are you changing dental schools? Indiana's school is highly regarded and closer to Greencastle."

Scott sensed another challenge to his credibility, so his answer had to be believable, if not accurate. He paused, and slowly responded, "Since the Ohio Dental College has offered me a generous scholarship, I feel obliged to accept it. You see, my father was a naval officer who passed on when I was just fourteen years old. He left a sizable inheritance to my mother, but I cannot in good conscience expect her to pay for all my educational expenses, when I have an opportunity to lessen the financial burden for her. I am also working with Dr. Gillespie in his office to help pay for my dental education."

Alex nodded noncommittally, and thought fleetingly that the fancy duds that Scott was sporting must have cost plenty. "Perhaps I'll see you again in town, Mr. Jackson. But as busy as you are, I'm sure you won't have time to visit us here very often," Alex emphasized. With a challenging look, he stared keenly into Scott's eyes. There was a distinct message attached to his intense gaze, but Scott failed to grasp it.

That evening, Alex chatted with his son, Fred. "Will introduced me to Scott Jackson this afternoon," he stated. "I know he's a good friend of Will's, but he seems to me like a real 'dandy,' with his just so proper manners, flashy clothes, and self-importance. I'm firmly convinced you should never trust a man dressed in a cape. I also didn't like him talking down to me, and what a line he was feeding me about being too sick to stay in school! Besides, I don't appreciate him suggesting that Greencastle is a small town stuck in time."

Fred thought for a moment before answering. "I've not really known you to judge others unfavorably without having a good reason. I barely know this guy Jackson, but I agree with you. And what's more, I'm not so shot with Will, either. You know that his father sent him to stay with relatives in South Bend last fall so that they could keep an eye on him for a few weeks. He hoped that after being around some good folks for a stretch, a little of that 'goodness' might rub off on Will. As far as I can see, though, it didn't turn out that way. Apparently, Will did a few chores around the place, and was fairly pleasant during the daytime. But at night, he would disappear and head to the local pool hall. I have heard that one night he came home tipsy, missed the top step, and made a big racket as he tumbled down the stairs. That was enough for the relatives. Being good Christian souls, they felt obliged to send Will back home and tell the whole story to his Pa. Pastor Wood was furious that in spite of being such a prominent figure in the church, he had once again been humiliated by Will's escapades. A good preacher presumably helps people to reform, but in this case, he can't even get his son to behave properly!"

Fred seethed inside, thinking that he wanted both Scott and Will to stay away from his sister. There was something really distressing to him about those two.

CHAPTER SIX

After supper that evening, Fred stopped by Pearl's room to speak with her. He began with a few benign questions. "Did you see anybody that you knew in church? Was the service any different than in our church? Had Will behaved properly? Speaking of Will," he added, "Even though he's in our family, he's not like the rest of us. He's never grown up; he gives his parents no end of trouble; and he's lazy! And how about the latest? He was 'farmed out' to some kind-hearted relatives this spring, and was kicked out of their home after only a couple of weeks! After Will left here today, I got to thinking about him, and about my short meeting with Scott Jackson. Look, Pearl. I truly believe that birds of a feather flock together. I have major reservations about this Jackson fellow." Fred reflected on the similar feelings expressed by his father earlier in the day.

Pearl glared at her brother, "You don't know anything about Scott! Just because he is a friend of Will's doesn't mean that he's like Will. In fact, I think Scott can help Will become a better person." She said this impulsively and defensively, and recognized that this 'savior' image of Scott might be a stretch. But however well meaning her brother intended to be, he was butting into her business. In a frosty tone, she continued, "You apparently have forgotten that I'm not a child, and am fully capable of making my own decisions. Goodnight, brother dear."

Taken back by the fervor of her response, Fred replied, "Sorry! I'll try to limit my advice to you in the future, if that's what you want. I'm only thinking of what's in your best interest, Sis."

Pearl's tone softened. "All right, Fred," she declared. "I realize that you only want to protect me, but, remember. I'm 22 years old – an adult! If I can't make reasonable decisions about my life by now, it's too late and I never will. Please stop worrying so much."

As Fred left the room, he smiled at Pearl amicably.

Over the next 6 weeks, Will and Scott returned to visit the Bryan farm on several Sunday afternoons. On these occasions, Alex and Fred generally were not present. In contrast, Pearl's older sister, Jennie, enjoyed the young men's visits and especially looked forward to conversing with Scott. While Jennie was fully informed about Will's shenanigans, she didn't see Scott as anything like her wayward cousin. Scott seemed to her to be refined and thoughtful – a far cry from the bumbling, awkward males she had grown up with.

Jennie confessed to Pearl, "I wish I had a beau who looked at me the way that Scott looks at you." She gushed further, "He's just so sophisticated and interesting. How can you resist him?"

Pearl blushed, and nodded with a smile. Though her feelings for Scott were still ambivalent, she agreed with Jennie. She was struck by how articulate Scott was when he described his past sailing experiences and his adventures in Europe. He seemed very worldly, and his charm was magnetic. However, she had her entire life to think about. Scott was such a slick talker. Romance might lead to marriage, children, housework, and the sacrificial life of a wife and mother. Whether a girl married a farmer or a professional man, her life would still be centered on home and hearth, and pleasing her man. Still, she was fascinated with Scott. When he stared at her, as he often did, she became anxious, and her senses heightened. She even got sweaty hands. His eyes seemed to probe deeply into her soul. His was a gaze that both attracted and frightened her.

At the moment, Pearl was unaware that Scott had other female attractions. During the summer of 1895, he and Will were making the rounds, visiting a number of Greencastle's finest families. They were quite selective, honing in on the most vivacious and pretty young ladies. One recipient of Scott's attention was Pearl's longtime and closest friend, Ida Hibbitt. In loyalty to Pearl, Ida didn't take the bait. Pearl had previously told her about Scott and Will's Sunday visits. Living in town, she also knew about some of their other evening calls, but had said nothing about this to Pearl. Ida was convinced that Pearl would find out, soon enough. The thought of Scott toying with Pearl's emotions angered Ida, and her opinion of him plummeted.

Although he was often away on Sunday afternoons, Alex Bryan was aware of Scott's continuing attention to Pearl. Although a trusting man by nature, he was becoming increasingly mistrustful of Scott's intentions. Fred had told Alex about his touchy encounter with Pearl, whose passionate response concerned Alex. However, he kept his reservations to himself. There was no reason to worry Jane about it needlessly.

On the evening of July 4, Will stopped at the Bryan farm at 7 pm. Pearl was expecting him. He had promised several weeks earlier to take her to the town's Independence Day fireworks spectacle. He was early, even though the display wouldn't begin until dark. When Pearl came downstairs, Will was sitting in the kitchen with Jennie. One glass of iced tea later, he was ready to go. The fireworks display was to be held in a large rock quarry, northeast of the Bryan's farm adjacent to the Monon Railroad tracks. After they left in the buggy, Will drove northwest. Pearl, thinking that he might be momentarily confused about his directions, told him that they were going the wrong way. Will quickly corrected her, "We're going back to the edge of town to get Scott. I won't be going along. Uh, it will just be you two."

Pearl's indignation rose. "So you and Scott just made these bogus plans together, without even consulting me? Am I too delicate and unenlightened to participate in decisions directly affecting me? I feel like a piece of luggage being traded from one train to another. I am a person, Will, not a thing! How could you have done this?"

Will was dumbfounded and silent. "My God," he thought. "What man can ever read the mind of a woman? I thought she would be pleased, getting a chance to be alone with Scott. Now what do I do?"

Will finally regained his senses, and began his obligatory explanations. He told her that their plans had been made with only the best of intentions, and he apologized profusely. He assured Pearl that such an error in judgment would never be made again. By this time they had arrived at Seminary Street where they could see the clock tower of DePauw University's East College Building. Frustrated, she reflected on how different her life might be if she were a full-time student at the University. The evening remained warm, breezeless, sultry, and close. Pearl could see beads of perspiration on her companion's forehead and the back of his neck. She felt justified in having expressed her anger to Will, and yet she recognized how pleased she was that Scott wanted to be alone with her, and she thought how complicated communications with the opposite sex always seemed to be. Fleetingly, she considered how much more relaxed everything could be if such conversations could just be honest and straightforward. Then, silently, she began to devise an appropriate response to Scott when she saw him.

Vintage postcard (The Albertype Co., Brooklyn, N.Y.) displaying the Class Arch at De Pauw University. The brick and iron ornamental gateway is located on Locust Street and opens onto the lawn of East College. It was presented in 1910 as a gift from the class of 1890 at their 20ᵗʰ reunion.

Will pulled the carriage over and tied the horse loosely to a cast iron hitching post jutting upward from the ground. The evening was breezeless and sultry and Pearl could feel perspiration beginning to gather on her forehead. Scott came into view, sauntering toward them, anticipating that he would receive a warm greeting and a smile from Pearl. But Will's edgy demeanor told him that this was not to be. Pearl sat stony faced, while Will dismounted from the carriage, and walked back to Scott, out of her vision. Will quickly related to Scott what had happened. "You need a new plan, old buddy. Pearl is really aggravated that we hatched up this scheme without even consulting her. A heartfelt apology might be your best play right now."

Scott considered his options and thought, "This Pearl is one feisty character! I wonder if she is worth the hassle?" Looking chagrined and remorseful, Scott walked to Pearl's side of the buggy and asked humbly, "Miss Pearl, may I see you to the quarry alone?"

Pearl's nod in the affirmative was almost indiscernible, but she added, "I will not be taken for granted, Mr. Jackson. I hope you have learned that."

Knowing that he must be at his 'silver-tongued' best for the next several hours, Scott hiked up to the driver's seat, took the reigns, and pointed the horse east along Franklin Street and ultimately to the quarry. On the way, Pearl admonished him further regarding his and Will's ruse. He made no excuses and took his penance bravely, confident that this tempest would blow over. But he recognized that there might not be any romance tonight. Regardless, he wouldn't give up easily! Holding the reins, he drove east along Franklin Street toward the quarry.

Turning to Pearl, he spoke haltingly, "Pearl, I can't lie. I'm infatuated with you. I don't know how else to say it. I think about you all the time, and just had to find a way to be alone with you. I am very sorry if that offends you!"

"How many other ladies have you told that to recently?" questioned Pearl, with a slight twinkle in her eye.

"No one, Bert. Absolutely no one," Scott answered looking very serious.

"That's not what my friend Ida tells me," countered Pearl. "She says you have even called on her several times."

"Pearl," protested Scott. "I'm just trying to make some friends and acquaintances in my new hometown. Ida doesn't mean anything to me, and I've never told her that she does."

The twosome drove on in silence as Scott directed the mare toward the quarry. Suddenly, he steered the buggy north onto a little traveled grassy lane and reigned in the horse.

"Well, Pearl. Finally I can be alone with you, and I think we should commence your introduction to new excitement and pleasure in your life" said Scott, sliding his right arm around her shoulders, and pulling her toward him. Leaning toward her, he brought his lips forcefully upon hers. Pearl was taken aback, but in spite of her self, she responded and settled into his arms.

Suddenly, Scott placed his hand at her waist, and then slid it upward along the cloth of her dress just under her breast.

"Scott!" she gasped, jerking out of his embrace. "What are you doing? Stop it!"

"Pearl," he answered. "We both know that this is what you want. Just enjoy it!"

Struggling out of his embrace, she barked, "I mean it Scott! Take your hands off of me this minute!"

Scott looked at Pearl incredulously, his face contorted in anger. "For God's sake, you naïve little bumpkin. You must be joking. If you'd just relax a little, I know you'd be grateful for what I can do for you."

Tears welled up in Pearl's eyes. "You're no gentleman. You simply masquerade as one. Take me home, right now!"

"I'd be happy to you little tease," Scott replied with a sneer. "I thought you were a grown woman! I didn't realize you were such an immature child!" he snapped.

For 10 minutes they rode in silence, interrupted only by Pearl's occasional sob. Finally, the Bryan farm came into view.

"Let me out right here," her voice quivered.

Scott obliged, and watched her stumble as she left the cab, and then headed toward her house. He shook his head, and smirked while thinking, "There'll be a different outcome next time, Miss 'Pure Pearl.' I always get what I want, and I'm going to play you like a fiddle. You can count on it."

Pearl bolted from the carriage in tears, and dashed the 50 yards to her front porch. Angry, disappointed and puzzled, Scott wheeled the buggy around in the direction of Greencastle, and spurred the horse to a gallop. Pearl burst into the house, and rushed upstairs toward her room. As she passed Jennie's open door, she saw her sister in her bed, propped up with pillows. She was in her nightclothes.

"Pearl," called Jennie, "what's wrong?"

Pearl smoothed her clothing, took a deep breath, and went to Jennie's bedside. It was not typical of her sister to retire so early. As Pearl looked down at the young woman, she noticed that Jennie's eyes looked glassy and her brow was dotted with beads of sweat. Touching her forehead, Pearl exclaimed, "Jennie, you have a temperature! Is that why you're in bed so early?" she asked, leaning down to look in her ailing sister's eyes.

I'm not feeling well," Jennie replied hoarsely. "I have a headache, and I just feel exhausted. I'm all played out, so I thought I'd just turn in early this evening. Maybe I just need a good night's sleep to feel better. Tomorrow I'll probably be back to my old self again." Wanting to field no more questions regarding her health, she shifted the focus to Pearl: "I can see that all is not well with you either, dear sister. Tell me why? What happened tonight?"

Pearl hesitated, and seemed to be struggling for the right words. "Let's just say that Scott Jackson is no gentleman, and I won't be seeing him again!"

Jennie was puzzled. "But you were with Will, tonight, not Scott. Right? How did you wind up in Scott's company?"

Pearl, now crying softly, lay down next to Jennie. "I did leave with Will. I understood that just the two of us were going to the fireworks display. But, he and Scott apparently made other plans behind my back. One the way there, Will took the buggy down a side road to a lane where Scott was waiting, and departed, leaving just the two of us alone. Even then, things were fine until Scott kissed me and put his hands all over me. That's when I made him bring me home."

Jennie sat up in bed. "Sis ... you've got to calm down and get control of your emotions. Maybe you misunderstood Scott's intentions. There's absolutely no excuse for his behavior, but he's just a man, and you know how they can blunder along without quite knowing what they're doing. But you're home now, and evidently, nothing horrible has happened to you!"

Pearl sat on her sister's bed and smiled through her tears. "You're right Jen," she said as she kissed her on the forehead. "I'll take your advice. Now you just lie back down and get better, you hear?"

Pearl slept fitfully that night, replaying the episode with Scott repeatedly in her mind and examining the event from every conceivable angle. At daybreak, she arose, feeling better about what had happened the previous evening, and even rationalized, "Well, at least he must find me attractive." She ate breakfast alone at the kitchen table, consuming ham, biscuits, a soft-boiled egg and tea. After concluding her meal, she suddenly remembered that she had to help her mother churn butter this particular Friday. Just thinking about that chore made her arms ache. The Bryans had a wooden barrel churn and a vertical plunger they used to make the butter. After placing the cream into the cask, the Bryan children had to take turns raising the plunger and then pushing it down quickly and with force, repeating the process in one-second cycles until the butter began to form. This might take 30 minutes or longer. Jennie, Pearl and Jane had been scheduled to share this task today, but with Jennie ill, there would be only two sets of arms to complete this arduous task.

On tiptoes, Pearl quietly climbed the stairs to Jennie's room and peeked in, but her sister was still asleep. After a moment, she saw Jennie stir and gently touched her forehead. It was quite warm. As her sister awakened and raised her head, Pearl exclaimed, "Jennie! Your fever is worse! I think we'd better call the doctor."

Jennie shook her head negatively and rolled over on her side. "Don't worry, Pearl," she whispered huskily. "I'll be fine by tomorrow."

Pearl countered, "I'm going to make you some willow tea. Remember how much that tea helped lower Mama's fever last winter?" Pearl went down to the kitchen, and removed some pieces of willow bark from a sealed jar in the cabinet. She boiled the bark in water for 15 minutes, added lots of honey, and took the beverage up to Jennie, who grimaced as she took her first sip of the bitter tea.

"Not that I've ever drunk any, but I think this stuff must taste worse than cat urine, but if it will help me feel better, I guess I can drink it. Thanks Pearl. You are a gem! And it looks like you are feeling a little more chipper this morning."

Exiting the room, Pearl smiled and replied, "Well, yes. Maybe just a little bit."

That evening, Dr. Blades made a house call at the Bryan home to examine Jennie. Afterwards, he told the family that she seemed to have a bad cold, or perhaps a touch of "the grippe." He prescribed bed rest and the intake of lots of fluids. Pearl retired that evening feeling more optimistic concerning Scott's intentions toward her, and hopeful that her sister's health would soon improve.

Regrettably, when the next morning dawned, Jennie had developed aching joints and muscles, as well as a sore throat. Her parents grew visibly worried about their daughter, and Jane prepared an asafidity (camphor) bag to pin to Jennie's nightgown. Such a remedy had been widely used in America since colonial times. To serve as a treatment for influenza and the like, asafidity, a herbaceous perennial plant, was soaked in camphor, made into a paste with goose fat, wrapped up in a little bag, and worn around the neck. Jennie obediently placed the odiferous bag around her neck, but suggested that this treatment was worse than the disease. She discarded it under her bed within the hour.

On Monday July 8, Jennie was stricken with a dry, hacking, unproductive cough, and her father presented her with a mixture of hot water, honey and a small amount of whiskey to drink. Predictably, this concoction did not lesson her symptoms nor provide her any relief. In the meantime, Pearl anticipated that Scott would contact her with an apology, or at least express some regret for his inappropriate past behavior. However, he made no effort to speak to her at all during the following week. She began to think that she had been hasty in her reaction to Scott's advances, and discovered that she couldn't even clearly recall the exact details of their encounter in the carriage. Perhaps Scott's actions were normal for a healthy young man who was experienced in love, and somehow she was to blame for their quarrel. She couldn't deny that she wanted Scott to have feelings for her, and she hoped that she hadn't destroyed those feelings by her negative reaction to him. When she searched her heart, she knew she was feeling something for Scott that she had never experienced before.

But Pearl was worrying less about Scott, and much more about Jennie, who couldn't seem to shake off her illness. On Sunday, July 14, Jennie took a turn for the worse. She developed a severe, unrelenting cough, a worsening fever, and bouts of chills, which made her shake violently. Her breathing was becoming labored and Dr. Blades was again summoned, but he could neither make a definitive diagnosis, nor suggest effective medications. Having already lost 4 siblings to early deaths, Pearl was becoming frantic.

On Tuesday, July 16, Jennie's skin began to take on a yellow hue. Dr. Blades was clearly alarmed, and told the family that the "jaundice" could be indicative of liver damage and possibly failure. The next day, Jennie's extremities began to swell noticeably. The doctor feared that her kidneys were also compromised. On Friday, July 19, Jennie fell into a coma, with each breath accompanied by a raspy rattle emanating from her lungs. Family and close friends were swiftly summoned to the Bryan home, and sadly arrived just in time to witness Jennie's death on Saturday morning the 20th of July. News of the latest Bryan child to die swept through Greencastle that evening and the entire community was distraught.

CHAPTER SEVEN

Although the Bryan family was devastated by Jennie's sudden death, Pearl was absolutely disconsolate. Her sister was merely two years older than she, and had been her closest confidante in the family. For the first four days after her demise, Pearl retreated behind her bedroom door, and showed no interest in either food or communication. Following Jennie's public viewing, funeral, and burial at the family plot, Pearl felt completely empty and angry. Each time that she had lost a close family member, her religious faith had been severely tested. But this time was different. Pearl began to question God's existence, and thought that even if there was a God, she wanted no part of a supreme being who repeatedly took delight in the death of the people who meant most to her. Silently, she thought, "If life is repeatedly so unfair and brief, why not live it fully and without heed to society's arbitrary and often absurd dictates?"

On Saturday morning, July 27, Scott and Will met for lunch at a local diner, and discussed Jennie's unexpected death. Scott commented, "Pearl and Jennie were real close. I figure that Miss 'Pure Pearl' will need some serious consoling of her grief right about now." Will took on a puzzled countenance and shook his head in amazement at Scott's gall. "Something tells me that you are about to enter the 'hands-on' compassion business, my young chum," he quipped.

Two days later, Scott borrowed Will's horse and buggy and drove out to the Bryan farm to pay a call. Pearl was alone in the house at the time and initially was very cool in her response to him.

Pearl asked with a slight frown, "You haven't contacted me for weeks. Why are you coming around now?"

Scott responded, "Pearl, I apologize for my past behavior, but if you would just listen to what I have to say for 5 minutes, I would be much obliged."

Pearl silently led him into the parlor, and somberly declared, "Well, go on. Let's hear it."

"My dear Miss Bryan. I truly regret hurting you, and am very sorry for your loss. I know what a wonderful person Jennie was, and how much you miss her. No one will ever replace her, but we both know that she would want you to move on with your life and not cut yourself off from those who care about you most. Can't you and I start again with a clean slate? I am simply offering you my friendship. It will be your choice. You can see as much or as little of me as you like. What do you say?"

"I don't know, Scott. I can't answer you this very moment. I appreciate your concern, and will certainly consider what you said and let you know my thoughts at a later time" Pearl said guardedly. She bid Scott farewell, and watched his buggy recede down the road. She noticed the dust arising from behind it, and pondered, "Who is the real Scott Jackson? The clod who insulted me on the 4th of July, or the gentleman I just spoke with?" Several times over the next couple of weeks, Scott, sometimes accompanied by Will, visited Pearl at the Bryan home. On each occasion, he was extremely supportive, and behaved impeccably. Pearl's trust in the young man was gradually being restored.

In mid-August, a touring Chautauqua came to Greencastle. Chautauqua was a community-based cultural and social movement that permeated rural America during the latter part of the 19th century, and the first part of the 20th century. These touring productions offered lectures, comedy, music, dance, drama, and other forms of education and artistic enrichment. Dozens of these touring groups flourished in the Midwest during the summer months when they performed under the protection of gigantic tents, and presented their diverse entertainment choices to their rapt audiences. Pearl and Ida Hibbitt had made plans to attend the Chautauqua together on a Friday evening.

As they waited to enter the tent, Scott Jackson sauntered by and tipped his cap, "Good evening ladies. It's my extreme good fortune to see Greencastle's two prettiest ladies right here in the same spot." Looking directly into Pearl's eyes, he whispered, "Please meet me outside at the back of this tent in about an hour." Scott quickly entered the tent, and Ida asked Pearl with a quizzical look, "What did he say to you?"

Pearl replied with a shake of her head, "Oh, nothing much. I'll tell you more about it later."

As they found their seats, Ida whispered to Pearl, "Be careful of that Scott Jackson, Pearl. I'm not sure you can rely on him. He's a slippery one!"

Pearl's cheeks flushed, and her neck turned a splotchy red. She was silent for a moment, and then, plunging into the discourse, she replied, "Granted that Scott has some faults, but he also has lots of good points. He carries himself with the air of a sophisticated gentleman, unlike most of the immature boys who live around here."

"I don't know, Pearl," Ida continued. "Scott is quite a dandy, but can you really trust him? I have a feeling there are many women in his past."

Pearl looked about her to see that no one was listening, and murmured, "But Ida, even if you are right, people can change. If Scott realizes that I really care for him, he'll become more responsible and less wild. I just know he can change. Don't you think so?"

Ida smiled sadly, and answered, "Pearl. I know you've thought a lot about this, but please don't ask me questions for which you don't want a truthful answer."

Pearl hesitated, then slowly shook her head. "You may be right, Ida, and I am probably being silly. At this point I don't even know how much I care for Scott, but let's talk about something else now."

Pearl grew silent, but her mind was racing as she watched the slapstick comedy routine that was developing on stage. What should she do when the time had elapsed; ignore Scott's request, or excuse herself and go outside to meet him? The minutes dragged by, and when an hour had finally passed, Pearl took a deep breath, told Ida that she would be back shortly, and slipped out into the warm, humid night. As she made her way to the back of the tent under the starlight, she saw Scott waiting for her with a broad smile playing on his lips.

"What is it, Scott?" a puzzled Pearl immediately asked. "What do you want to tell me?"

Scott replied, "I have something for you that my father brought back from one of his trips to Europe. It is a blue opal ring. I've had it for years, and have been waiting to give it to someone really special." Pearl stood in stunned silence, so Scott pressed on. "It is said to be a healing stone; a stone of hope. There are no obligations in accepting it,

79

but you are very dear to me, so I want you to have it and I pray it will help heal some of your grief."

Pearl struggled with her reply. Her brain wanted to say that she couldn't accept such a gift; her legs wanted to escape into the Chautauqua tent; but her heart wanted to throw her arms around Scott and kiss him. A few words finally tumbled out of her mouth, "Scott, I just don't know how to respond."

Scott countered, "Look, Pearl. If it would make you more comfortable, let's just say I'm loaning you the ring to help you deal with your sorrow. You can certainly return it to me later, if you wish. Allow me to put it on your finger, and let's see how it looks." Obediently, Pearl held out her right hand, and Scott slipped the ring on her little finger.

"It is lovely, Scott," whispered Pearl.

"I hoped you would like it," Scott replied, gently placing his fingers on her cheek for a moment. "I have to go now, but I will see you again very soon."

During the next two weeks, Scott borrowed Will's horse and buggy for several clandestine meetings with Pearl. The first took place in Pearl Bryan's parlor on a Sunday afternoon. The majority of Pearl's family had gone to the adjacent county to visit relatives, and the rest of them were not at home. Pearl and Scott had a lengthy but innocuous conversation about assorted topics, including mutual friends and acquaintances, Greencastle politics, a circus which was coming to town soon, and many of Scott's travel experiences in Europe. The conversation then shifted and Scott began encouraging Pearl to evolve from her predictable life in Greencastle, and to "sprout her wings and fly." He ended by saying, "Pearl, if you don't get a little adventure in your soul, a decade from now you will still be teaching Sunday School and caring for the orphans, just as you are now, but you'll be ten years older."

Pearl protested, "I can think of far worse things I could be doing!"

But, she was thrilled to hear Scott's next words, "You, know, Bert, since coming to Greencastle, I've been thinking more and more of settling down, and eventually getting married and starting a family." Scott said no more about the topic, but the two parted with Pearl's hopes soaring.

Their next meeting took place at an abandoned farmhouse known to Scott and located some 5 miles southeast of Greencastle. He drove the little buggy to the rear of the dull gray, dilapidated house, which was fully shaded by a stand of elm trees, beneath which flowed a small, gurgling brook. Scott again told Pearl that she needed to make some changes in her life. He told her that French women were much more liberal in their behavior than were women in America. He added that someone as beautiful as she would be wasting her life simply sitting in Greencastle waiting for romance that might never come. He kissed her tenderly, and she responded. He smiled at her and said he had never met anyone as enticing as she, and suggested that she might be the young lady he would like to spend his life with some day.

They made plans to meet surreptitiously for a picnic on Sunday, September 1. Pearl told her mother that she would be with her friend, Ida, who would be picking her up. Instead Pearl walked to the end of the driveway and met Scott, who once again had borrowed Will's horse and buggy. It was a cloudless, sunny afternoon. Pearl had packed sandwiches, and Scott had a blanket and two bottles of French wine that he had been saving for a special occasion. They sat down on the blanket behind the ramshackle farmhouse at their usual meeting place. Pearl tried to be cheerful, but thoughts of her recently deceased sister crept into her memory. She could not stop thinking about Jennie, and the pain associated with her loss. Scott placed his arm around her, and asked what he could do to help.

Pearl cried softly. "Nothing. Just hold me a while."

After she had stopped crying, Scott poured two glasses of wine, handed one to her, and smiled, saying "This will help you feel better."

They sipped their wine and chatted intimately for the next hour, and Pearl's good spirits gradually returned. She hesitated, and then consented to a second glass of wine. As she slowly sipped from the glass, Scott told her he thought he was falling in love with her, and that it hurt him to see her so sad.

"Scott, please don't say things you don't mean, nor make promises that you can't keep," she murmured.

Scott looked into her eyes, placed his lips on hers, and Pearl surrendered to his strong embrace, the intoxicating spirits, and the tide of emotions that swirled within her. As she lay back on the blanket, the sun shone brightly in her eyes, forming a pinwheel of color and blinding her temporarily. As she yielded fully to his advances, Pearl thought, "I'm not going to postpone living my life any longer." She was at least fleetingly confident that she had found the source of her future happiness, and she was going to hold onto it.

"East Washington Street Drive" Greencastle, Indiana.

Vintage postcard circa 1900 showing East Washington Street Drive,
Greencastle, Indiana. Some of Pearl and Scott's surreptitious buggy rides were
taken along this dirt road, which today is a busy east-west thoroughfare.

Published by the Indiana News Company, Indianapolis, Indiana

When he returned Will's horse and buggy after being with Pearl, Scott promptly bragged about his conquest, describing the entire event in graphic detail. Will was both saddened and impressed by his friend's revelation, pressing Scott for even more of the particulars. "The little bimbo actually thinks I'm interested in marrying her, " Scott said with a smirk. "But it will be a cold day in hell before I settle down with a wife in some little frame house and become a Hoosier for the rest of my life," he added in a very sarcastic tone.

A week passed before Scott next borrowed Will's horse and buggy to call on Pearl, at a predetermined time when they could be alone. Picking her up at the end of the driveway, he suggested that they take a short ride again out to the abandoned farmhouse.

Pearl said, "We made a big mistake the last time we were together, and that's not going to happen again. My family would be mortified if they knew what I had done!"

Scott replied, "Well let's at least take the short ride out there so that we can talk privately."

Pearl finally consented, and he held her arm as she mounted the buggy. Once they reached their destination, Scott produced the blanket and they walked arm-in-arm to the site of their past indiscretion. Scott's sweet-talk, charm, and scheming soon lead Pearl to do the unimaginable once again. Dusty had learned one lesson quite well at an early age: that with many of the women in his life, a small lie or two accompanied by an engaging smile and the right words invariably produced the outcome he wanted. As he held the reins on the way back to Pearl's house, she looked at him with a mixture of affection and anxiety.

"Dusty. We've got to begin some serious discussions about our future together. I can't continue this way, deceiving all the people I really care about. Besides, it's just a matter of time until someone catches us. That would be a disaster for both of us!"

Scott frowned and said nothing for a long moment, and then replied, "I don't know, Bert. Let me think about it a little while. I've got a lot on my mind right now, and I'll be leaving town to attend dental school in just about three weeks."

Once he had dropped Pearl off at the entrance to her driveway, and was back in Greencastle, Scott made a decision. It was unfortunate, but the pleasure he was deriving from being with Pearl was not worth the hassle and risk to his future. He would simply avoid seeing her until he departed for Cincinnati, and then maybe she would just gradually forget about him. Yes, he thought. That was exactly what he would do.

As luck would have it, Scott encountered Pearl outside a Greencastle shoe store on Friday morning, September 20. She looked distressed as she whispered to him, "Why haven't you come to see me? Is something wrong? Don't you care about me?"

Scott answered curtly, "I've been very busy."

Pearl insistently pushed on, "I've got to talk to you about our future, Dusty. Pick me up Sunday afternoon about 3 pm at my driveway."

Scott glared. "What exactly do you want from me? Are you listening? I'm a very busy man right now."

Pearl snapped, "Just be there! Unless you want me to tell my brothers that you seduced me," she added.

Jackson agreed reluctantly, and found himself with Pearl two days later at the abandoned farmhouse. As they talked in the buggy, she was adamant that they needed to make marriage plans, or at least become engaged. But Scott was unwavering, reiterating that his only immediate goal was to attend dental school in Cincinnati.

Pearl glared at him, protesting, "You lied to me Scott! You've been misleading me all along, whenever it's convenient for you."

Unflustered, Scott replied, "A lie is just the truth which has been slightly disguised. Your problem is that you only hear what you want to hear!"

In response, Pearl started crying softly, and asked, "So you don't really love me?"

Scott answered, "I didn't say that, but I need to take you home now. I have some business to take care of, but we can talk more about this later."

Pearl sighed deeply, and tried using all her guile and charm to dissuade him from leaving, and Scott gradually weakened in his resolve to leave. Later in the afternoon after taking Pearl home, Scott returned to Greencastle deep in thought. He decided that his dalliance with Pearl must end immediately. He felt as though she was suffocating him. He didn't need this and vowed to not see her again.

On October 3, 1895, Scott left home to begin his first semester of studies at the Ohio College of Dental Surgery, traveling the 175 miles southeast to Cincinnati by train. At the time, Cincinnati was a booming steamboat port located on the Ohio River, but widespread corruption was flourishing in its political system, and George "Boss" Cox was in the midst of his 30-year run as the leading political force in the city. Much of the downtown area was wide open and crime-infested. The neighborhood teemed with saloons, gambling joints, pool halls, and brothels. Pedestrians were obliged to watch their steps very carefully, because piles of horse manure often littered the streets, accompanied by hordes of buzzing flies. Many of the residents in the area were of questionable character, and rowdiness and disorderly scuffles often erupted in the streets. But this kind of background suited Scott well. It created a milieu in which he could satisfy his hunger for gambling, boozing and womanizing.

His mother fervently hoped that his academic endeavors in the Queen City would prove more fruitful than they had been at the Indiana Dental College a year earlier. As she had done on many prior occasions, Sara Jackson cautioned her son, "This may be your last chance to be the success your father would have wanted. Don't waste the opportunity."

Immediately upon arriving in Cincinnati, Jackson settled briefly at a local YMCA, while he looked for a more permanent place to live. He soon rented a room in a local boarding house at 222 West Ninth Street, across the street from City Hall. His elderly landlady, Mrs. McNevin, raved to him about the high quality of the other gentlemen living in her establishment, and assured him that she always took very good care of her boarders.

Meanwhile, Scott's chum, Will Wood, had made plans to move north to South Bend, where in January he was to begin the study of medicine under the tutelage of his uncle, a physician there. The two young cronies had agreed to carry on a written correspondence while they were living apart in different cities, and they began to exchange letters on a fairly regular basis.

On Friday, October 11, Scott left his boarding house and walked the few blocks to the dental school, where he was to register for classes. Entering the 3-story, gray stone building, he glanced around, seeing many other students gathered there. Across the room, and leaning against the opposite wall, he spied a familiar face: Alonzo Walling, a former classmate of his at the Indiana Dental College. Lonnie was a full seven years younger than Jackson, stood about 5'9", and weighed 150 lbs. On this day he was clean-shaven, and had dark hair and hazel eyes that were housed under heavy eyebrows that almost met in the middle of his forehead just above his pug nose. His distinct eyebrows and general facial morphology gave him both a somewhat eccentric, yet serious appearance.

Like Scott, Alonzo had attended the Indiana Dental College program in Indianapolis in 1894-1895, but had been forced to withdraw after only one year of study due to insufficient financial resources. Prior to his dismissal from the Indiana dental program, Dusty had attended classes with Lonnie for two months, and was well acquainted with him. Lon had discovered that Scott was a very worldly 26 year old, who had lived in the New York City region many years, had traveled to the European continent many times, and who frequently bragged of his many affairs with assorted women. Walling hoped that some of Jackson's worldliness might rub off on him, and as a result, he eagerly sought his company. The two men had a history in downtown Indianapolis of gambling, drinking, partying, and general carousing. Sometimes, Scott would mesmerize Alonzo with tales of his past exploits and feminine conquests. It was in "Naptown" that Scott had introduced Alonzo to several of his woman friends, some of whom were "ladies of the night." Lon was less experienced than Scott in these sorts of escapades, but was eager to learn, and soon became an apt student.

When Alonzo was forced to leave Indianapolis because of his accumulating debts, he returned to Greenfield, Indiana, and for six months, was employed by Dr. Rothenbush, a local dentist. By October 1895, Walling could afford to resume his dental studies, this time at the Ohio College of Dental Surgery, and so he had moved to Cincinnati to register for the fall semester. Meanwhile, his mother rented rooms in her home in Greenfield in order to earn extra money to help finance Lon's education.

Alonzo was born in 1875 on a small farm near Mt. Carmel, Franklin County, Indiana. His father, Samuel, was a physician, and his mother, Sarah, was immersed in her role as homemaker and mother to three rambunctious young boys. The Wallings were devout Methodists, who attended church regularly and supported it financially. Moreover, they had been sufficiently absorbed in church life to name their third son after their minister, Alonzo Murphy.

At the time, Brookville was the largest town in Franklin County, and claimed a number of noteworthy individuals who were either born, or had lived there. These included four pre-Civil War Indiana governors;

as well as Lew Wallace, Civil War General and the author of Ben Hur; and famous Midwestern artist, T. C. Steele, who frequently stayed in Franklin County to paint its lovely, scenic landscapes.

In the 19th century, poet Mary Louisa Chitwood was another well-known Mt. Carmel resident. Born in 1832, Miss Chitwood was raised and lived her entire life in Franklin County. Her first poem was published when she was just 12 years old, and by the time of her unexpected death at age 23, she was considered one of the premiere writers and poets in the Midwest. Sarah Walling particularly enjoyed poetry, and sometimes read some of Chitwood's poems to Alonzo when he was a young lad. Although he had never especially cared for it, he remembered well one of his mother's favorites, entitled *"The Graves of Flowers."*

> *"Upon no stone is carved the name,*
> *Of April's children fair;*
> *They perished when the sky was bright,*
> *And gentle was the air.*
> *To the soft kisses of the breeze*
> *They held half trembling up.*
> *Full many a small transparent urn*
> *And honey-ladened cup."*

When Alonzo was 3 years old, his father had died after a lengthy illness, and was buried nearby in the Mt. Carmel Wesley Chapel cemetery. Alonzo's two older brothers, Charles and Clinton, were forced to work part-time as farm hands to supplement the family income. Although the four surviving Wallings managed to eke out a living in Mt. Carmel for several years, Sarah eventually moved her family northwest to Greenfield, Indiana. When Alonzo was 13, he was employed part time in the Greenfield Fruit Jar and Bottle Company. He worked there for 4 years while attending Greenfield high school, ultimately saving enough money to enter the Indiana Dental College in the fall of 1894.

After spotting Alonzo across the room, Scott walked over to him, slapped him on the back, and grinned.

"Hello, Wally, old man. I didn't expect to see you here."

Alonzo smiled, reminisced for a moment, and asked where he was staying.

Scott answered, "I'm boarding at a place just a few blocks southeast of here. It's right next door to Robinson's Opera House.* Look, if you don't have a place to live yet, move in with me. We'll have some good times together and we'll both save some money."

Alonzo thought for a moment before replying, "Well, why not?"

A day later, the two dental students were lounging in their room about 4 pm, when Scott looked up suddenly and asked Alonzo, "You like music, don't you? Maybe you'd like to go with me to hear the Rev. Dwight Moody** preach tonight. He has a famous Gospel singer with him, and I've promised my dear mother to mend my ways and 'find religion.' I just received a letter from her, telling me all about this Moody fellow. She really wants me to attend."

Alonzo looked at him quizzically. "Are you serious? I ain't going to listen to some ole preacher, tonight or any night!"

Scott nodded and smirked irreverently. "We won't go then. Let's just don't and say we did. My mother will never know the difference. Besides, I need to wet my whistle at the tavern a lot more than I need to listen to some Bible-thumper's sermon," he added, chuckling. "What of any importance could I learn from Rev. Moody?"

In mid-November, Pearl Bryan had major concerns back in

* *Robinson's Opera House was positioned immediately across the street from City Hall near the intersection of Ninth and Plum Streets. John Robinson, a celebrated 19th century circus manager constructed the building in 1872. The four-story brick and stone edifice contained a large auditorium on the ground floor which could seat up to 1500 people, and frequently hosted performances of opera, drama, and Sunday church. A cellar and sub-cellar extended under the entire building, and had been designed to house Robinson's circus animals and menagerie in the winter months. There, costumes, wagons, cages, props and other equipment were made and repaired, and posters and programs printed for the new season. During these periods, it was not unusual to detect the unpleasant odor of the throngs of circus animals housed in the bowels of the building. Each April, a new circus season opened with a week of shows presented in the city. On October 15, 1898, at 8:30 pm, two years after Jackson had been living next door, the dome of the building suddenly collapsed into the interior, killing three people and injuring more than thirty. The establishment ultimately fell into disuse, was demolished and replaced with a filling station in 1936.*

** *Mr. Dwight L. Moody (1837-1899) was a well-known American evangelist who had founded the Moody Church, and had an international reputation. He partnered with the famous gospel singer and composer, Ira D. Sankey for 30 years as they toured the U.S. and Europe. Some claimed him to be the greatest evangelist of the 19th century.*

Robinson's Opera House on West 9th Street looking east. Scott Jackson and Alonzo Walling roomed together in the boarding house thought to be just to the right of the building.

Courtesy of the Public Library of Cincinnati and Hamilton County.

Greencastle. She was suffering from low back pain, frequent nausea, and chronic fatigue, and wondered what health issue she had. What really petrified her was that she had missed her last menstrual period. She briefly ignored this fact, but was wholly familiar with the symptoms of expectant motherhood from observing her older sisters during their pregnancies. As time passed, she was forced to accept the reality that she was pregnant, and that Scott Jackson was the father. All she could immediately think of was, "What am I going to do?" Although having an abortion was not initially an option in Pearl's mind, she immediately resented the fact that such an operation was illegal.

Young women from respectable families who were unmarried and pregnant in the 1890s faced total disgrace in society, and had few options. In Pearl's case, if Scott Jackson chose not to marry her, her choices were quite limited. Pearl had known of certain young ladies in Greencastle who had undergone an abortion. But she also knew it was an expensive, painful, and dangerous process. Anesthesia wasn't customarily used, for it took too long for the women to recover following the procedure.

Once she surrendered to her unthinkable condition, Pearl wrote to Scott, informing him of their impending desperate predicament. She prayed that Scott would agree to marry her, but he responded with anger and disregard to her shocking news. In her anguish and panic, Pearl confessed her shameful secret to Will Wood, imploring him to convince Scott that the couple should marry. Will wrote Scott about Pearl's wishes, but he was unyielding and related to Will that he had no intention of ever marrying Pearl.

Rather, he was emphatic that they must find a way to abort the pregnancy. Another missile from Scott instructed Will to privately obtain various chemicals and herbs from the local pharmacy in Greencastle, and to administer them to Pearl, hoping the agents would induce an abortion. The young woman was not thrilled with this proposal, but in light of her desperate situation, she acquiesced to Scott's demand. After a week's intake of the purported chemical remedy, the desired result did not follow. To everyone's dismay, the chemically-induced abortion effort had failed.

In December, Jackson advised Wood to help Pearl arrange for a visit to Cincinnati, tentatively to take place in late January. Will was told to inform Pearl that Jackson wasn't ruling out the possibility of marriage, but that the prospective parents needed to discuss their options and plan accordingly while she was there. In reality, Scott was openly considering two main paths of action. One was to arrange for a criminal abortion; the other was to get rid of his dilemma permanently.

Just prior to the Christmas holiday school break, Jackson and Walling were discussing Scott's "problem" in their boarding house room.

"You know, Wally," Scott said. "If Bert somehow were to die in this city, one could cut her body into small pieces, and dispose of them in the sewer system." Walling arched his bushy eyebrow, smirked, and said, "Yeah … right. I also believe that the moon is made of cheese!"

"I'm quite serious," Scott said, frowning intently. "I'm NOT going to ruin my whole life just because that stupid bitch got herself pregnant!"

Scott returned to Greencastle to visit his family during the Christmas-New Year's school break, and on January 2, he arranged to briefly meet Pearl in Greencastle. He greeted her with a scowl, saying, "This news of yours could wreck all my future plans. We've got to get you an abortion as soon as possible, and don't talk to me about marriage. That's not going to happen!" Pearl responded strongly against this proposal, but after he had departed, she recognized that this might be her only recourse.

A few days later, Pearl's waistline seemed to be expanding exponentially, and she knew her condition would soon be obvious to any interested party. She sensed a wave of desperation encompass her and was both conflicted and paralyzed about her future course of action. At times, she considered informing her mother about the pregnancy, but she was reluctant to do so because of the overwhelming shame that she knew would descend upon her family with this kind of news. It was at this point, that both Scott and Will strongly encouraged her to take a trip to Cincinnati, and see if she and Scott could devise some plan to solve her problem. Hoping that she might still convince Scott to marry her, and assuming that he wanted to do what she felt was the right thing, Pearl agreed to their suggestion.

In mid-January, Jackson and Walling were drinking with several other medical and dental students at Wallingford's Saloon. Scott had long been intrigued with poisons and their effects on the body, and he read whatever he could about them. This particular evening, he inquired of his companions as to which poison might produce death the most rapidly. Much discussion ensued, but the consensus was that hydrocyanic and prussic acid were the most deadly, with cocaine also being high on the list. Jackson was later described as being "fascinated by the conversation." Three days later on January 20, Jackson legally purchased several doses of cocaine at Koeble's drug store located a few blocks from his boarding house.

On January 23, Wood received another letter from Scott imploring him to convince Pearl by whatever means were necessary to travel to Cincinnati for an abortion. Jackson promised that he would take good care of her there, and the message concluded, "I have got a nice room for Pearl." Wood showed the letter to her, and Pearl considered the idea for 24 hours, and then reluctantly concluded this was her only course of action. She would simply invent some story to explain the journey to her parents, but must do so at once.

CHAPTER EIGHT

On Tuesday, January 23, Pearl informed her parents that she was planning to visit a high school friend, Jane Fisher, who had recently moved with her family from Greencastle to Indianapolis, where they now resided at 75 Central Avenue. Both Alex and Jane were quite fond of Jane and her parents, and they encouraged Pearl to make the trip. Their reasoning was that aside from enabling Pearl to renew an intimate friendship, the relatively short sixty mile train ride between the two communities would also allow their youngest daughter to experience the ambiance of urban life, far away from the influence of Scott Jackson. The unsuspecting parents wanted Pearl to expand culturally beyond the narrow confines of Greencastle society. The Bryans understood that Pearl would depart on Tuesday, the 28th, and return ten days later.

Will Wood offered to drive Pearl to the train station, where he was already planning to meet his father as he returned from a quarterly church meeting in Terre Haute. On the duly appointed day, Will arrived at the Bryan home in his buggy, ready to make the short trip to the "Big Four" train depot. Pearl climbed up into the carriage, with plenty of good advice and motherly counsel still ringing in her ears. As the horse clip-clopped in a northerly direction through the cold, damp morning air, conversation was in short supply between Pearl and Will and both sensed an uneasy tension existing between them.

In a matter of ten minutes, they arrived at the one-story brick and stone depot. Will stopped the buggy, looped the reins through the hitching post, helped Pearl dismount and grabbed her luggage. Fully aware of the sordid details of Pearl's dilemma and what must be running through her mind, he told her, "Try not to worry, Bert. When you get back to Greencastle, all your troubles will be over."

Pearl nodded her head unenthusiastically, and said, "I certainly hope so" in a barely audible voice.

She entered the station, and silently took a seat with her baggage at her feet. She was wearing a fashionable, plum-colored Henrietta dress; a large black felt hat decorated with velvet pink roses and black ostrich feather tips; a medium length fur cape with a high collar; and was carrying two pieces of luggage: a chocolate-brown, alligator leather grip and a smaller, light brown bag.

Thirty minutes passed, and the conductor announced the arrival of the Indianapolis-bound train. Shortly after, Pearl boarded it, entered a passenger car, and slid onto a seat next to the window. She sat silent and motionless until the steam locomotive began to tow its eight cars away from the station, its smokestack billowing exhaust in its wake. Pearl waved lethargically to Will through the window, and slumped despondently into her seat. Descending into a mental fog, she was besieged with an array of emotions. Her intense feelings of vulnerability, anxiety, and uncertainty were only slightly alleviated by one small ray of hope. If Scott would simply agree to marry her, the stigma and shame surrounding her pregnancy would gradually dissipate. She knew a number of girls who started married life while "in the family way." The town gossips would soon tire of pointing their fingers at her, and she'd settle down into the typical role of wife and mother. But before any of that could happen, Scott must acquiesce to her wishes.

Ninety minutes later, the train stopped briefly at Union Station in Indianapolis, and then departed, heading in an easterly direction toward Cincinnati. A few passengers had departed, but many more had boarded. Pearl took no interest in either group, but merely tried to escape her mental doldrums and take notice of the passing landscape. Her friend Ida had once mentioned that the train-ride between Indianapolis and Cincinnati was breathtakingly beautiful in the autumn, when the trees were displaying their intense changes of color. Ida had described miles and miles of rolling hills, forested with countless shades of green, gold, yellow, orange, and red.

Now, in late January, the trees were bare, and the countryside looked drab and dreary. As Pearl gazed out the window, she felt increasingly consumed by the omnipresent grayness. Her somber mood was intensified as the train passed by Rushville. The small town, inundated with mud and dark slush, offered even more gloom. Only when the sun peeked out from behind the clouds a half hour later, did Pearl's spirits began to lift slightly. The landscape had changed, and the stark allure of the surrounding terrain, which was blanketed with a thin dusting of pure white snow, now engaged her. Horses and cattle meandered about in the fields, and numerous windmills were silhouetted in the distance. Pearl was becoming mesmerized by the gentle swaying of the coaches and the rails' rhythmic clattering: *CHUNKA-chunka-chunka-chunka-CHUNKA-chunka-chunka-chunka.*

As the train continued its easterly trek, impressive limestone cliffs rose about fifty feet on either side of the tracks. Some minutes later, the parade of engine, coaches, and the caboose entered Connorsville, an inviting small city with wide paved streets and well-maintained homes. For a moment, Pearl imagined living happily in such a community complete with a husband and children. However, her wishful thinking was quickly dashed. The town and its homey atmosphere were quickly left behind. As the locomotive moved on, the train whistle broke Pearl's reverie with its shriek: *TWEEEEEEEEE! TWEEEEEEEEE!.* Crossing the Indiana border, the train sped on into Ohio, stopping briefly in Hamilton, and, proceeding to Cincinnati, Pearl's final destination. At Grand Central Station, it screeched to a halt as the train's Westinghouse air brakes gave a high-pitched hiss..

After the platform attendant put down the stepping box, Pearl exited the coach. As she walked toward the depot in front of a porter who toted her luggage, she looked around intently expecting to see Scott. She was perplexed. Although Will had assured her that Dusty would be there, he was nowhere to be seen! A wave of apprehension flooded over Pearl. "Where is he? Why isn't he here? What should I do now?" she thought. She waited nervously in the terminal for almost an hour, and then was forced to accept that Scott wasn't coming. As though her overriding dilemma for being in Cincinnati in the first place wasn't traumatic enough, now she must contend with this new predicament.

Meanwhile, two bristly-whiskered, uncouth-looking men were seated nearby attempting to gain her attention. Periodically, they would leer at, snicker, and even brazenly swear.

"You all alone, missy? Are all the little girls down on the farm as pretty as you? How grateful would you be if I helped you with your luggage? Maybe you'd be a damn sight friendlier if I came over and sat next to you. Would you like that?"

Although Pearl attempted to ignore the remarks, she was deeply disturbed by their crude, suggestive behavior. For a moment, she almost panicked, thinking, "What am I doing here?" Then, she took a deep breath and willed herself to continue the task at hand. Taking in tow both her anxieties and her luggage, she walked outside the huge four-story, stone station complex. At the curb, eight horse-drawn cabbies awaited fares. She selected the first in line, and announced to the driver her destination: the Indiana House Hotel on Fifth Street.

As they approached 5th and Vine streets, two bright yellow electric cars whizzed past their buggy, while numerous pedestrians scurried by on all sides of them. "Greencastle was never like this," she thought with wonder. Pearl was suddenly confronted by a 45-foot vertical structure facing her: a large brass statue of a woman with outstretched arms. The reddish-yellow cast configuration was positioned on a large granite pedestal, and overlooked a plaza, which at the moment was full of pedestrians.

The driver called out, "That's Fountain Square, ma'am." The horse and buggy stopped in front of the Indiana House Hotel, while on inquiry, Pearl learned that the driver's name was John Belli. Resolute in her desire to find Scott immediately, Pearl turned to the driver, saying, "Mr. Belli. After you have helped me drop off my bags, if you would be so kind, I would to like to commission you to take me to a second destination."

Belli nodded his assent, "Certainly, madam. I am at your disposal. Where would you like to go next?"

"Let's stop by the Ohio College of Dental Surgery. While I wait in the carriage, you may enter the building and deliver a message to a student there, named Scott Jackson. I'd like you to tell him that 'Mabel' is in town to see him, and is staying at the Indiana House Hotel." The driver nodded his agreement, carried her luggage into the hotel, and left the two grips at the front desk.

Exiting the hotel, Pearl observed dynamic action all about her: horses, carriages, trolley cars, and pedestrians were all in seemingly feverish motion and producing a clamor of discordant sounds. The backdrop for this beehive of activity included saloons, pawnshops, hotels, pool halls, clothing stores, and millinery shops. Many people scurried about the area, and numerous seedy-looking individuals were simply loitering about. Pearl shook her head in alarm and wonder;

*Photograph circa 1907 of the Tyler Davidson Fountain in Fountain
Square Plaza as Pearl Bryan might have seen it. Courtesy of the
Public Library of Cincinnati and Hamilton County.*

Contemporary photo of the Tyler Davidson Fountain in Fountain Square. Although streams of water typically flowed out of the figure's hands during the warmer seasons, they were turned off during the winter months.

this was the most frenetic setting she'd ever observed! The driver turned onto Central Avenue and drove a few blocks north to the dental college located on Court Street. Telling Pearl he would return shortly, Belli entered the building, and soon after, located Scott Jackson in a basement laboratory. Jackson was not overly receptive to the news the driver brought to him, and said to advise Pearl that she should return to the Indiana House Hotel where he would call for her either during the evening or the following morning.

When she returned to the hotel, Pearl registered at the front desk using her sister's name, Mabel Stanley, and was then escorted to room #114. After closing and locking the door, Pearl surveyed her living quarters and frowned. She deemed the room to be nice enough, but felt it was cold and uninviting. Her surroundings extended the somber mood that Scott's absence had initiated, and Pearl was consumed with homesickness. Once she was settled inside, she ate the sandwich her mother had prepared for the trip, and waited patiently throughout the evening, hoping somehow that Scott might come ….. but he didn't.

Although she was typically a very cheerful and optimistic individual, Pearl cried herself to sleep that evening. She had never before felt so totally alone, and her position seemed utterly hopeless. It was doubtful that Scott would agree to marry her. Good Lord! He hadn't even been willing to meet her at the station! What were her choices? She could get back on the train in the morning and return to Greencastle, to face the mortification which she knew would rain down on her family when the news of her pregnancy came to light. Her expanding midriff would soon be obvious to everyone.

She resisted the idea, but perhaps the illegal operation that Scott had exhorted her to undergo was her only reasonable course of action. Yet who would conduct the operation? Could they find a willing physician? Might a midwife do it? How much would it cost? Who would pay for it? Would it be a safe procedure? What would be the health risk to her? Could she live with herself after sacrificing her unborn baby? Could she forgive herself for committing both a sin and a crime? She had no immediate answers for any of these questions.

In the United States in 1896, the majority of abortions were illegal. Not only were there ethical and moral concerns, but the entire process constituted a major health risk. There were few antiseptics available, and the procedure carried a high mortality rate. Many physicians were in favor of antiabortion legislation. It was a time when many physicians, who were primarily male, wanted more control over their profession. Midwives, who attended births and performed abortions as a regular part of their practices, were viewed as a threat to physicians' economic and social power, as well as to their patients' well being. Much of the growing antiabortion sentiment in the country reflected a backlash to women's suffrage and other women's rights issues. Unfortunately, Pearl's pregnancy seemed to have occurred at the wrong time and the wrong place. Regrettably, making abortions illegal had neither eliminated the need for them, nor prevented their widespread use. It had merely forced the entire process to go underground, where the quality of care provided was greatly diminished, and the risk to the patient substantially elevated.

After what had seemed for Pearl to be an interminable evening, Scott finally arrived at her hotel about midmorning on Wednesday, and the two of them left the Indiana House together. Alonzo Walling was waiting for them outside the establishment, and Scott introduced his classmate to Pearl, adding that Lonnie was going to be very helpful to them. The trio walked east toward a district of town where Scott had rented an inexpensive room for Pearl. Walling left for a moment to purchase some cigars. Pearl grabbed Scott's arm and begged him, "Dusty! Why can't we just get married? I'll make you a very good wife, and I know we can be happy together as a family."

Scott shook his head negatively. "You can't be serious. We've already discussed this. I'm in no position to support a wife, much less a child. I don't want this kind of commitment yet, Bert. Now you just listen to me, and do as I say, and everything will turn out fine. We've reserved a room for you, and we have some herbs and chemicals to give you that often induce abortions. We'll try that method first, and if it doesn't work, Lonnie has an acquaintance who has performed abortions, and we'll use that method. One way or another, this problem is going to be resolved before you leave here." He looked into Pearl's eyes and smiled icily. "You can trust me to take care of you and your situation," he added.

"But, Scott,….." implored Pearl.

"You're not listening to me Bert," Scott interrupted, growling, "This is how we are going to handle this situation. Period!"

Pearl was heartsick. An abortion was against the law, and for her it was an absolute last option. She frowned and screamed at Scott, "I'm just going to catch the next train to Greencastle and then tell my brothers about your lies and deception!"

Scott attempted to calm her by promising to consider other options first. She managed to regain her composure shortly, and for the remainder of the day, Jackson and Walling took turns escorting Pearl around the city. The two men took her luggage, clothes, and money, and kept her under close watch. Whoever was not accompanying her at any given moment was focused on obtaining the chemical agents that might promote a miscarriage.

When Pearl arrived in Cincinnati, she was shocked by the "rough-and-tumble" nature of the downtown area. In many citizens' views, the southwest corner of Fifth and Vine Streets was the seediest area of all. It came to be known and described as "Nasty Corner," based on the large number of saloons concentrated in the area, and the offensive nature of many of the men often loitering about. Courtesy of the Public Library of Cincinnati and Hamilton County.

Early in the evening, Scott and Pearl sat in the small, barren room he had found for her. It was located in the midst of Cincinnati's "tenderloin" district. In the 1890s, this city in the southwest corner of Ohio was a booming steamboat port on the Ohio River and the region teemed with saloons, gambling joints, pool halls, brothels, and disreputable characters. Moreover, the "Queen City's" political makeup was synonymous with corruption at the time, and George "Boss" Cox was in the midst of his 30 year run as the leading political force in the city. The area was also well known for an exciting new type of music that was developing in black neighborhoods all across urban America. "Ragtime" was a hybrid of African rhythm and Western European tonality, and it attracted its own fraternity of pianists, composers, and other musicians. This wildly popular music poured from many of the saloons during the time of Pearl's visit there.

While they sat in the dreary little room, Pearl insisted that Scott return her money. But he was adamant that he must watch over all her funds in order to defray either the cost of chemicals to be purchased, or any surgical procedure she might need. Mortified, Pearl silently acquiesced. Jackson urged Pearl to ingest a herbal mixture of pennyroyal and tansy. Within an hour, she was retching in the chamber pot in the corner of the room, but no spontaneous abortion occurred. Extremely disappointed, Scott told her that he was leaving and would return early the next morning. Pearl sighed, and quickly fell asleep on the cot.

Jackson's next stop was at Koeble's Pharmacy on 6th street between Plum and Elm, where he purchased 17 grains of cocaine from the druggist. Later that evening he told Walling,

"You know, Wally, my friend. In a worst-case scenario, we may need to rent a horse and carriage and take Pearl out in the country somewhere. Where's the closest livery stable around here?"

Walling thought for a moment and replied, "Why would we want to transport her out in the country?" Lacking any response from Scott, he continued, "There's one north of here a mile or so, in Walnut Hills."

Meanwhile, back in her room, Pearl slept fitfully, and dreamed that her sister Jennie's spirit was warning her of imminent danger.

On Thursday morning, Jackson, Walling and Pearl took a carriage ride across the Ohio River to Bellevue, Kentucky, a small community just northeast of Newport. The two men were searching for additional chemicals to induce an abortion. They made their way to a drugstore at the corner of Washington and Fairfield avenues, just a quarter mile from the river. While Pearl waited outside at the front of the store, Jackson and Walling entered the establishment. A cold wind blew Pearl's cape against her body, and she grasped her hat firmly, resisting the gusts of wind blowing its ribbons outward, and bending its feathers. Inside the store, Jackson quickly scrutinized the shelves looking for oil of savin or croton oil to supplement the meager supply he had managed to acquire for his perceived needs. Scott had heard that this Bellevue pharmacy might be a source of these substances, but there was no evidence of their presence, Although disappointed, Jackson purchased some ergot (a cereal grain fungus thought by some to induce abortions) and Walling a flask of Jamaica ginger and whiskey as well as his customary cigar.

Before departing, Walling quizzed the druggist whether there was a ferry at the foot of Washington Street to return them to Cincinnati. Foertmeyer replied that there wasn't, so Walling asked about the most direct way to Walnut Hills from Bellevue, and was told to take the Dayton ferry. Walling and Jackson then joined Pearl outside. The trio walked northeast in the direction of Dayton, a small Kentucky town which lay about one half mile in the distance. An hour later, the three of them were on the ferry headed back to Cincinnati.

Back in Ohio, Walling confessed to Jackson that his 'friend' who they wanted to perform the abortion on Pearl was now demanding $200 for the task, a sum that they did not have. Walling told Jackson that he had heard of a clairvoyant in Cincinnati who knew of a midwife who performed abortions much more cheaply. While Jackson ate lunch with Pearl at a 4th Street saloon, Walling inquired at several nearby taverns as to where such a spiritualist might be located. He was told that a medium lived just a few blocks from the dental school on 9th street, and that she might be able to help them.

After lunch, Scott and Pearl continued their dialogue about possible abortion plans as they walked north toward West Ninth Street. Once there, they stopped and knocked at the door of Mrs. Plymouth Weeks, the seer who they hoped might help them. Scott and Pearl were unsure how to approach the topic, so they initiated the conversation by asking her for a 'spiritual sitting'. The clairvoyant quickly informed them that she could conduct a sitting for only one person at a time. Jackson consented to Pearl being the subject, and he and Mrs. Weeks agreed on the price. Mrs. Weeks then lead Pearl to a small room in the back, and the two closed the door. Almost immediately, Pearl sensed that she was a kind and sensitive lady, and shortly after the séance had begun, Pearl began to pour her heart out, while Mrs. Weeks simply listened.

Pearl confessed that she was from Greencastle, Indiana, and that she was pregnant, but not married. Approaching hysteria, Pearl sobbed, "I have seen the spirit of my dead sister Jennie. She told me that I should go home to my parents. I told her that I couldn't, because they wouldn't let me stay with them anymore after what I had done." Pearl began to wring her hands in anguish and begged, "Oh, please won't you help me? Dusty will never marry me and I am going to be disgraced. Can't you let me stay with you until this is all over?" Mrs. Weeks patted Pearl's shoulder, and gently replied, "That's just not possible, dear. I can't keep you here, and I won't assist you with any kind of criminal act. However, I do have some motherly advice for you." Pearl stopped crying and listened intently.

Mrs. Weeks leaned toward her and grasped her two small hands in her own. "Honey," she said. "My mother once recited a quotation to me that I have never forgotten. And it has applied to my life many times. I'm going to tell it to you, and I hope that you listen carefully." Mrs. Weeks continued, ***"Oh what a tangled web we weave, when first we practice to deceive."*** The clairvoyant waited a moment, and asked, "Do you understand what I am saying, child? Whenever you tell the first lie, and try to deceive those who care about you, it never ends there. You'll have to lie again, to cover the first lie, and then again for the next lie, and again and again. As a result, the problems simply escalate, and nothing is ever solved. Eventually, you wish that you had never told the first lie. But by then, it's often too late. So, my heartfelt advice to you is to get on the train as soon as you can, and go straight home to your mother and family. It will be very difficult at first, but everyone will eventually forgive you. Confess what you have done; tell them how sorry you are for your poor judgment; and let their love comfort you. It's the only thing you can do. Promise me you'll do that, and forget this nonsense of getting some kind of operation."

Pearl nodded numbly, dabbed at her eyes with a handkerchief, and returned to Scott who waited in the front room. It was obvious to both that Mrs. Weeks would play no part in any abortion effort. As the two left, Scott muttered under his breath, "Damn! What a waste of money that was!" At the same moment, Pearl silently resolved that she was going home by rail the following day.

Jackson and Walling had previously agreed that after the séance had concluded, Scott would take Pearl to a convenient public place (the immense Cincinnati post office was selected) and would leave her there for a few hours while the two men planned their future course of action. Walling would return to the post office later and rejoin Pearl.

Yet again, Scott and Pearl argued heatedly about the abortion plan as they walked to their destination at 800 Vine Street. Firmly at loggerheads, Jackson left her at the postal building around 3:00 pm. Pearl was alone, and possessed neither money, nor identification. All she could do was wait. At 5 pm, Walling returned and found Pearl still seated inside the building. He told her that the three of them were going to a nice restaurant that evening, and in that environment, they could discuss the next step regarding their dilemma.

The vast Cincinnati Post Office and Government Building, circa 1895. Pearl Bryan waited for Jackson and Walling inside this building for more than two hours on Thursday afternoon. Courtesy of the Public Library of Cincinnati and Hamilton County

A waiter at Heyden's Restaurant seated the threesome in a booth at 7 pm. This dining establishment had a first-rate reputation, and serviced a family-oriented clientele, often including some of Cincinnati's best citizens. On this particular evening, Attorney A.T. Root and his wife were having an enjoyable evening dinner at the supper club. Their table was situated near the booth where Jackson, Walling, and Miss Bryan had been seated. The Roots were intrigued by the rather unsophisticated behavior of the two young men and the young blonde woman sitting with them. The light-haired man sported a beard and mustache, and had intense blue eyes, which flashed angrily as he spoke intently with the wholesome-appearing young woman. He seemed to be lecturing her. Periodically, the third member of the party, a black-headed man having a dark complexion, joined in the conversation. Occasionally, the woman wiped her eyes and nose with a handkerchief. The subject matter of the exchange appeared to be rather grim, although the Roots could not hear any specifics of the conversation. When they left the restaurant at 8 p.m., the threesome remained and was clearly engrossed in their animated discussion.

After dinner, Jackson and Pearl returned to her room, where he provided her with yet another concoction of chemicals that he hoped would cause her to miscarry. However, she once again became ill after ingesting the mix of croton oil and oil of savin, but did not abort the fetus. His hopes dashed, Scott stormed out of the room and returned to his boarding house, once more leaving Pearl alone for the remainder of the evening.

The following morning, Scott Jackson visited his barber, Fred Albion, to shave off his beard. Meanwhile, Alonzo Walling was eating a leisurely breakfast at Heider's Restaurant one block away. The two dental students then opted to stop at the dental school to complete some laboratory work in preparation for patient visits the following Monday. Upon completing this chore, the duo dropped by Pearl's room to take her to lunch at the Atlantic Garden at 513 Vine Street. This building served as a concert hall, and in fact, concerts were held there every evening, as well as on Sunday afternoons. However, the premises offered far more than mere music. The establishment's long, well-stocked bar and connected billiard room made it a haven for beer drinkers and their friends. The local draft beers were the favorite drinks, although some customers also drank wine and whiskey. In addition to the liquid refreshments, choice meats, vegetables and cheeses were readily available to encourage the customers to stay longer and drink more. John Lederer, the proprietor, claimed to have the only genuine electric orchestrion (generic term for a machine which plays music and is designed to sound like a band or orchestra) in the country as well as the best food in town.

Many of the beer gardens and saloons of the day covered their floors with sawdust, since tobacco chewing was an almost universal habit. Although brass spittoons were strategically placed throughout the premises, the chewers only spat their juices in the general direction of the receptacles, and unfortunately, seldom hit their targets. The heavy scent of tobacco smoke also permeated these sites at all times.

This was the environment that Jackson, Walling, and Pearl encountered as they entered the Atlantic Garden for lunch on Friday, January 31. The three of them each ordered bologna sausages placed on thick slices of rye bread with dollops of mustard applied liberally. The two men drank beer; Pearl ordered her usual sarsaparilla. Their conversation once again focused on possible ways they might terminate Pearl's pregnancy. However, during the previous 24 hours, Pearl had become much more insistent about the matter. The more that Scott exhorted her to stay in Cincinnati until the pregnancy was terminated, the more she asserted that she was going to leave on the train to Greencastle that very afternoon at 3 pm. Jackson railed against Pearl, exhorting her to change her mind, but to no avail.

Following 20 minutes of fruitless pleading, Jackson stormed out of the beer garden in disgust. Shortly later, Pearl also departed the site in the company of Walling, who trailed behind her a few steps. The two paused at a street corner for a moment, when Jackson approached them once again. He stood in front of the pair talking and gesturing with great vehemence for several minutes. An employee of the John Church Company, who was eating his lunch nearby, listened to the squabble with avid interest. Suddenly, Pearl snapped at Jackson, "No, I tell you! I won't do it!" She stomped her foot, tossed her head in the air, and marched southeast toward the railroad terminal. A moment later, Walling followed her.

The two of them arrived at the lower waiting room of the depot at about 2:15 pm. Pearl and Lonnie sat on the last seat of the row and talked quietly. Pearl began to cry softly as Walling entreated her not to board the train for Greencastle, but to remain in Cincinnati for one more day. During the next 45 minutes the discussion proceeded, as Pearl continued to weep and occasionally wring her hands. The train to Greencastle was announced, but she did not move from her seat. Rather, she and Walling continued talking quietly for another hour, with Pearl periodically daubing her downcast eyes. Several more trains were announced, but neither Pearl nor Alonzo budged. Finally, at 4:10 pm, Walling got up, and Pearl hesitantly followed him. They departed the station at the 3rd Street exit. At least for the moment, Lonnie had changed Pearl's mind about leaving the city.

Jackson joined Pearl and Walling about 5 pm, and the two men conferred briefly in hushed voices, excluding Pearl from the conversation. Walling then departed, walking north to a livery stable located in Walnut Hills. There he talked with Chester Mullin, the stable keeper. Walling agreed to rent a horse and a coupe rockaway for the evening for the payment of three silver dollars in advance.

This rockaway was a light, low, four-wheeled vehicle very popular in the U.S. after its introduction at Rockaway, N.J., in 1830. The driver's seat was separated from the coach, but was built into the body, with the top projecting forward to protect the driver from inclement weather. The top was fixed with open sides that were covered with waterproof curtains. Walling drove the vehicle to a hitching post north of the dental school and left it there for the time being. Meanwhile, Pearl and Jackson had purchased a couple of "corn in the husks" from Simon, the Hot Corn vendor whose cart was located on Fountain Square. They sat silently and ate their chewy, buttery snack, each contemplating their course of action.

At 6:30 pm, Scott and Pearl entered Wallingford's Saloon at George and Plum Street. Jackson and Walling frequented this saloon almost every evening together, and they were acquainted with all the employees working there. Pearl turned a lot of heads as she entered the establishment. She was clearly not the usual floozy that Jackson often accompanied to the saloon. Pearl was wearing a blue checked dress, a dark cloak trimmed in fur that struck her just below the hips, and a large hat decorated with large plumes.

Doc and Bert immediately walked to the so-called 'wine room'. This chamber was composed of 6 cubicles, often called 'stalls', which had been separated from the main room by partitions extending up toward the ceiling. In lieu of a door, each cubicle had an outer curtain, which could be tied up with tassels to remain open, or be untied if the patrons wanted privacy. Jackson escorted Pearl by the elbow into cubicle #4, and closed the curtain. He spent the next 15 minutes verbally hounding her, wanting to convince her to remain in Cincinnati indefinitely until they could find a proper abortionist. But Pearl remained steadfast and the impasse continued.

Changing tactics, Scott asked her, "Well, Bert, do you want a 'real' drink, or another one of these 'sissy sarasparillas' you always order?"

Without looking at Scott, she replied quietly, "Sarasparilla."

Jackson smirked, "Wow. What a surprise. Why don't we just name you 'Predictable Pearl'?"

Pearl raised her eyes, and glared at him. "I don't know. Why don't we just call you 'Despicable Dusty'?"

With that, Scott left the cubicle and hopped up on a nearby barstool. He spotted Allen Johnson, who worked at the saloon as a waiter.

Johnson called over, "How are you doing, Doc?"

Jackson replied, "Good to see you, sport."

Johnson came closer and asked to borrow fifty cents from Scott, who responded that he didn't have any money and was going to have to borrow some money himself. Scott then sidled up to the saloon's owner, David Wallingford, and implored him to loan him a few dollars, promising to repay him the following night. Wallingford complied, handing him four silver dollars. It wasn't the first time he had loaned money to the man he called "Doc," but in his experience, he always repaid him. Jackson and Walling each ordered a whiskey and asked for a sarsaparilla for their young lady friend. From a distance, Johnson saw Scott pour something out of a vial into Pearl's drink; he then told Johnson to "take this drink back to the blonde lady in stall #4." Johnson did so, and then went about his business serving other patrons. At about 7 pm, Johnson held the George Street door of the saloon open for Jackson, Walling, and Pearl as they exited the building and he observed the three entering a cab.

They immediately returned to Pearl's room, where she began to feel groggy and disoriented from the dose of cocaine that Jackson had slipped into her drink. Jackson insisted that she drink some whiskey, literally forcing her to gulp down a couple of swallows. He informed her that Walling had previously observed an abortion being performed, and that the two of them were going to use dental and medical instruments, and conduct the operation themselves. She was in no position to resist effectively. Over the next hour, the two dental students, who had vastly overestimated their surgical skills, bungled the job. It was a much more difficult procedure than they had anticipated, and all that they accomplished was to leave Pearl bleeding, languid and incapacitated.

Meanwhile, a mile to the northeast, Mr. George Jackson left his home at 263 McGregor Street and walked to a nearby field where he put the Caldwell Guards (an African-American militia company) through its paces from roughly 9 pm until after 11 pm. Such drills were frequently conducted on Friday evenings after typical working hours. When the marching routine was concluded about 11:30 pm, Jackson and a group of four other men left the field and walked downtown to the corner of George and Elm Streets. While the group huddled in the raw, rainy evening air debating what they wanted to do next, a man in a light colored cap approached them and asked,

"Who wants to make five dollars?"

"Doing what?" asked George Jackson.

The man replied, "Driving a carriage across the Newport Bridge into Kentucky and back."

George Jackson asked the man, "Where's the five dollars?"

The man in the cap answered, "You'll need to do the job first, and then you'll get the money."

George Jackson replied, "You've found your man. I'll do it." He was told that he would be driving a physician who was accompanying a sick patient to her home in Newport, Kentucky. The man added that George should wait at the corner for about half an hour or so until he returned with a cab and the two passengers.

George paced up and down Elm Street for about 45 minutes, until the man who had hired him finally drove up in a surrey. George could only faintly see a man and a woman riding inside the coach. He got up on the seat next to the fellow with the cap, who was now wearing a long dark coat, and took the reins. The man ordered George to drive across the Newport Bridge; then told him to travel three squares to the right, turn south on Licking Pike, and eventually turn back north on Alexandria Pike.

George replied, "Whatever you say, mister."

The horse was gray and very high-spirited, repeatedly tossing his head in the air and pawing at the dirt with his hooves while he whinnied emphatically. George discovered he had to hold him with a very tight rein. The vehicle passed the tollbooth at about 1 am, but the toll-collector failed to appear and receive the fee. In reality, Mr. Tarvan was dozing inside the booth and awoke only in time to see a surrey driven by a black man transporting a white man with a cap and wearing a long coat up on the seat next to him, and containing a man and a woman riding inside.

After the carriage had crossed the Ohio River and passed into Kentucky, George Jackson heard a strange and frightening moan within the surrey. It was the kind of muffled cry that a woman with severe and unrelenting pain might make. It made him uneasy, but he remembered that one of his passengers was a doctor, and presumably, the other a sick patient. After making several turns, and traveling a piece further in the dark night, the man seated next to him told George to stop the carriage, since the house where they were taking the woman was only a short distance away.

The man with the cap then climbed down from the seat, and the two passengers got out of the surrey. The passengers and dark haired man began walking down a blind lane, which lead away from the road.

Vintage postcard showing the Central Bridge crossing the Ohio River leading to Newport from Cincinnati. This was the route taken by the carriage driver, George Jackson, and his passengers, Alonzo Walling, Scott Jackson, and Pearl Bryan on the evening of January 31, 1896. Courtesy of the Public Library of Cincinnati and Hamilton County

One of the men called back to the driver and said, "Turn that damn carriage around, and walk back down the road away from it! We'll whistle for you when we are ready to leave."

The woman staggered, slumping forward, and leaned heavily on both men. She acted as though she was drunk or violently ill. The threesome walked away from the carriage into the darkness. George heard a noise that sounded like a deep groan. He couldn't see anything that was happening, but a terrifying sense of fear disseminated over him. He jumped into the carriage and removed a heavy piece of railroad iron that was on the floor, and dropped it on the ground. It was over a foot long, and contained two holes, with a leather strap fastened to one of the holes. He quickly hitched the horse to it, and then heard what sounded like a fierce struggle occurring in the general area where his passengers had disappeared. His blood ran cold as a deep moan briefly permeated the night sky, and he discerned a prolonged, chilling wail that didn't sound quite human.

George could see absolutely nothing in the murkiness, and was petrified. He bolted in the direction of town, and didn't stop running until he had reached the Newport Bridge. He walked the rest of the way to his home, finally arriving at 3 am, with the horrifying cries of the previous night still resonating in his ears.

CHAPTER NINE

Jack Hewling stumbled across the decapitated body of a woman lying on John Locke's property near Ft. Thomas, Kentucky early on the morning of February 1, 1896. The corpse lay on a slope, with its chest down, and arms extended upward and outward, as though in a posture of surrender. A large collection of blood had pooled under the stump of the neck. Horrified by the sight, Hewling propelled himself into action, sprinting uphill to the nearby Locke farmhouse. Mr. Locke's parcel of land, triangular in shape, was bordered by the Army Post to the north, and included the area between Fort Thomas Avenue on the east and Alexandria Pike on the west. A deep, narrow, meandering ravine ran across the property, and in the bottom of this gully, a board fence defined the southern boundary. Adjacent to the fence, a long, narrow, wagon road overgrown with bluegrass intersected the Pike roadway, ascended to the top of the hill, and ended at the Locke farm. On the north side parallel to the fence was an embankment, whose crest was lined with an almost impenetrable line of privet bushes. It was here that Hewling had discovered the headless corpse near a gap in the hedgerow.

When he reached the white, wood-framed residence, Jack exploded through the back door and into the kitchen where John Locke, along with his son, Wilber, and hired hand Mike Noonan, sat at the table, drinking their morning coffee. Startled by the sudden intrusion, the three men leaped to their feet, spilling their coffee all over the table in the process. Before they could speak, a wild-eyed Jack blurted out his horrific finding,

"There's a headless body out by the apple orchard!"

Needing no further prompting, the three men quickly followed the fleet-footed teenager to the spot where the prostrate, decapitated form of what appeared to be a woman, lay.

Distant view of Fort Thomas, Kentucky, which was only a few hundred yards from the murder site. Courtesy of the Kenton County Public Library, Covington, KY.

Sickened by the scene, and feeling his heart pounding wildly, John Locke quickly took charge of the situation.

"Calm down, boys, and follow me. We're going to the Army Post to get help!"

The men raced the few hundred yards north, passed the 100-foot Stone Water Tower*, and finally turned into the Post Headquarters. There, they breathlessly described their appalling discovery to an

---

* In 1887, General Phillip Sheridan of Civil War fame, was instrumental in the governmental purchase of 125 acres of northern Kentucky land needed for construction of the Ft. Thomas army post. By 1890, erection of the military base and its 90 foot tower had been completed, with Col Melville Cochran appointed as its first commanding officer. In 1896, Colonel Cochran was an esteemed officer, and local figure. Aside from his military career, he had two strong passions: baseball and gardening. His highly disciplined post baseball team, drawn from the barracks personnel, was known as Cochran's Champs, and had the reputation of being almost unbeatable. However, when not devoting his energy to the national pastime, the Colonel took great pride in beautifying his surroundings, and by 1896, he had planted rows of trees, shrubbery, and flowerbeds throughout the grounds. He was known to freely utilize any military prisoners detained in the guardhouse to provide unflagging care for his flowerbeds. It was duty that most of the involved men grumbled about openly, but in which they secretly took great pleasure. But on this day when a beheaded body had been found, botanical concerns were of a very low priority.

aide posted at the front desk. The latter immediately notified Post Commander, Colonel Melville Cochran, who promptly telephoned the Newport Police Department.

After receiving the Colonel's call, Newport Sheriff Jule Plummer, Coroner W.S. Tingley, and several other County and City officials arrived at the murder site. It was approximately 10 a.m., some two or three hours after the body had been discovered. The investigators viewed the corpse, examined the crime scene intently, and following some animated discussion, agreed that the remains would be taken to undertaker W. H. White's establishment in nearby Newport.

The inspectors noted that the subject's fingers were half-closed and frozen in a claw-like position, with dirt embedded under the fingernails, as if they had been clutching at the underlying earth. The blood beneath her neck cavity had congealed in a dried, jelly-like veneer, now extending laterally for some distance. Nearby, blood had splattered on the grass and also hung in crimson, dew-like drops on last season's dried leaves, which still clung to their overhanging branches. On other surrounding vegetation, splotches of blood could be detected up to three feet high.

Photograph of the headless body discovered on the morning of February 1, 1896 near Ft. Thomas Ky. The man standing in the picture may be Campbell County Coroner, W.S. Tingley. From the Kentucky Explorer, June, 1996, (abridged from an article in the Louisville Courier-Journal, March, 1897).

Campbell County Sheriff Jules Plummer was the initial investigator on the scene, but was soon aided by two detectives from Cincinnati, Cal Crim and John McDermott. Courtesy of the Kenton County Public Library, Covington, Kentucky.

Cincinnati's Superintendent of Police Phil Deitsch, pictured in his office after reading his morning mail circa 1900. Deitsch was considered one of the top police officials in the Midwest and was in charge of the murder investigation.

D. CALVIN CRIM,

Sergeant of Detectives of the Queen City Detective Department—A Noted Sleuth-Hound With a National Reputation.

Cincinnati Detective, Cal Crim

JOHN J. McDERMOTT,

Mayor's Private Detective, who has Won Fame for Himself by Hard and Unremitting Labor in His Chosen Calling.

Cincinnati Detective John McDermott

These three images are from the Police and Municipal Guide, Cincinnati, 1901, published by the Ohio Book Store, 726 Main Street, Cincinnati, Ohio

On the ground near the corpse, the sheriff had also found several strands of blond hair. The victim's clothes were in marked disarray, suggesting that her body had been hurriedly searched. The upper part of her knit, union-type undershirt and blouse had been ripped open, exposing one of her breasts. Her blue and white checked wrapper was gathered up around her waist, and her blood-stained corset, with several protruding stays, lay a few feet away. A woman's glove and a torn piece of white fabric were caught in a nearby bush. Her shoes, still on her feet, were partially covered by a worn pair of rubber overshoes. The lower half of a man's right shirtsleeve, spotted with blood, was also discovered near the body. This evidence suggested that the attacker might have sustained scratches during the assault, particularly on the right arm. It was clear that a fierce struggle had occurred just before the murder.

After the initial wave of inspection and inquiry had subsided, the body was removed, and the investigators departed, while relative calm prevailed at the site for several hours. However, the reprieve was brief. Back at his office in the Cincinnati jail, Superintendent of Police, Philip Deitsch, dispatched detectives Cal Crim and Jack McDermott to the murder scene. The two men, each of whom cut handsome figures, were first rate as an investigative team. D. Calvin Crim, a native of Maryland, had a full head of neatly parted, brown hair. He sported a dark mustache, and his prominent chin was marked by a pronounced cleft in the middle. John J. McDermott had short, black hair, silver at the temples, and a full, dark mustache that turned up on both ends. Because Cal and Jack had been recently investigating houses of ill-repute located in the Cincinnati area, their initial thoughts regarding the current case were that the victim might be a local prostitute who had come from a Cincinnati brothel. They speculated that perhaps while servicing one or more of the soldiers stationed at Fort Thomas, she had met her untimely end; but both men acknowledged that these were merely conjectures.

The two Cincinnati detectives encountered absolute chaos when they arrived at the crime scene early that afternoon. Hundreds of souvenir-hunters and soldiers from the army post had descended on the locale, pillaging whatever items had caught their interest and trampling down the grass and bushes throughout the area. Meanwhile, heavy rains began to fall, further limiting the search for any clues, which might have helped to identify either the victim or the killer(s). At the army post, Col Cochran immediately launched an investigation to determine if any military personnel had been involved in the homicide. Neither he nor the local police found any evidence to substantiate this possibility. As a result, those suspicions were quickly put to rest.

Hoping to find some viable leads, Crim and McDermott exhaustively studied the crime scene that day, and continued to scrutinize the area during the next 3 days. Their initial task was to force any curiosity seekers on the premises who had collected relics or souvenirs related to the atrocity to immediately surrender them, and to then vacate the premises. The Cincinnati detective's continued assistance was sorely needed, for at the time, Sheriff Julius Leonard "Jake" Plummer was the only officer in all of Campbell County who was available to investigate the murder. Plummer was a dapper 36 year old father of seven, who was a highly respected lawman in northern Kentucky. As a competent and confident investigator, he welcomed the additional help from across the river in Ohio.

It had rained until 10 pm on Friday night, and investigators observed a muddy path near the body. Since the dead woman's clothing was relatively dry, the time of death was set at sometime after that hour, either late on the evening of January 31, or early in the morning of February 1. The police officers had carefully examined the footprints leading to the body, and concluded that two sets of tracks were present. They hypothesized that the smaller imprints belonged to the murder victim, and the larger, to the unknown assailant. The initial horizontal pattern of the tracks suggested that a man and woman had first walked side-by-side. However, after a short distance, the woman had sprinted forward, as if in a dead run. The man's footprints followed, and quickly caught up to hers. Clearly, an intense struggle had ensued. The victim's left hand had sustained three deep gashes, suggesting that she had grabbed the assailant's knife in a desperate attempt to protect herself as he attacked her. Her valiant effort had obviously failed.

Meanwhile, upon hearing news of the murder, crowds of inquisitive people descended upon the Newport mortician's Fourth Street establishment. Several anxious visitors asked permission to view the corpse, explaining that they knew of a missing woman who might fit the description of the victim. If their detailed accounts seemed plausible and might possibly lead to a positive identification of the body, they were allowed to view it.

Late that morning, the authorities contacted Arthur Carter of Seymour, Indiana and requested his help in the investigation. Mr. Carter owned three bloodhounds (Jack, Wheeler and Stonewall), who several years before had gained great publicity when they helped track down a murderer. The case had taken place near Washington, Indiana on the night of September 18, 1893. While sleeping, Elizabeth Wratten and five members of her son's family were viciously attacked and murdered by an unknown assailant who wielded a corn knife, a machete like weapon used to clear corn stalks from farmers' fields. The perpetrator was subsequently tracked down and captured with the help of Carter's competent canine companions.

When Carter and his dogs arrived by train in Cincinnati that evening, he proudly told journalists that more than 20 criminals were now serving time in the penitentiaries of Indiana and Illinois as a result of his hound's successful pursuits. Later that evening, County Judge Bennett authorized a reward of $200 for information leading to the apprehension of the murderer(s), and $20 for recovery of the body's missing head.

Early Sunday morning, the dogs were taken to Newport, where they were given a sniff of the victim's clothing. This breed of dog is thought to follow the scent of human skin cells, which have been sloughed off. However, because hundreds of people had traipsed around the murder site the previous day, Carter doubted that his hounds could effectively perform their duties. Sure enough, when released at the scene, the trio of bloodhounds ran aimlessly about with their noses to the ground, apparently confused by a mingling of numerous scents. Eventually, however, the animals made their way a mile northwest of Ft. Thomas. Arriving at the water-storage reservoir #2 in Covington, Kentucky, they stopped, barking and baying exuberantly, and refusing to travel any further. Only with difficulty were they removed from the spot. This led officials to believe that the murderer's grisly trophy had been deposited in the water. Thus, investigators agreed to drain the reservoir, and carefully search the resulting dry bed for the corpse's missing head. On Monday, February 3, the water was pumped out, but neither the head nor any significant clues were found. Lacking any tangible result, authorities seemed to have arrived at a dead end.

The only clue of potential value to the police was the size and style of the victim's shoes: they were very small and dainty, almost doll-like in appearance. As soon as he heard about the description of the footwear, Mr. L. D. Poock, a shoe merchant of Newport, offered his help in the investigation. With Sheriff Plummer's blessing, he studied the tip of the shoe's inner lining, and noted that it was stamped with the number 22-11-62458 (size 3). Further examination of the interior showed an imprint, "Louis & Hays, Greencastle, Indiana." Pursuing this lead, detectives contacted the Greencastle shoe store on Saturday night, and inquired about any shoes of this description that had been sold from their stock. After the clerks had examined all of their records, the owner reported that two local women had each purchased a pair of that style of shoe, and they had each paid by check. One was a cleaning lady, and the other, a student at DePauw University. Both individuals were found to be living in Greencastle, alive and well, and still in possession of their shoes. The store theorized that at least one unrecorded sale of that specific foot ware style might also have been made.

Local newspapers agreed to publish a notice requesting information from any reader who had either bought this type of shoe, or had any knowledge regarding such an item. On Tuesday, February 4, an issue of the Greencastle Daily Banner Times printed the following announcement:

Notice

Any person or persons who have purchased or know of anyone purchasing a pair of shoes from Louis & Hays answering the following description would confer a great favor by reporting same to this firm. The shoes are made on a heart shaped vamp, with a silk cashmere top. The body is of kid, and the tip of the shoe is pointed, and tipped with almond shaped patent leather. On the inside of the top of the lining in silver letters are the words "Louis & Hays, Greencastle, Ind." The following figures appear near the name: 22-11-62458.

The murder of the unknown woman, and the search for her killer were front page news in most Midwestern newspapers. Any leads being pursued by the police were of keen interest to the local journalistic community. Early Tuesday morning about 3 am, three investigators arrived in Greencastle by rail. These officials included Sheriff Jule Plummer, and Detectives Cal Crim and John McDermott. Accompanying them were three Cincinnati newspaper journalists, Frank Crawford of the *Tribune*, Theodore Mitchell of the *Enquirer*, and C. E. Lambertson of the *Post*. The six men, who registered for the night at the Commercial Hotel, had arrived to follow a lead that the murder victim might be Mrs. Charley Kesterson, a local woman who had been reported missing in the northern Kentucky area. The lady in question preferred to wear cloth-top shoes, which she typically bought at the Louis & Hays store in Greencastle.

On October 29 1895, Mrs. Kesterson had left her husband and eloped with Peter Cooper, a tin worker who was employed at a shop in Greencastle. Her mother, who lived in Saltilloville, Indiana, later disclosed that her son-in-law was a physically abusive husband. She believed that in desperation, her daughter had run away with the sheet metal laborer to a site somewhere in northern Kentucky. Because the young matron had not been heard from for several weeks, and because her physical description generally matched that of the dead woman in Newport, the detectives began to investigate this possibility.

The morning after their arrivals, they extensively questioned Charley Kesterson, who stated that his wife had written to him from Kentucky shortly after leaving town, admitting her fling with Cooper, and that he believed that she still was in the man's company. However, after questioning Mrs. Kesterson's Greencastle friends and acquaintances, the investigators learned that the missing lady's mother and father had failed to report her more current whereabouts, hoping to avoid retribution from their daughter's soon-to-be ex-husband. She was, in fact, now living in Saltilloville with her parents. These assertions were confirmed by telegram the following morning, and thus by noon on Tuesday, there was no further investigational interest in Mrs. Kesterson as the possible murder victim.

One of the first embalming schools in the country was established in Cincinnati in the 1880s. Although this well recognized institution was selected initially for the unknown victim's burial preparation, the authorities opted instead to bring the body to the Newport funeral home. On Monday afternoon, February third, the remains were closely inspected by a team of physicians, and then subsequently embalmed. Dr. Robert Carothers, a Professor at the Ohio Medical College, was in charge of the post-mortem examination. Carothers was assisted by Coroner Tingley and four other physicians who, at the conclusion of their evaluation, were unanimous in believing that the woman had not been raped. Their most notable finding was the presence of a fetus in her womb. The victim also displayed an anomaly presenting on the toes of her left foot, where small webs of flesh existed between these digits. This condition, known as syndactyly, involves the joining together of adjacent fingers or toes by soft tissue. She also had a scar on the back of her left hand, a small amount of scar tissue on the thimble finger of the right hand, and fresh hand wounds that she had suffered during the attack. Dr. Carothers concluded that the victim was approximately 20 years old, four and a half months pregnant, and had been decapitated while still alive. He hypothesized that the murder had been premeditated, and that the victim's head had been severed from her body and then hidden to prevent her identification. When asked about the relative difficulty of decapitation in this specific case, Carothers quickly responded,

"It would be very easy for a man to cut a woman's head off with a sharp knife, even if he had no knowledge of anatomy. I could do it with a small penknife and it wouldn't take long."

The murder victim's stomach and its contents were removed and sent to Dr. W. H. Crane of the Medical College of Ohio, to be tested for the presence of any foreign substances. Several days later, Dr. Crane submitted his initial report to the authorities and subsequently to the media, announcing that he had found a significant amount of cocaine in the dead woman's stomach.

As publicity regarding the crime became more widespread, additional suggestions regarding the victim's identification began emerging from the public. Two friends of Mrs. Eva Markland, of Cincinnati, had not seen this lady for several weeks and were increasingly concerned about her wellbeing. When the intimates discovered that neither Eva's parents, nor any other family member had heard from her in more than a month, they postulated that she might be the woman in question.

Eva's parents, Mr. and Mrs. Hart, immediately went to the Newport funeral home where they were allowed to examine the body. As Mrs. Hart stared at the corpse and wept softly, she told Chief Dietsch that she believed that this was her poor, mutilated daughter. The Harts had last seen Eva on New Year's Eve. The investigators eagerly seized upon this information, and instituted a search for Mrs. Markland across the

Cincinnati area. Within 24 hours, they located Eva who was working as a maid on Ninth Street. Although she gave no excuse for the lapsed communication with her mother and father, Eva agreed to contact them immediately. The authorities happily cabled the distressed parents with their good news.

During the same period that this clue had surfaced, another more promising possibility emerged. Mrs. Anna Burkhardt, of 1317 Vine Street, visited the Cincinnati police headquarters, imparting a bizarre story. She stated that on the previous Tuesday morning, fearing that the headless body might be Francisca Engelhardt, a former boarder with her, she had been allowed to visit the morgue. Francisca, who had moved to Anna's boarding house in September 1893, had remained there for two months. In late November, she had gained employment at a local hospital as a telephone operator, and thus moved closer to her work. However, having become friendly with Anna and her daughter, she returned periodically to visit them.

In the spring of 1894, Francesca ran an advertisement in a Cincinnati newspaper, seeking a marriage partner. Among the ad respondents was a Dr. Kettner from South Dakota. On April 13, Kettner came to Cincinnati to meet Miss Englehardt. In short order, he asked her to be his bride. Francesca immediately accepted his 'proposal', and the next day, they were married. Francesca vacated her apartment and the newlyweds stayed at Mrs. Burkhart's boarding house for the following 10 days. In late April, they moved out and Anna had not seen Francisca since that time. Through mutual acquaintances, she learned that Dr. Kettner and his new bride had changed residences several times over the next few months, but had remained in the Cincinnati area

Meanwhile, according to Mrs. Burkhardt, word had made its way from Cincinnati back to the small town of Mitchell, South Dakota, that Dr. Kettner had acquired a new wife. No one was more surprised at the news than his original wife, from whom Kettner had never been divorced. Implausible as it seemed to the conservative townspeople of Mitchell, Dr. Kettner was a bigamist! After the proper Mrs. Kettner had fully absorbed this shocking revelation, she filed for divorce and then traveled to Cincinnati to confront her husband. Kettner's cowardly response to the news of his legitimate wife's arrival was to flee the city with his latest missus, seeking refuge first in Louisville, and then shuttling between several small towns in Indiana, including Batesville.

Unable to proceed with the divorce in the absence of her husband, the South Dakota matron decided that her best course of action was to prosecute him for bigamy.

When Anna Burkhardt learned of Dr. Kettner's villainy, she feared for the safety of her friend, Francisca, whom, by now, she had not seen for months. Anna already knew that Francisca had grown suspicious of her new husband's past, for shortly after their wedding, she had hidden their marriage license between the folds of her corset, and later divulged this information to Anna. Now fearing that the worst had happened, Mrs. Burkhardt reasoned that if Kettner was to murder his second, illegal wife, and then render the body unidentifiable, he could elude any bigamy charge. When Anna had inspected the body in the morgue, she concluded that its size and stature strongly resembled that of Francisca, as did the arms and legs and, in particular, the strangely shaped toes. Anna convincingly presented her concerns and speculations to the police. Chief Deitsch was so intrigued by the entire story that he immediately dispatched detectives to investigate. The police sent a flurry of telegrams to numerous communities where they speculated that Dr. Kettner and Francesca could have been staying. Late Wednesday afternoon, they discovered and documented that the "newlyweds" were still together and living peacefully in Marquette, Michigan.

The detectives also learned that the "good doctor" was wanted by the police in several additional locales, where he had been charged with a variety of other nefarious activities. Soon, Dr. Kettner's troubles with the law were duly addressed, and he was held accountable for his offenses. A hefty fine left him financially strapped, and further legal action rendered him officially divorced from his first wife and alienated from his second. In spite of the uproar, Francisca still gained some solace in the fact that at least Dr. Kettner was not a vicious murderer.

Meanwhile, the Bryan family's anxiety and concern about Pearl's safety was growing. After fervently following the newspaper accounts of the vicious murder at Ft. Thomas, they had concluded with great apprehension that descriptions of the dead girl's body resembled that of their youngest daughter, whom they had not heard from for a week. Pearl's brother, Fred, fearfully telegraphed Miss Jane Fisher in Indianapolis, asking her if Pearl was still visiting her. He was stunned to learn that his sister had not been to see Jane at all! When A. W. Early, the manager of the Western Union Telegraph Company at Greencastle, examined the two telegrams, he realized that he possessed personal information that might be vital in shedding light on the murder investigation. Even though it implicated one of his good friends, he knew that he had to tell the truth. His conscience demanded it. Rushing to the hotel where the sheriff and detectives were staying, Early related to them the following story:

On October 4, 1895, after I had moved to Greencastle, and gotten a job at Western Union, I knew few people in the town, but struck up a friendship with Will Wood. Over time, we began to confide in each other, and one day Will showed me a few letters from his friend, Scott Jackson. In one of them, Scott talked about how he had been having ... ahh, you know ... intimate relations with Pearl Bryan, and wouldn't you know it, she got pregnant. Since they were good pals and Pearl was Will's cousin, Scott expected him to help rectify the situation. You know ... to save Pearl's honor and all that sort of thing. Well, anyway, Scott sent several chemical "recipes" which he believed would end the pregnancy, and he asked Wood to obtain the required ingredients at a pharmacy, and make sure that Pearl swallowed them. So, Will, loyal buddy that he was, talked Pearl into taking the stuff. She was reluctant to do so, and wanted to marry Scott and have the baby, but Will finally convinced her. When no abortion was induced, Will informed Scott of the failure, and then received a new assignment: to convince Pearl to visit Jackson in Cincinnati. Early added, "Wood told me afterward that he had talked Pearl into going to Cincinnati to see Scott, but the reason for the trip was kept open. Pearl still saw this reunion as perhaps a chance to again consider marriage. Will felt a momentary pang of guilt that he was not leveling with her, but he figured that his job was to simply get Pearl to Cincinnati. After all, she was a grown woman and didn't need his input. Early added one more piece of information, "Will said that a few days before Pearl left for Cincinnati, she had lied to her parents, telling them that she was going to Indianapolis for a week to visit an old friend."

By the time that the detectives had listened to this entire disclosure, it was past midnight. Disregarding the late hour, they rushed to the residence of Lou Spivey, manager of the Louis & Hays Shoe Store. Awakening him with their vigorous knocking, they asked for permission to reexamine the sales records that he kept at the store. He agreed and accompanied them to his place of business. This time, their more meticulous inspection proved fruitful: Pearl Bryan had purchased a pair of size 3B shoes the previous November. Thus, at 2 AM on Wednesday morning, the police officers dutifully visited the home of Alex and Jane Bryan, taking the clothes and hairpins that they had recovered from the body of the deceased woman. Mrs. Bryan immediately recognized the items and wailed,

"My Pearl! My Pearl!"

In shocked disbelief, the entire family sorrowfully and reluctantly concluded that the murder victim must be Pearl.

Without delay, the detectives sent a telegram to Philip Deitsch, Cincinnati's Superintendent of Police. The communiqué read in part:

> *"Arrest and charge with murder of Pearl Bryan, one Scott Jackson, student at the Dental College .... Arrest if in Cincinnati, William Wood, friend of Jackson. Charge as accomplice"*

CHAPTER TEN

The full text of the telegram sent by the three law officers in Greencastle to Philip Deitsch, Superintendent of Police in Cincinnati, read:

> *"Arrest and charge with murder of Pearl Bryan, one Scott Jackson, student at Dental College, about 24 years old, 5 feet 7 or 8 inches high, weighs about 130 pounds, blonde, nearly sandy mustache, light complexion, may have beard of about six months growth, effeminate in appearance. Have positive identification of clothing by family. Arrest if in Cincinnati, William Wood, friend of Jackson. Charge as accomplice. About 20 years, 5 feet 11 inches, light blonde hair, smooth face, rather slender, weighs 165 pounds. We go from here to South Bend after Wood as he left here for that place."*   Crim, McDermott and Plummer

Chief Deitsch immediately dispatched three detectives to find and arrest Scott Jackson. The officers, informed that Scott was also frequently called 'Dusty' or 'Doc', promptly discovered that Jackson was living at a boarding house at 222 West Ninth Street, next door to the Robinson's Opera House, where he shared a room with fellow dental student, Alonzo Walling. However, Jackson was not in his room when the investigators arrived. Hoping that he might return soon, one detective remained inside the entryway to the boarding house, while the other two men stationed themselves in a saloon across the street. During the next 16 hours, however, police could not locate Jackson anywhere in the city.

Shortly after 9 pm, Deitsch was informed that Jackson had been seen at the Palace Hotel on the northwest corner of Sixth and Vine streets. Detectives were sent at once to this address where they searched the lodging and its surroundings, fanning out in all directions. Detective Bulmer soon spotted a young man fitting Jackson's description strolling west on Ninth Street. The suspect paused in front of Mrs. McNevin's boarding house, stared for a moment at the upstairs windows and then, cautiously continued walking toward Plum Street. Once there, he stopped again, glanced back at the house and turned north. After he had taken only a few steps, officer Bulmer, a large, burly fellow, intercepted him, declaring,

"Your name is Jackson, right?" The startled man looked at the detective incredulously, turned pale, and nodded affirmatively.

Bulmer barked, "I want you!" Jackson nervously exclaimed, "My God! What is this about?"

The detective seized Jackson firmly by the elbow, informing him that he was wanted for murder and that both Mayor John A. Caldwell and Superintendent of Police, Philip Deitsch, were waiting to question him. Bulmer promptly steered his dazed captive south toward City Hall, where Cincinnati's government center was housed. This majestic building, completed just 3 years earlier, had walls of red granite and brown sandstone. Occupying one entire city-block, and reaching 4½ stories high, it featured a nine-story clock tower on its front façade. The detective and Jackson climbed the stairs of the Plum Street entrance, where Superintendent Deitsch was awaiting them. With thinning hair and a heavy mustache, he was a solid 165-pound man carried on a 5'8" frame. Prior to the onset of the Civil War, Deitsch had fought against the Plains Indians under Phil Sheridan's command. During the War Between the States, Deitsch was a member of the Army of the Potomac, participating in the battles of Antietam, Chancellorsville, Fredericksburg, and was wounded at Gettysburg.

Now the highest-ranking police officer in Cincinnati, Deitsch was well respected in his community. Looking straight into Jackson's eyes, he proclaimed, "Well, Dusty, we have got you!" As Jackson's shoulders slumped dejectedly, he responded, "Yes, it looks like it."

Pivoting briskly, Deitsch entered the building with Bulmer and Jackson, turned left past granite columns and a marble stairway and strode to Mayor Caldwell's office. He rapped on the door, and the party of three was granted entry. As the men crossed the threshold, Jackson paused for a moment and looked anxiously at his surroundings.

The Palace Hotel in Cincinnati, located on the northwest corner of Sixth and Vine streets. Scott Jackson was seen walking by this building at 9 pm, February 5, 1896. The police were contacted and Chief Deitsch informed. An hour later, Jackson was arrested a few blocks north of this site on Ninth Street near his boarding house. Courtesy of the Public Library of Cincinnati and Hamilton County.

CINCINNATI CITY HALL.

Cincinnati's City Hall, an imposing structure which filled an entire city block and housed the Police Department, City Jail, and the Mayor's Office. From the Police and Municipal Guide, Cincinnati, 1901.

Published by the Ohio Book Store, 726 Main Street, Cincinnati, Ohio.

The suite contained a number of ornate rooms interconnected by tall, arched doorways topped by clear, glass transoms. The main chamber, large and imposing, was made to look even more spacious and grand by its 12-foot ceilings. On the east corner of the decorative tile floor sat six upholstered, wingback chairs and an ample couch, positioned around a heavy, circular oak table with a granite top. A potted palm plant adorned the center of the table. Directly above this elegant, yet comfortable collection of furniture hung a massive, sparkling chandelier, which housed twelve luminous electric globes. Nearby, the mayor sat at his desk in an oak swivel chair, puffing vigorously on a Cuban cigar. Seated nearby were: Chief Clerk Cliff Lakeman; Coroner Haern; three detectives; and several representatives of the local press.

Vintage postcard of the Mayor's Office in Cincinnati's City Hall, circa 1908, where Scott Jackson was initially interrogated by Mayor Caldwell and other officials. Courtesy of the Public Library of Cincinnati and Hamilton County.

As Jackson entered the room, His Honor remained seated, but spun around swiftly to face him. Grimly, he motioned Scott to sit in the middle of the davenport between Superintendent Deitsch and Detective Bulmer. Glancing at the occupant of the swivel chair, Jackson asked tentatively, "Is this Mayor Caldwell?" His Honor responded, "It is." Shifting his gaze back to Deitsch, Jackson inquired, "The officer said you wanted to see me?" Deitsch leaned toward Jackson and replied, "Yes, indeed. We definitely want to speak with you, and have a number of questions that you need to consider very carefully and answer truthfully."

Mayor Caldwell, a past prosecuting attorney of the Cincinnati police court, began the interrogation:

"What is your name?"

"Scott Jackson."

"You are also known as Dusty?"

"Yes, sometimes."

"Where is your home?"

"Greencastle, Indiana."

"Do you know Pearl Bryan?"

"I do."

"When and where did you last see her?"

"It was during the Christmas holidays. I think on January 2nd."

"Have you seen her since?"

"I have not."

"Do you know William Wood?"

"I do."

"What is his business?"

"I don't know. He used to be connected with the school at Greencastle (DePauw University). I saw him last about January 6th."

Turning to retrieve an official looking paper from the top of his desk, Deitsch read aloud the dispatch under which Scott was arrested. "What have you to say to this accusation?"

"That charge is entirely false. I know nothing about the murder!"

"That's what everybody says after they're arrested. But the identification of the clothes and other facts point directly to you as the man who took Pearl Bryan - or her body - to Ft. Thomas. Where were you last Friday evening?"

"I must have been in my room."

"What time did you go to your room?"

"I believe I had supper about 7 pm, and went home around 7:30."

"And what did you do there?"

"I studied for my classes."

"Was your roommate there?"

"I think he was."

Over the next hour, Deitsch and others continued to pepper Jackson with questions. After he had been thoroughly grilled and still refused to admit any involvement in Pearl Bryan's murder, he was escorted from the office by Detective Bulmer, and walked down a long corridor, leading directly to the Central Police Station. As they reached their destination, Night Chief "Iron Neck Sam" Corbin and a dour looking Sergeant Billy Borck were seated behind the main desk. As Corbin began the registration process, a curious group of employees gathered in the hallway, watching the proceedings.

"What is your name?"

"Scott Jackson."

"Where do you live?"

"I live here in Cincinnati now."

"Whereabouts?"

"Number 222 West Ninth Street."

"Old or new number?"

"I don't know; it's next door to Robinson's Opera House."

"What is your occupation?"

"Dental student."

"How old are you?"

"Twenty-six."

"Married or single?"

"Single."

"Where were you born?"

"In Maine."

Looking up, Corbin inquired,

"What's the charge against this man?"

"Murder," replied Bulmer.

"Is that right?" Corbin asked, looking fixedly at the prisoner.

"I believe that's what they say," replied Scott.

At this point, three police officers ushered Jackson to a small room located behind the receiving desk, where a thorough search was conducted, yielding two carriage tickets for the Central Newport Bridge present in his pants pocket. Additionally, on the right sleeve of his undershirt, they noticed several spots resembling dried blood. On closer examination, it appeared that the stains had been moistened, perhaps in an attempt to wash them out. After the policemen had ordered the accused to remove all of his clothing and had inspected him from head to toe, they noticed two prominent, elongated, red abrasions, trailing down his right arm.

"Where did the blood and these scratches come from?" demanded Lt. Corbin.

"I was bothered by bugs the other evening, and I scratched myself raw until it bled. I also seem to have suffered some kind of allergic reaction to them."

In response to this lame and seemingly rehearsed explanation, Detective Bulmer and Officer Jake Bernhart glanced at each other, rolled their eyes and snickered. Regaining their composure, they asked Jackson a few more questions and then lead him to a cramped jail cell in the basement. As he stepped into the dim, dank cubicle, the heavy iron door clanged shut behind him.

Chewing nervously on his lower lip, and twirling his mustache with his thumb and forefinger, the prisoner turned and gripped the cold, iron bars with both hands. Pleadingly, he asked the departing jailer, "Mind sitting up all night in front of my cell?" The turnkey smirked, "Why? Are you afraid of getting lynched?" This was exactly what Jackson feared, and his apprehension was certainly warranted, for lynching was relatively common during this era. In fact, an angry crowd demanding justice for this heinous crime had already begun to gather outside the jail.

Defensively, Jackson replied, "Never mind about that. I just prefer to be well guarded, whether I'm in danger or not." Now suddenly consumed with exhaustion, he lay down on his bunk to rest, but sleep would not rescue him from his apprehension.

At about 2 am, Jackson blurted out, "Hasn't Walling been arrested yet?" The jailer (posted nearby as his prisoner had requested) quickly responded, "Why should he be arrested?" Jackson did not answer. The dutiful guard immediately reported this remark to Lt. Corbin, who took quick action: he walked to Alonzo Walling's boarding house, entered the front door, found Jackson and Walling's room and knocked repeatedly. Stumbling to the portal still half asleep, the occupant looked drowsily at the officer, who sternly returned his cloudy gaze with a volley of pointed questions. "Were you in Wallingford's saloon with Scott Jackson and a girl last Friday night?"

"Uhh, yes, I was."

"Who was the girl you were with?"

"I don't know who she was."

"Listen! You'd better tell me everything you know about this matter! Now let's start over. Tell me who was in the party at Wallingford's last Friday evening?"

"I don't know anything more about it."

"If that's your story, so be it, but consider yourself under arrest. Come along with me." Seizing Walling by the arm, officer Corbin roughly escorted him the short distance to police headquarters, where he was locked up at 3 a.m. Jackson was not informed of his roommate's arrest until several hours later.

At 6:30 the following morning, Superintendent Deitsch was handed a telegram from Detectives Crim and McDermott announcing that they had arrested Will Wood in South Bend, and that he had confessed to arranging Pearl Bryan's trip to Cincinnati for a "criminal operation." Wood had also implicated both Scott Jackson and Alonzo Walling in the overall scheme to rid Pearl of "her burden."

After receiving this communication, Deitsch was becoming troubled by the unparalleled scene unfolding at police headquarters. Hundreds of individuals were converging on City Hall to catch a glimpse of the murder suspects. Throngs of people had not only massed on the streets outside of the building, but also filled the hallways. By mid-morning, the expanding crowd had become so aroused and unruly, that an additional contingent of police was called out to restore order.

As the day drew on, Jackson continued to disregard all questions that might implicate him in Pearl's murder. However, when Walling was quizzed, he readily acknowledged his friendship with Jackson, and, in the face of intense grilling, disclosed that he had, in fact, seen Pearl on one occasion during her four-day visit to Cincinnati. Walling then abruptly stunned his interrogators by divulging that, sometime around the Christmas holiday, Scott taken him aside and confessed that he and Will Wood had gotten Pearl Bryan into trouble, and that he now must dispose of her.

Walling recalled several schemes proposed by Jackson to accomplish this end. One plan was to lure the young lady into a cheap hotel room in the tenderloin district, kill her, and abandon her body there. Walling further recalled that after proposing this potential plan, Jackson had paused suddenly, narrowed his eyes as though receiving some kind of revelation, and corrected himself. "Wait a minute!" he had said. "I have a better idea. I always get a surge of insight when I'm on the wrong track. I wouldn't just leave her body in the room. Instead, I would cut it into small pieces and drop them into different sewers scattered throughout the city. That way, she could never be identified if segments of her body were eventually found!"

Walling proceeded with his story, "One Friday evening when Dusty and I were in Wallingford's saloon drinking a few beers with a bunch of medical students, Jackson quizzed those fellows intensely about which poison would kill a person the most quickly. A lively discussion of this topic ensued and continued for some time, until the consensus emerged that either hydrocyanic or prussic acid would likely cause the quickest death, although cocaine was also fast acting and perhaps the most deadly. A few days later, Jackson stopped at Koeble's drugstore on Sixth Street and purchased cocaine (not a legally controlled substance until 1970)."

Investigators peppered the two suspects with questions for the remainder of that day. Jackson finally admitted to having been with Pearl during her visit to Cincinnati, but vowed that he had not been involved in her murder. Rather, he insisted that Walling must have done it. Meanwhile, Walling steadfastly maintained that Jackson was the killer. He claimed that in mid-January, Scott had once again spoken to him about Pearl's pregnancy, and had requested his aid in getting the girl "out of trouble." Dusty said that the girl would be coming here in about a week. Last Monday, he announced that she would be arriving that night. The next day, he told me that Pearl Bryan was now in Cincinnati at the Indiana House, and he insisted that I go down there with him, so I did. He went up to her room, while I waited downstairs. After some time, I tired of just hanging around doing nothing, so I left and attended to other matters. Later, he never even asked why I had departed. The next day, he wanted me to meet the young lady at Fourth and Plum Streets. I was to convey his apologies for not showing up himself, and to inform her that he would be waiting for her there at seven that evening. I did what he asked, and that was the last I ever saw of her."

After another hour of questioning, Walling was dismissed and returned to his cell. However, less than 30 minutes later, he suddenly asked to speak with Superintendent Deitsch once again. During this second session, he made a fascinating disclosure:

"I want to tell you something else that may have a big bearing on this case."

"What is it?"

"Well, yesterday afternoon, Jackson got some paper and envelopes and told me he was going to the Palace Hotel to compose a letter. I asked him who he was writing it to and he said the letter was for Will Wood in Greencastle. He told me that he planned to enclose a note for Pearl Bryan's mother, disguised as if Pearl had written it, and that he would ask Will to send it, I think first to La Fayette to Will's friend who could then re-mail it to Mrs. Bryan. He said he was going to do this in order to throw the Bryans off track."

"Do you know that for a fact, that he sent the letter?"

"Yes, he told me last night just before he was arrested that he had mailed it."

Deitsch immediately shared this revelation with Mayor Caldwell, who responded by firing off a telegram to South Bend, while Deitsch took a break in his interrogation of the prisoner. Caldwell's communiqué read:

Cincinnati, Ohio, February 6, 1896

Postmaster, South Bend, Indiana: Kindly send all mail addressed to Wm. Wood from this city to me.

John A. Caldwell, Mayor

Thirty minutes later, Deutsch continued his questioning of Walling. "Jackson still puts all the blame for the murder on you."

"He does, does he? Well, he is the one who is guilty. I know nothing of the crime."

"What do you think became of Pearl's head?"

"I never saw her head, but Jackson told me he threw it into a sewer."

By first claiming to know nothing of the crime, and then stating that Jackson told him how he had disposed of Pearl's head, Walling had literally "hung himself" with his contradictory statements. During the rest of the day, both Scott Jackson and Alonzo Walling were questioned intermittently, but neither man admitted any involvement in Pearl's murder; rather, each continued to accuse the other.

At 9 pm, Crim and McDermott arrived in Cincinnati by train, and quickly escorted their prisoner, Will Wood, to City Hall. The suspect was accompanied by four men: his father, Reverend Demos Wood; his uncle, Reverend A. A. Gee; an Indianapolis attorney, Mr. A. N. Grant; and a friend of the family from Michigan City. Mr. A. R. Colburn, a wealthy lumber merchant who had agreed to furnish bond for Wood, should it be needed.

Upon their arrival, Crim and McDermott immediately joined Mayor Caldwell and Superintendent Deitsch at the jail, where they aggressively interrogated Jackson, and then, Walling. Jackson continued to profess his innocence of the murder, contending that he was not even the father of Pearl's unborn baby. Rather, he claimed that Will Wood was "the author of her ruin."

At 11:30 pm, Wood, in the presence of both his father and his uncle, was subjected to an oral examination in the Mayor's private office. Following some preliminary questions, the inquiry grew more pointed.

"Were you ever intimate with Pearl Bryan?"

"No, Sir."

"Did you know of anyone else who was?"

"Yes Sir. Jackson told me that he had been intimate with her in September."

"Did you receive any letters from Jackson about Miss Bryan's condition?"

"I did, on about the 10th of January. He said he was going to have an operation performed on her if he could get a hold of enough money (to pay for it). He said he had gotten a room for Pearl in Cincinnati, and that the operation would be performed by a doctor and chemist who was an old hand at that kind of business."

"Did Miss Bryan know about this scheme at the time?"

"She did, because I told her about the plan myself."

"Was the letter you received from Jackson the only way that you knew that he and the girl had been intimate?"

"No. Pearl told me herself when I was out at her house several weeks ago."

"And so, you dropped Miss Bryan off at the Greencastle depot on Monday, January 27, and she took the train to Cincinnati?"

"Yes Sir. That's correct. I also met my father at the depot right after I said "goodbye" to Pearl, because he had just arrived on that same train from a quarterly meeting at Terre Haute."

"Have you ever been in Cincinnati before?"

"No Sir."

"Do you know Alonzo Walling?"

"No Sir. I've never seen him in my entire life."

As the questioning proceeded, it became obvious that Wood had not been in that city at the time of the murder, and thus could not have directly participated in the crime. Subsequently, he was taken down to the Central Police Station and registered. After he had provided his name, age, and place of residence, he was charged with aiding and abetting an attempted abortion and was released to his father under a $5,000 bond. A short time later, the elder Wood and his son joined their small entourage at the Grand Hotel, where they spent the night.

Meanwhile, Dr. Crane, the Campbell County medical examiner, had notified authorities that he had detected the presence of cocaine in Pearl Bryan's stomach. The following day, the leather valise, which was suspected to have carried Pearl's head from the murder site, was discovered in John Kugle's saloon. It was promptly delivered to Police Headquarters.

Several additional pieces of evidence related to the case also soon emerged. Detectives found Jackson's coat, spotted with what appeared to be bloodstains, in the sewer at Richmond and John streets. Shortly after, Mrs. Plymouth Meeks of Cincinnati came to the Police Station and identified Jackson as the man who had been at her home with Pearl Bryan on Thursday afternoon January 29 for a séance session. She methodically related to the officials what she had remembered about that visit, including the circumstances surrounding it and the conversation which occurred among the three of them.

Just before noon on Friday, Frank and Maude Bryan, along with several family friends, arrived in Cincinnati from Greencastle. Frank promptly made arrangements to return his sister's body to her hometown.

Now, for the first time, Jackson and Walling were interrogated in each other's presence. However, this session revealed little additional information, as the two suspects simply clung to their prior stories, adamantly accusing each other of the crime. As a result of this deadlock, the decision was made to charge both men with Pearl's murder. When Jackson and Walling appeared in court, they stoically received the murder indictment, displaying little emotion. Wood, also present, was accused of making illegal arrangements for Pearl's abortion. His arraignment was delayed for future consideration.

On Friday, February 7, one day after Mayor Caldwell's dispatch had been sent, the South Bend postmaster intercepted the letter that Jackson had so hurriedly written and mailed to Wood just before he was arrested. On Saturday, February 8th, the communication was surrendered to the Cincinnati investigators, who immediately realized what formidable evidence against Jackson it represented.

It read:

> *"Hello, Bill ---*
>
> *Write a letter home signed by Bert's name telling the folks that he is somewhere & going to Chicago or some other place -- has a position etc -- and that they will advise later about it -- Say tired of living at home or anything you want. Send it to someone you can trust -- How about Will Smith at LaFayette -- tell the folks that he has not been at I but at LaFayette and traveling about the country. Get the letter off without one second's delay – and burn this at once. Stick by your old chum Bill – And I will help you out the same way – sometimes. Am glad you are having a good time –*
>
> > *D.*
> > *Be careful what you write to me"*

The Mayor, police, and prosecutor were elated, now confident that the fragmentary and cryptic message which they now had in their possession, directly implicated Scott Jackson in the murder of Pearl Bryan. They had quickly surmised that "Bert" referred to Pearl; that "I" meant Indianapolis; and that "D" stood for Dusty. Undoubtedly, Jackson had contrived this deceitful scheme to cast doubt on the evidence that Pearl had been murdered.

Meanwhile, early on Saturday morning, Will Wood and his party left Cincinnati for Greencastle. However, shortly after they arrived in town, City Marshall Starr approached them and ordered Will to leave immediately, warning that if he stayed, his personal safety would be at risk. Apparently, a plot to lynch Wood was brewing among a band of young men in the community who were passionate in their desire to gain revenge for the Bryan family. Will responded quickly, departing on the 2 pm train bound for Indianapolis.

Among the various biological theories of crime causation that were formulated during the 19th century, phrenology was the most popular. In essence, this premise suggested that the shape of an individual's skull and underlying brain could reveal his/her personality, psychological development, and propensity to become a criminal. On the afternoon of Saturday, February 8, both Jackson and Walling underwent phrenological examinations in the Bertillon Room at police headquarters. These tests were conducted by Dr. Hyndman, who served as a consultant for the Cincinnati police department. Having been trained in Chicago to use phrenology as an aid in criminal investigations, Dr. Hyndman was confident in the efficacy of his medical specialty, and had been eager to examine the two suspects.

Hyndman began his evaluation using calipers to measure the skull size of each captive. After noting this information, the physician carefully and repeatedly ran his fingertips and palms over the men's skulls. He was particularly interested in identifying and charting any bumps, enlargements, indentations, fissures or other anomalies. During his examinations, he utilized a large drawing of the human skull for reference and he paused periodically to record his findings.

At the conclusion of his extensive cranial inspections, Hyndman wrote two individual summary reports of his findings. In the Sunday, February 9 issue, the Cincinnati Enquirer published his interpretations (in today's world, a violation of the HIPAA Privacy Rule, protecting the privacy of an individual's health information). Jackson was described as "nervous, with good, quick reasoning power ... a bold, fearless, intense organizer, with a perverted amativeness (amorousness) ... who would mislead anyone to assist himself and who has strong perceptive power ... a good planner, and a fearless executioner."

Walling's skull pronounced him as "easily led in the direction of friendship," in whose cause "he would often do things which his better nature would revolt against ... His standard of morals is not of a high order, his perceptive powers are small, and if he would be influenced, he would have to be managed through his self-approbation (need for approval). He is susceptible to flattery and would make a confidant of one who would flatter him in this manner."

It is difficult to assess the credibility level given to such phrenological evidence during this era. However, after the Enquirer's publication of the cranial data, the public increasingly perceived Jackson as the instigator and principal leader in carrying out Pearl's murder, and Walling, in all likelihood, as simply his pawn and follower.

As time passed, additional witnesses came forward, who presented assorted pieces of information, helping to clarify the events occurring on the night of Pearl Bryan's murder. Although the accumulating evidence against Jackson and Walling was largely circumstantial, it was, nevertheless, quite compelling. Officials in the prosecutor's office were increasingly confident that their case was taking shape

On Friday morning, a reporter for the Indianapolis Sun conducted an interview with Miss Nellie Crane. She had been Jackson's 'call girl' friend in Indianapolis while he was a student there. Now a self-described "reformed woman," Nellie currently lived with her aged parents on Hermann Street. Recalling her relationship with Jackson, she stated that when sober, he was a stimulating conversationalist and fun to be around, but when he was drinking, he "was one of the orneriest men I ever knew."

Nellie also divulged that when Scott had worked at *The When Store* during the holidays, he had stolen a ring, several silk handkerchiefs, and additional merchandise, all of which he had presented to her as gifts that he had purchased. When Nellie was asked if she thought Scott could actually commit the kind of horrific crime with which he was charged, she quickly responded, "Yes, I do. He was a very dangerous man when he was drunk and appeared to be capable of many cruel things. One night, when we were together in Jake Crone's Saloon, he got mad at me, and threatened to kill me with a razor." She went on to say that after he was arrested on New Year's Eve and dispatched to the workhouse, she had never again seen Jackson.

The Sun also published some heartfelt thoughts that Mrs. Alex Bryan had provided regarding her deceased daughter. The 64 year old lady stated that she would rather see Pearl dead than lead the life of sin and shame into which her murderers had lead her.

Meanwhile, Mrs. Sarah Jackson apparently had relinquished her initial conviction of Scott's innocence, and commented, "If my son is guilty of this terrible crime, let him meet justice and the full extent of the law. I have no hope now of his changing his life. I have done all that a Christian mother could. May God be merciful to him, and may he have time, even yet, to repent and be saved!"

In contrast, Mrs. Demos Wood was more confrontational. She refused to accept the notion that her son carried any guilt in the wretched affair, and she ridiculed and denied the reports that her boy had previously led a reckless and dissipated life. However, it was strongly rumored around Greencastle that the Bryan family believed young Wood to be the major villain responsible for Pearl's downfall and her subsequent death. Her father emphatically stated that his daughter would be at home, alive and well if it were not for her association with Will Wood. The rift between the two biologically related families would never be healed.

During the afternoon of Saturday, February 8, Pearl's body was discreetly moved from Newport to Eppley's morgue in Cincinnati across the street from City Hall. A very dramatic scene occurred later that evening in this establishment. Mayor Caldwell, Superintendent Deitsch, and Sheriff Plummer, accompanied by several newspaper reporters, met Pearl's sister, Mrs. J.T. (Maude) Stanley and her brother, Fred Bryan, at the funeral home. In their midst, Pearl's remains, attired in her silk high school graduation dress, were laid out in a pure white casket.

After a few somber moments had passed, Detectives Crim and McDermott ushered the two accused men into the room, where they abruptly and unexpectedly encountered Maude and Fred, mournfully looking down at Pearl's body. Jackson was directed to stand at the head of the coffin, and Walling, near the foot. In the presence of Pearl's brother and sister, the two captives nervously glanced down at her remains. Moments later, Deitsch began to interrogate them.

"Look at me, Walling! Do you recognize the corpse which lies in this casket?" resonated Deitsch.

"I have every reason to believe it is that of Miss Bryan," responded Walling in a clear voice.

"And how do you know that?"

"From what Scott has told me."

Turning toward the other defendant, Deitsch sternly asked,

"Jackson! Do you recognize this corpse?"

"I suppose it is that of Miss Bryan," was the noncommittal reply.

Turning back to Walling, Deitsch asked bluntly, "Alonzo, did you kill this woman?"

"I did not, but I have every reason to believe that Jackson did."

Turning to the other prisoner once more, Deitsch repeated, "Jackson, did you murder this girl?"

"I did not, sir."

"Can you actually look upon this corpse and deny that you committed the crime?"

"I can, and I do most emphatically," was the response.

Keeping his eyes riveted on Scott, Deitsch dourly demanded. "Who did kill her?"

"I have every reason to believe that Walling did."

Although additional probing questions were hurled at the prisoners by the vexed interrogators, the curt and one-dimensional responses yielded no viable indications of what had actually transpired during the murder. In a last desperate attempt to break their resolve, Deitsch turned to Maude Stanley and Fred Bryan and invited them to quiz the two men, but the two despondent siblings both quickly declined to ask any questions.

As Jackson and Walling were marched back to their cells, Deitsch once again invited Maude and Fred to question the suspects face-to-face, but this time in a nearby isolated room. Retrospectively, he realized that such a gut-wrenching confrontation was not best conducted in the presence of Pearl's body. Regretting his initial impulsive move, he hoped to rectify the situation. Hesitantly, the two shaken siblings conferred, and moments later, Maude agreed to participate in such a meeting.

She entered the designated room into which the two prisoners had been steered moments before. A guard was stationed at the open door, and stared fixedly at the men, his eyes following their every gesture.

Holding back her tears, Maude first approached Scott: "Mr. Jackson. I come to you and ask, where is my sister's head? For the sake of my poor mother and the others in our grieving family, I beg of you to tell me. This is our only chance to send Pearl's complete remains home, and give her a proper, Christian burial. Won't you please tell me?"

Jackson looked at her, and coolly replied, "I don't know where it is."

A moment later, she approached Walling, and nervously pleaded with him to reveal the same information. But Walling, like Jackson, denied having any such knowledge. Concluding that nothing would be gained by interacting further with the two prisoners, Maude quickly exited the room.

Chief Deitsch, who had waited in he hall during the brief interchanges, stepped aside as the guard took the two men away. He briefly expressed his sympathies to Maude and thanked her profusely for her brave efforts. She sniffed in acknowledgment, and then hurried down the corridor to rejoin her waiting brother. At this point, Deitsch returned to the anteroom, where he gloomily told his associates and expectant journalists, "I've been in many trying situations before, but have never seen anything to equal this. How they could refuse to tell that poor woman where her sister's head is hidden, I cannot understand!"

Later that evening, amidst the snorts and snores of the sleeping jail guards, the two defendants discarded their cigar stubs and crawled onto their cots to sleep. Jackson hoarsely whispered to Walling, "Lonnie! I think things are looking pretty good, as long as neither of us admits to anything." Lonnie responded, "Well that won't be a problem. There's nothing to admit to, is there?"

The next morning, accompanied by Maude, Fred, and several family friends, Pearl's body was returned home to Greencastle by rail. It was eight days after her mutilated body had been discovered near Ft. Thomas.

Throughout 1896 and 1897, news related to Pearl Bryan's murder and the subsequent arrests and trials of Scott Jackson and Alonzo Walling continued to dominate the front pages of many Midwestern tabloids. Having ready access to the jail's donated newspapers, the two defendants spent much of their time reading. While awaiting their fates during their period of confinement, they delighted in following every published detail regarding their case. Reading these scandalous reviews clearly broke the tedium of their imprisonment, and also allowed them to revel in their notoriety. Occasionally, the news prompted them to think that they might be found innocent, or at the least maintain hope for a reprieve or pardon. In Walling's case, reading these articles must have on occasion caused him to relive the entire tragic scenario involving the murder, and to lament his foolhardy involvement with Jackson.

Aside from engaging their minds in this nefarious fame, they were also entertained by some of the more mundane published stories. With lighthearted amusement they read that on February 9, President Grover Cleveland had returned from a bird-hunting trip to the lakes of

Quantico, Virginia, where he had bagged 82 waterfowl. "Wonder how long it will take our President to eat 82 ducks?" mused Jackson.

They sometimes read tragic news reports as well. In Springfield, Illinois, a serious outbreak of diphtheria had occurred; and in Middletown, Connecticut, several residents of an Italian boardinghouse who had contracted smallpox, were transported to a nearby pest house (euphemistically referred to as an 'isolation hospital'). As the days passed, keeping in touch with outside news events provided at least a modicum of normalcy to the two captives' lives. To stir their imaginations, Jackson and Walling discussed the relative merits of being housed in the Newport jail, as opposed to being isolated in the aforementioned Connecticut pest house.

In addition, an entry in an Indianapolis newspaper reported that "a 10 year old boy was found lying unconscious on a city street, yesterday, suffering from the effects of smoking cigarettes." Walling snorted, "Well, Dusty … it looks like our cigars may be the death of us, yet!" The irony was not lost to Jackson.

Observing the current on-going congenial interactions of these two incarcerated murder suspects, their captors were confounded as to how two men who had so repeatedly and emphatically accused each other of an atrocious crime, could now be jailhouse buddies. Their current relationship was a total enigma! How could this forgiving attitude arise so quickly between two apparent adversaries, especially within the participant who appeared to be far less guilty?

On Tuesday, Feb 11, Coroner Tingley and six jurors began to deliberate concerning the manner, the cause and the location of Pearl Bryan's death. The next day, the Coroner's Inquest concluded that the young woman had died from decapitation on the Locke farm near Newport. This report had great practical implications, for if Pearl was murdered in the Cincinnati area and her body then transferred across the Ohio River, the state of Ohio would claim jurisdiction in the case. In contrast, if she had died in the orchard at Ft. Thomas, Kentucky would have the authority to try the case. The governmental authorities and the general populace of Kentucky were determined that the trials be held in their state.

On Saturday, February 15, amid the legal haranguing over the issue of jurisdiction, a major break in the case had transpired. An African-American coachman, George F Jackson, came forth to reveal that on

Friday night, January 31, he had carried two men and a woman in his cab from Cincinnati across the Ohio River to a spot near Ft. Thomas. There, the three passengers had disembarked, with the men flanking the apparently disoriented woman. The hack driver stated that the dark-headed man had told him to wait for their return. However, minutes later, when he heard chilling sounds of a fierce struggle from the darkness, he feared for his own personal safety, and ran away from the site, leaving the horse and buggy behind.

As George continued his disclosure of the events of that evening to the authorities, he identified Alonzo Walling as the dark-headed man in his cab, and Scott Jackson as, very likely, the other. The following day, the rig which George H Jackson claimed to have driven on the night of the murder, was identified as having been rented to Walling by Walnut Hills liveryman, Chester P Mullen. Meanwhile, on Thursday morning, March 5, Sheriff Plummer traveled to Frankfort, the Kentucky state capital, hoping to obtain the requisition papers required for relocating the prisoners from Ohio to Kentucky. However, attorneys representing Jackson and Walling had filed the necessary forms to at least temporarily block this action. Legal haggling ensued, as the two states battled for custody of the two men and for the right to try them for their alleged crime. On Saturday, March 7, Judge Buchwalter ruled that the requisition papers necessary to move the two prisoners from Cincinnati to Newport were valid. Nine days later, the appropriate Circuit Court sustained Judge Buchwalter's action and held that the two prisoners must be extradited to Kentucky as quickly as possible. At last, the blue grass state was going to get its wish!

CHAPTER ELEVEN

On Tuesday, March 17, after clearing all the legal hurdles blocking the transport of Jackson and Walling to the Newport, Kentucky jail, the two prisoners were remanded to the custody of Kentucky authorities. As a precaution, Kentucky's governor mobilized the state militia based in Frankfort. Their mission was to prevent any prospective scheme to seize and 'string up' the prisoners while they were en route to their new residence. Officials of the Commonwealth were also admittedly concerned about their captives' safety during their period of incarceration in the "rickety" Newport jail, for it was an old wooden structure with poor ventilation, unsanitary living conditions and questionable security.

Regardless, on St. Patrick's Day 1896, the two inmates, securely handcuffed to detectives, were whisked into a large patrol wagon drawn by a team of horses led by "Old Ned," the splendid white stallion and skillfully driven by Captain Mike Walsh. They were transported across the Ohio River to Newport while being closely pursued by 15 other horse-drawn vehicles, carrying both news reporters and a number of irate citizens who possibly had lynching in mind. The twenty-minute chase was frenzied and culminated in a full-fledged gallop to the jail door. Crowds of inquisitive onlookers had assembled along the travel route, and several hundred others were waiting at Newport's Central Police Station, which lay amid a stand of grand old forest trees, still barren from the past winter. Upon their arrival, Jackson and Walling were quickly hustled into the local jail. To restrain the insistent crowd of advancing reporters and onlookers, the door was immediately slammed and bolted.

The Newport jail, a later addition that had been tacked onto the rear of the courthouse building, was constructed of both wood and brick. In July 1896, a visitor described it as "a most wretched looking pen about 45 by 30 feet on the outside." He further noted, "An old, dilapidated stairway lead to the second floor. No wonder prisoners (who were housed there) were afraid of potential mob violence!"

Beneath the stairs, a door directly opened into an 8' X 12' starkly decorated office, containing only a desk, a chair, and a filing cabinet. Opposite to the outside entryway was the wall containing a second door, which had a small hole positioned at the top through which one could peek and observe the entire layout of the remainder of the first floor. An adjoining corridor, about 30 feet long and five feet wide, lay behind the door, with the prisoners' cells situated on either side. The floor, constructed of stone, was black and greasy, and the walls and roughly hewn rafters had once been whitewashed, but were now drab and heavily stained. An unpleasant odor emanated from the 7 cells, each about 7 feet tall.

As Jackson and Walling surveyed their latest incarceration site, they noticed that wooden planks, positioned above the individual jail cells, served as ceilings for each small enclosure. On top of the planks, beyond the prisoners' range of vision, was a crawl space strewn with thin mattresses and blankets. This cramped area served as sleeping quarters for the guards. This layout held one advantage: close proximity between the captors and their captives (much could be seen and heard through the widely spaced planks). Jackson eyed the sleeping arrangements critically, and snorted, "Well, Lon ... let's hope our guards don't get too frisky up there at night. We'll never get any quality shut-eye!"

Jailer Kushman retorted, "Shut up, smart-mouth! You have far bigger issues than your sleep to worry about," as he directed Jackson into the first cell next to the door, and then Walling into cell #3.

Both men desperately needed to find legal counsel for their upcoming trials. Colonel Robert T Nelson was well known in northern Kentucky as a highly reputable and competent defense attorney, and the Jackson family was eager to retain him to defend Scott. They arranged to have a preliminary meeting with Nelson, and during that session, the lawyer unabashedly stated his position: he was outraged by the horrible nature of the crime, and as a result had no interest in defending Scott. In fact, shortly after his pronouncement, Nelson offered his services pro bono to the Commonwealth of Kentucky to help pursue Jackson's prosecution.

As an alternative selection, Jackson chose a young local attorney, Colonel Leonard J. Crawford, to prepare his defense. Meanwhile, Walling retained Colonel George Washington of Newport as his counsel, and Mr. Richard Shepherd of Hamilton, Ohio, who served as Washington's assistant.

The Courthouse in Newport, Kentucky. A wooden structure had earlier been attached to the rear of this building and served as the jail. It was here that Jackson and Walling were incarcerated following their extradition from Cincinnati. This illustration is from a vintage postcard which was mailed in 1906, with the owner's message written on the same side as the photograph.

On a windy Monday morning, six days after their arrival in Newport, the two defendants exited their current jail cells for the first time. From there, they were escorted to the front door of the courthouse for the preliminary arraignment. The prisoners and their guards entered the building, stepped in unison across a wide, wood-planked floor, and walked down a narrow hall flanked on each side by a set of stairs. Jackson and Walling slowly trudged up the stairway on the right and crossed the threshold into the courtroom, a large chamber, where their attorneys and Judge Charles T. Helm awaited them at the bench.

Common newspaper depictions of Jackson and Walling at the time of their trials

After both men entered pleas of "not guilty," the Judge asked their legal representatives if the defendants were to be tried separately, or together. As Jackson's attorney hesitated, Walling's lawyer immediately stated that he wanted a separate trial for Walling. Judge Helm responded, "All right. Let the order be entered accordingly. This court will begin the case against Scott Jackson first, and I am setting his trial for April 7."

"But Judge," Crawford swiftly protested, "I have only known my client for a few days, and our witnesses are scattered over three states. The prosecution appears to have many surprises in store for us, and we need to have time to prepare for whatever they intend to do!"

Colonel* Lockhart stood, smiled mischievously, and responded, "We have no 'surprises' in store. All we intend to do is prove that Scott Jackson killed Pearl Bryan." This remark drew a number of chuckles from the gallery.

Crawford continued to press for a postponement of the trial date, but

---

* A "Kentucky Colonel" is an honorary title bestowed upon individuals by approval of the Governor of Kentucky. These Commissions were given in recognition of noteworthy accomplishments and outstanding service to a community, state or the nation. It was not a military rank, required no duties, and carried with it no pay, nor other compensation other than membership in the Honorable Order of Kentucky Colonels. These commissions continue to the present time.

Judge Helm cut him short. "I think you have ample time between now and April 7 to become adequately prepared. If you have an objection to make, do it then, but it had better be a good one in order to receive my attention. Looking to his left at Plummer, Helm nodded and said, "Sheriff, please remand the prisoners."

That afternoon, Sheriff Plummer was provided a list of 100 prospective jurors to contact and summon for Jackson's trial. Over the next several days, Judge Helm, Colonel Crawford and Prosecutor Lockhart interviewed and evaluated numerous individuals from the jury pool. Ultimately, the following men were secured: William Motz (merchant); Philip Mader (carpenter and builder); Louis Scharstein (grocer); Murty Shea (retired merchant); William White (plumber); John Ensweiler (grocer); David Kraut (coal merchant); Fred Gieskemeyer (grocer); John Backsman (cutler); George P Stegner (grocer); John Boehmer (teamster); and Willard Carr (carpenter).

Following the capture of the two murder suspects in Cincinnati, newspapers throughout Kentucky, Indiana, and Ohio promptly and unabatedly published a stream of stories about the murder, the victim, the defendants, their families and friends, and any other topic even remotely related to the case. Since the public's hunger for any details related to Pearl Bryan's murder seemed boundless, newspaper sales boomed both during the murder investigation and the subsequent trials. As readers devoured the deluge of daily newspaper accounts, many concluded that a major difference in the degree of culpability definitely existed between Jackson and Walling.

Both newspaper editorials and public opinion ran strongly against Jackson, presuming that he was undeniably guilty and therefore, should receive maximum punishment. His motive for the crime seemed to be obvious, since he had been identified almost certainly as the father of Pearl's future child. Labeling him as a man with a heartless, self-serving intent, the public tended to despise Jackson.

In contrast, they were inclined to perceive Walling as a puzzling almost pathetic figure, and much more difficult to hate. After all, he had never even met Pearl before she had arrived in Cincinnati. Was it possible that he had helped Jackson commit a gruesome murder simply as a friendly favor? Yet this became the sole motive that the prosecution would advance during his trial.

As time went on, interested citizens increasingly perceived Jackson as "far more guilty" of the crime than was Walling. He was seen as the brains behind the operation, while Walling was generally viewed as merely a subservient follower. According to published reports, they were "unequal partners" in the crime. Scott Jackson, "the principal agent in the crime," was actually "much brighter than Lonnie," whose features "betrayed the ignorance and the innocence of a weak mentality." What's more, they reported, Jackson's "head has a striking resemblance to that of H. H. Holmes," a merciless serial killer who had been executed just a year earlier.

But others judged Walling as harshly as they did Jackson, speculating that both men were equally homicidal, and had ruthlessly murdered for the sheer pleasure of it. Pinkerton wrote, "There seems to have been a strong affinity between these two young men (Jackson and Walling), and it arose from a common lack of all moral principle, a fiendish and most unnatural disposition that cannot well be doubted. The light regard in which they held human life and the brutal manner in which they consummated the terrible crime, argue that they were both victims of the homicidal impulse." Still others theorized that Walling's involvement simply resulted from a progression of illogical and self-destructive courses of action that he had undertaken. His downward spiral had initially begun when he agreed to help Jackson with "his problem," and it had culminated when he was duped into becoming an accomplice in Pearl's murder and decapitation.

The trial was scheduled to begin on April 7. Meanwhile, Sheriff Plummer had spent several weeks anticipating and planning for any problems that might arise during the judicial proceedings. In addition to his efforts to assure Jackson's safety throughout this legal action, Plummer had also meticulously carried out Judge Helm's orders concerning the conduct of the trial. He had designed the physical layout of the courtroom, and had devised contingency plans should any disturbances or violent acts erupt during the legal sessions. He felt prepared for any eventuality.

At 9:30 am on that Tuesday, Plummer glanced around the courtroom and was pleased with the arrangements he had made. Minutes later, he left for the jail to accompany Jackson back to Court. Scott was in good humor as he walked out the back door, handcuffed to the Sheriff and flanked by Jailer Bitzer and another deputy. Instantly, he was confronted with a crowd of rowdy onlookers, who taunted him contemptuously. One man called out, "Hey Jackson! What's it feel like to be a condemned man? How much longer do you figure you'll live?" The prisoner, whose airy demeanor was now replaced with a scowl, was hustled upstairs and temporarily placed in the witness room where he awaited the opening of his trial.

At 9:40 am, Judge Helm entered the courtroom amid the hum of conversation among the spectators, which instantly ceased. With every seat in the spectator's gallery taken, the magistrate turned to the business of the day. Calling out, "Case #2296, the Commonwealth vs Scott Jackson," he directed the Sheriff to bring in the prisoner. All eyes turned toward the doorway as Jackson jauntily sauntered forward with a smile playing on his lips. However, his cavalier attitude belied a degree of nervousness, which was quite apparent to any careful observer. After the Sheriff had announced the names of the twelve summoned jurors, Judge Helm asked, "Is the Commonwealth ready?"

Prosecutor Lockhart replied, "The Commonwealth is ready, sir."

Instantly, Mr. Crawford rose for the defense, saying, "May it please Your Honor, Scott Jackson is not ready. We desire to file a motion for postponement."

Crawford then proceeded to read an affidavit, stating that presently, he was the sole lawyer representing his client, and he had been sick with 'la grippe' for the last 10 days. Moreover, he was caring for one of his children who was currently very ill, and under a physician's care. As a result of these difficult circumstances, Crawford claimed that he'd had insufficient time to interview potential witnesses for the defense. He concluded his statement by requesting another month to more thoroughly prepare the defendant's case.

Mr. Lockhart rebutted, "The State is ready **NOW** to present its case, and I see no reason why the Court should allow a month's additional time for the defense."

Judge Helm thought for a moment and then responded, "It seems to me that the difficulties in preparing the prosecution's case are infinitely greater than are those for the defense. The defendant knows everything with reference to himself concerning this case, whereas the prosecution has to find out everything."

The Judge looked intently at Col. Crawford and continued, "The fact is, you are not entitled to any continuance at all, but I am going to give you the benefit of the doubt, and allow you an extra two weeks to prepare. That certainly should be more than enough time, so this case will be continued until Tuesday, April 21." The Court subsequently proceeded to the next order of business, while three officers led Jackson back to his jail cell. Scott, now smiling smugly, felt confident that he could not be convicted of murder, for currently there was insufficient direct evidence against him. Also, the two extra weeks of preparation granted to his attorney should further enhance the chances for his acquittal.

As the prisoner and his guards departed the premises, surreptitiously, a young woman, appearing to be a curious bystander, slowly proceeded to the edge of the group. Suddenly, without warning, she leaped forward and fiercely kicked Jackson twice on his right leg. In a flash, she darted away and quickly disappeared into the crowd without being identified. Since no one who was present acknowledged knowing her, the police were stymied and soon dropped the matter completely. Nevertheless, the unknown assailant's actions were heartily applauded by many who had observed the entire incident.

When Sheriff Plummer was informed of the bungled security effort, he frowned in frustration and immediately realized that his carefully conceived plan to keep Jackson out of harm's way called for some quick revision. He shuddered to think what might have happened, had the attacker possessed a more deadly intent than simply delivering two kicks on the shin.

In contrast to the unknown assaulter's desire to inflict injury and pain on Jackson, there were other young ladies in Newport who not only seemed to bear him no ill will, but seemingly were mesmerized by his notoriety. One such woman was a Newport schoolteacher, who, feeling sorry for Scott, provided him with clean linens throughout his period of incarceration in Newport. Another lady brought him candy and frequently sent him encouraging notes. She was often seen in the general vicinity of the courthouse, using any possible excuse to be in close proximity to the young defendant and hoping to establish a relationship with him.

The local authorities were both astonished and intrigued by the behavior of these "groupies," and puzzled over the motivation for such action. Educated observers surmised that the ladies merely wanted attention, or perhaps saw a "little boy" in Scott Jackson, and wanted to "mother" him. Perhaps they felt compelled to try to change someone as dangerous and cruel as a murderer who had decapitated his victim. No doubt, contemporary mental health experts could propose a whole array of possible explanations for similar groupie behavior directed toward present-day serial killers.

Shortly after Jackson and Walling were arrested, both law enforcement agents and members of the press descended upon many of their former classmates and faculty acquaintances at the dental school in Indianapolis. Their queries gushed forth in torrents: "How well did you know the two defendants?; Did they fit in with their classmates?; What were they really like?; Were they dedicated students?; What kind of grades did they earn?; Did they seem capable of committing such a heinous crime?"

In response to the myriad of questions thrust at them, most of the respondents had something to say about each of the accused. They typically described Walling as a peculiar sort of fellow, and somewhat of a 'loner'; however, they had little to offer regarding his inner nature. They called him 'secretive' and not inclined to socialize much with his classmates. "He was a pretty good student," said one faculty member, "but I never had much confidence in him. He seldom looked you in the eye, and always appeared sort of devious, as if he had been involved in something that made him ashamed. I was not confident that he would ever provide capable care for his patients."

Two former classmates related a story about Scott when he was in dental student. "One time, Jackson had shown an interest in a fellow student's girlfriend. This attention was unwelcome, and it angered her boyfriend, who immediately challenged Dusty to a fight. Scott quickly backed down, and attempted to calm the irate young man with his glib tongue." Although he had avoided any fisticuffs, Jackson lost the respect of many of his classmates thereafter. They always perceived him as a cowardly sort of a fellow and noted, "He often allowed himself to be insulted, and no one had a very high opinion of him. You know, we students don't have much use for a man who *shows the white feather.*"*

On April 13, Scott's attorney petitioned Judge Helm to remove Sheriff Plummer as the Court Bailiff, and to appoint a different official

---

* *The white feather (showing cowardice). This phrase perhaps dates back to the 18ᵗʰ century, when gamblers believed that fighting cocks with white tail feathers would invariably run away from their opponents, thereby revealing their pale posteriors.*

in his place. Crawford argued that Plummer was biased against his client, and thus, it would be prejudicial for him to serve in this capacity. As a means to justify his claim, Crawford cited an incident following Jackson's arrest when the Sheriff ostensibly smirked at him and said, "You must realize, Scott, it's pretty safe for you here in Cincinnati, but once you're extradited to Kentucky, things will undoubtedly change. I'll do my very best to protect you against any violence or lynching, but you know how Kentuckians are. They don't take too kindly to murdering pregnant ladies, so . . . . . ." Crawford continued, "Sheriff Plummer merely shrugged his shoulders slowly, and allowed his voice to trail away without finishing the sentence, but his intent was obvious." Crawford added, "Your Honor, the sheriff is clearly incapable of being an impartial agent of the Court, and must be replaced as bailiff."

Judge Helm listened carefully, and hesitated only briefly before responding, "You have only hearsay and no real evidence to support your claim of bias by the Sheriff toward your client. Your petition is denied." Crawford slowly shook his head from side to side, signaling his disapproval of the decision.

On Sunday, April 19, His Honor was satisfied that all the proper preparations to ensure a successful trial had been completed. However, on Monday, attorney Crawford expressed dissatisfaction with some of the arrangements. He wanted the public to have free admittance to the courtroom without any restrictions. Perhaps he hoped to pack the gallery with Scott's friends and acquaintances. In contrast, Judge Helm absolutely wanted to solely determine who would be present in his courtroom. After the two had wrangled over this issue for some time, Helm finally threatened to charge Crawford with contempt if he continued to pursue the matter. Thus, the attorney ceased his objections, and the prosecution proceeded to present the defense with a complete list of its witnesses. This inventory produced very little surprise coming from the defense. In less than forty-eight hours, the much heralded murder trial of Scott Jackson would commence.

CHAPTER TWELVE

On Tuesday, April 21, Jackson's trial began. It was to last 23 days. Colonel Lockhart made a lengthy opening statement for the prosecution, outlining his theory of the events surrounding Pearl Bryan's murder, and emphasizing Jackson's role in it. He began with the initial meeting between Scott and Pearl in Greencastle in 1895, and continued through the time of Pearl's murder near Ft. Thomas. Concluding the presentation to the jury with great zeal, Lockhart pointed to the defendant with his index finger and thundered, "Let me summarize. We will show that this man has been a veritable Dr. Jekyll and Mr. Hyde; that a week before the murder, he showed a dissecting knife to many of his acquaintances and then practiced with it until he became adept in using it for his evil purposes. We will show that after ruining Pearl Bryan's life in Greencastle, Mr. Jackson deliberately enticed her from her safe country home, and forced her to Fort Thomas, where he took her head, and took her life!"

The first witness called was John Hewling, the teenager who had discovered the headless body on John D. Lock's farm. His testimony was cogent and orderly as he described the condition of the ground beneath the body, which was saturated with blood. To rapt listeners, he related in detail the exact location of the decapitated corpse, noting the general disorder at the murder site, including the presence of a nearby corset, which appeared to have been torn away from the victim's body.

Campbell County Coroner, Dr. W. S. Tingley, was the second witness to appear. He stated that Pearl had been murdered at the same site where her remains were found. He recounted that at 9 am, Feb 1, he had been contacted and told of the grisly discovery. He continued, "I prepared to go to the location immediately, and arrived there about 10 am. As I drove down the lane, I could see a headless body lying prone at the bottom of a rise in the ground, a short distance east of the

Alexandria Pike. The deceased was clad in cloth shoes and stockings and a blue skirt, and nearby lay a corset and a brown kid glove. Her feet were at a higher elevation than her torso. The top of her body was drenched in blood, which had soaked through her dress. The ground was covered with dead leaves, which had blood splattered over them, as though it had spurted from the woman while she was still alive. The victim wore muddy rubbers over her shoes. There were several very deep cuts across the fingers of her left hand, suggesting that she had grasped the blade of a knife while defending herself. Drs. Carothers and Pythian both helped me conduct an internal examination of the body which showed the young woman to be about 5 months pregnant. We also saved the stomach and contents to be tested for the presence of poisons."

A crucial contention for the defense was that Pearl Bryan had died before she was beheaded. If so, the premeditated murder charge might have to be modified. However, two physicians then testified that blood could not spurt from blood vessels after the heart had ceased to beat. Thus, the discovery of blood hanging from the lower sides of dead leaves on the privet bushes at the murder site was stark evidence that Pearl had been alive at the time her neck was being severed from her body.

On the second day of the trial, the prosecution produced the clothing worn by Pearl at the time of her murder. In a most dramatic manner and without prior warning, a headless dummy dressed in Pearl's blood stained apparel was brought before the jury. As the twelve men stared at the spectacle, they gasped in repulsion. Immediately, Scott Jackson turned his gaze away from the display, the Bryan family dropped their heads in horror, and Colonel Crawford leaped to his feet, objecting strenuously to the 'cheap theatrical trick.' Following a lively exchange between the two rival attorneys, Judge Helm ordered the dummy removed from his courtroom, but allowed the bloodied garments and shoes to be returned. Subsequently, Pearl's sister, Maude Stanley, was called to the stand, where she carefully examined each of these items and tearfully attested that they had all belonged to her murdered sister. At the end of her testimony, she broke into deep, inconsolable sobs.

The next witness was Cincinnati's Mayor, John A Caldwell, who meticulously recounted his interrogation of Jackson. While the courtroom remained silent, many observers appeared to lean slightly forward in order to catch the Mayor's every word. Caldwell disclosed that when Scott Jackson was initially arrested and brought to his office for questioning, Col Deutsch had thrust a telegram in front of him. "Read this aloud," he had instructed the accused man. Once Jackson realized it was the communiqué from Greencastle ordering his arrest, he sighed and said, "My God! What will my poor mother say?" Caldwell then described how Jackson had leaped from his chair, and began pacing back and forth, muttering, "Oh, what am I going to do? What am I going to do?"

The mayor continued, "I told him to just tell the truth, and Jackson replied, 'This doesn't mean I'm guilty of anything. You must know that many an innocent man has been in as serious trouble as I am tonight.'" Caldwell stared coldly at the accused man from the witness stand, and then elaborated, "When we first asked Jackson if he knew where Pearl Bryan was, he replied that he didn't know and had not seen her since the Christmas holidays when he was in Greencastle. He couldn't explain his whereabouts on Friday, the night of the murder. Nor could he clarify his location on Thursday evening before the murder. Before long, it seemed clear that he wasn't being truthful with us, so around midnight, we let the newsmen in, and they asked him the same questions that we had."

The Mayor took a deep breath, and pressed on, "I next saw Jackson the following morning in Col. Deitsch's office, where he continued to be very vague about where he had been and how he had spent his time during Pearl's visit to Cincinnati. He eventually admitted that Pearl had been looking for him at the dental college on Tuesday evening, and that he had met her at the Indiana House on Fifth Street on Wednesday morning. He also acknowledged having talked with her at the corner of Fourth and Vine streets on Wednesday afternoon, about one pm. But he swore that he had not seen her since. Jackson later acknowledged that he had 'taken care' of Pearl's luggage for her while she was in town, and on Saturday night had left her satchel at Legner's saloon across the street from his room."

The remainder of Mayor Caldwell's testimony centered on his interrogation of Jackson's purported accomplice, Alonzo Walling. Caldwell recounted Walling's claim that Jackson had planned and engineered Pearl's murder and subsequently had attempted to dispose of both her clothing, as well as much of his own. The mayor concluded by describing the scenario and conversation that had occurred near Pearl's coffin where, in the presence of two of the victim's siblings, Jackson and Walling denied any involvement in her murder. The members of the jury were visibly somber at the end of this graphic story, and veteran courtroom observers later noted that the declarations of the Newport mayor were likely instrumental in sealing Jackson's fate.

The following day's testimonies produced a wave of circumstantial evidence strongly implicating Jackson in the homicide. Allegations from medical and pharmaceutical personnel were particularly damning for the defendant. Dr. Littler, a physician who lived in the same boarding house as Jackson, stated that Scott and Alonzo both had quizzed him about the properties of cocaine and its potentially poisonous effects. H. C. Uhlen, a druggist on Sixth street, revealed that Jackson had purchased cocaine from him on the day before the murder; and then Dr. Crane, a Cincinnati physician and chemist, stated that the analysis of Pearl's stomach contents revealed the presence of several grams of cocaine. Crane was insistent that in spite of the fact that she had ingested the drug, the deceased was still alive and conscious when she was killed.

The prosecution next produced a brown, alligator grip, which Fred Bryan had previously identified as Pearl's. When they inspected the piece of luggage, the jury members were riveted by the presence of bloodstains on its interior. It was clearly an emotionally powerful piece of evidence. Colonel Lockhart proceeded to rage against the "heartless butcher" who had used the victim's own luggage to transport her head from the murder scene back to Cincinnati.

The senior author holds Pearl Bryan's brown, alligator grip (made available by courtesy of the Campbell County Historical and Genealogical Society, Alexandria, Kentucky). Bloodstains were found in the interior of the bag, which was purportedly used to transport Pearl's head from the murder site back to Cincinnati.

As the trial progressed over the next few days, presumptive evidence against Jackson accumulated. Another chemist (Mr. Dickmore) stated that the mud discovered on a pair of Jackson's pants which had been discovered in Walling's locker, closely resembled wet soil removed from the murder site.

On Friday, Allen Johnson's testimony placed Scott Jackson and Alonzo Walling in the company of a woman identified as Pearl Bryan on the evening of the murder. Johnson, a 26 year-old waiter at David Wallingford's saloon at George and Plum Streets, also worked as a professional boxer and handy man. The waiter stated that he had seated Scott and Pearl in one of the curtain-enclosed booths available for customers who wanted privacy. After he had served a sarsaparilla drink to Pearl, he observed Scott surreptitiously pouring a substance from a vial into her drink. Johnson distinctly recalled that Jackson and Pearl had left the establishment about 7 pm. As they exited by the George Street door, Johnson had seen Walling immediately outside awaiting the couple. Johnson proceeded to provide a description of Scott's female companion, and the clothing she was wearing. Pearl's mother verified Johnson's testimony regarding both her daughter's physical characteristics as well as the apparel she had with her in Cincinnati.

The next witness was David Wallingford who stated that he had gotten to know both Jackson and Walling quite well, because the two dental students had frequented his saloon almost every night for the past four months. He asserted that early on the evening of the murder, Jackson was with a young lady matching Pearl Bryan's description, and confirmed that Allen Johnson had poured a sarsaparilla and taken it to her in the wine room where she was sitting with Jackson. He added that a few moments earlier, Jackson had taken him aside and asked to borrow a couple of bucks. Wallingford consented and handed him two silver dollars. Scott then ordered a beer from the bar and sat with his female companion while they finished their drinks. Minutes later, he saw them leaving together right after Jackson had paid the cashier. In essence, Wallingford's testimony confirmed what Allen Johnson had told the court, and the specific details provided by each witness melded together to form a clear picture of that event.

Mr. Louis D. Poock, a leading shoe merchant in Newport, presented the next testimony, carefully explaining his role in discovering the victim's identity. After examining the footwear of the murdered woman he related that, "these shoes were marked with the factory stock number (62,458), and also with the French sizes (22-11, equivalent to 3B). I also found the name of Lewis & Hayes, Greencastle, Indiana marked on the inside of the lining, and discovered the shoes had been made at Portsmouth, Ohio. From there, the detectives were able to find that they had belonged to Pearl Bryan."

On Friday afternoon, a buzz of anticipation swept through the courtroom when the prosecution announced its next witness would be one of Jackson's closest friends, William Wood. The blond, 19 year-old medical student, sporting a perfect part down the middle of his carefully shorn hair, cut a handsome figure as he stood in front of the courtroom. Will denied having ever been intimate with Pearl Bryan, but swore that she had confided in him that Scott was the father of her unborn baby. He acknowledged that he had introduced Pearl to Scott Jackson, and that the two soon became close. He revealed that the couple had borrowed his rig and gone buggy riding together frequently, and that in the fall of 1895, Scott told him that they had become intimate.

The prosecution lawyers next turned to Will's written communications with Scott while the latter was attending the Ohio Dental School. Staring intently at Will's face, Colonel Crawford requested him to "recount for the jury everything you remember about your correspondences with Scott Jackson, and include what, if anything, he said to you with regard to improper relations with Pearl Bryan."

Will responded, "Dusty said that he had illicit relations with Pearl on three different occasions during the late summer before he left Greencastle to attend the Ohio dental school. However, I cannot show you any of his letters, since he instructed me to burn all of them after I had read them."

Crawford pressed on, "Why don't you briefly describe from memory the contents of his letters to you."

Will licked his lower lip, and looked about nervously and slowly replied. "His first letter to me in November simply asked about Pearl's condition. A week later, a second letter arrived, which gave me the recipe for a chemical/herbal concoction that he felt would cause Pearl to abort, but it didn't work."

Will paused, sighed, and continued, "Scott came back to Greencastle in late November, and he told me that a surgical abortion was the only solution to 'Pearl's problem.' He promised to make the arrangements in Cincinnati for the operation, and instructed me that after he had notified me that it was the right time, I should help Pearl make the arrangements for the train trip to Cincinnati. The next letter arrived about January 20, saying it was time for Pearl to come and see him."

Will kept his eyes averted from Scott as he resumed his story, "I also received a letter in early February in which Dusty said something like, 'I have made a big mistake, but please stand by me.' However, I never had the chance to read the very last letter he sent me. According to the newspaper accounts, he wrote it on February 5, but the Greencastle Postmaster's Office intercepted it, and immediately forwarded it to the police in Cincinnati."

After Will was asked to step down from the stand, Colonel Crawford read the contents of Scott's confiscated letter, which in essence asked Will to write a letter to the Bryan family, supposedly written by Pearl, informing them that she was tired of living with her parents in Greencastle, had gotten a job and moved to Chicago, and would contact them later. Jackson told Wood to sign the letter with Pearl's name, mail it immediately, and burn his letter, which he had ended by saying, "Stick by your old chum, Will, and I will help you out the same way or some other way sometime."

In talking among themselves, Cincinnati police department officials commented that Jackson must have been the consummate optimist to think that Wood could pull off such a complex bit of trickery. However, he had written the letter in desperation, just hours before his arrest in Cincinnati.

Dr. Gillespie, the Greencastle dentist who had let Scott Jackson work in his office during the spring and summer of 1895, then presented his testimony. He said that Jackson had told him in the late fall that he had gotten Pearl pregnant. Gillespie stated that his advice to Scott at the time was to "Go marry that girl." Following Dr. Gillespie's statements presented to the jury on Friday, court was adjourned until Saturday morning at 9 am.

The following day, two local witnesses related that they had seen Jackson and a young woman resembling Pearl in Bellevue, Kentucky on the Thursday morning prior to the murder. An additional witness testified to seeing Jackson, Walling, and Pearl eating together at a family restaurant in Cincinnati. After hearing this, Mrs. Bryan suddenly called out, "Thank God they took her to one decent place after dragging her around in the (filth) all the rest of the time!"

*This is the lobby and front desk area of the Palace Hotel. It was here that
Alonzo Walling testified that Jackson wrote the extremely incriminating
letter to Will Wood, who later referred to the letter in his testimony.
Courtesy of the Public Library of Cincinnati and Hamilton County*

Mrs. Weeks was the next witness called and she told of the séance
that she held in her home on the Thursday afternoon prior to the
murder. She was adamant that Scott Jackson and Pearl Bryan were the
two individuals with whom she had met. The following witness for
the prosecution was W. D. Pickard of Cincinnati, who swore that he
had seen Walling and Pearl exiting from the Atlantic Garden eating
establishment on Friday afternoon, January 31. When pressed by the
defense, however, Pickard admitted that he could not unequivocally
place Jackson with the two at that time.

Detectives Crim' and McDermott's detailed accounts of their roles
in solving the crime consumed much of Monday's sworn testimony.
At the end of the day, listeners were visibly impressed by the excellent
investigatory work accomplished by the two. On Tuesday morning,
Chester Mullen affirmed to an intrigued audience that on the afternoon
of January 31, he had rented a gray horse and a cab to a man he now
identified as Alonzo Walling. He added that the livery equipment was
clandestinely returned at approximately 4 am on Saturday, but Mullen

could shed no light on the identity of the person or persons who had brought it back to his establishment.

That afternoon, Coachman George Jackson chronicled his activities on the evening of the murder. In sequence, he said that he drove two men and a woman to Ft. Thomas in a rented hack; he described their exit from the cab; and he related his subsequent flight on foot when he heard screaming and sounds of struggling coming out of the distant darkness where he thought his passengers had walked. In spite of the defense's strong efforts to discredit his testimony, including presentation of racial stereotypes, the coachman held firm with his assertions. When he was excused from the witness stand, there was little doubt that Scott Jackson's claim of innocence had suffered a severe blow.

On Wednesday, the prosecution produced an independent local physician who had studied surgery in London several decades earlier. In spite of never having seen the body, Dr. Jaencon detailed the physiologic outcomes of decapitation, and expressed a strong belief that Pearl was beheaded while still alive.

On Thursday, the defense began its argument by calling Scott Jackson to the stand. Displaying an indifferent demeanor, his testimony came across as well rehearsed but lacking credibility. He strongly denied any knowledge of Pearl Bryan's death, and claimed that it was merely out of thoughtfulness that he had taken possession of her valise and clothing when she left the Indiana House. He hadn't wanted her to be burdened by lugging these items around while she searched for new lodging. However, after learning of Pearl's death, he claimed to have panicked and felt obliged to immediately dispose of all of her belongings. Although he was bombarded with tough questions by the prosecution during his testimony, Jackson remained composed and steadfast in his denial that he had any contact with Pearl after the Wednesday prior to the murder.

Following Jackson's testimony, the defense called several witnesses to speak on his behalf. In direct contradiction to the professional conclusions previously presented by Dr. Jaencan, a local physician stated his belief that Pearl was not killed at Ft. Thomas, nor was she alive when she was beheaded. Mrs. Minnie Post, Scott's step-sister, served as a character witness attesting to his generally good character. However, the prosecution was able to effectively rebut her claims.

When Scott's landlady, Miss Rose McNevin, swore that he was in his room during the entire evening of the murder, several jury members shifted in their seats and arched their eyebrows quizzically. She also claimed to consistently be knowledgeable concerning the whereabouts of any of her boarders at any given moment. The prosecution countered by pointing out how difficult that would be given the large number of boarders she had.

The next witness for the defense, William R. Trusty Jr., of Urbana, Illinois, took the stand on Monday, May 4, and related an outlandish story. He stated that on Friday evening, January 31, he drove a carriage containing a dead woman and an elderly man who he believed to be a physician, from Newport to the murder site at Ft. Thomas. He insisted that after the man and the corpse in his custody exited at this location, he drove the carriage back to Newport and delivered it to an unknown individual waiting in the street. He implied that the deceased woman was Pearl Bryan, and that she had died from a botched abortion attempt. The judge and attorneys immediately discerned that if this man's testimony was true, Pearl had died in Cincinnati, and Jackson should be on trial for murder in Ohio, not Kentucky. As Colonel Lockhart began his cross-examination of the witness, Trusty grew increasingly confused and repeatedly contradicted himself. It was late afternoon, and Judge Helm paused, furrowed his brow, and declared a recess in the trial until the following morning. Because of the numerous bizarre components to Trusty's story, he could anticipate a very difficult cross-examination on Tuesday morning.

Later in downtown Cincinnati, the engaging spring evening of Monday, May 4, was abruptly shattered by a massive explosion. The shock waves from the detonation disseminated throughout the city and across the river in Newport. The blast had originated in the basement of the 5-story Drask building located on Walnut Street between 4th and 5th streets. The edifice housed two saloons and a host of assorted occupants. The explosion completely demolished the structure and significantly damaged adjacent buildings. A passing streetcar was blown off its tracks and had crashed. Before the evening had concluded six people were dead, 10 were missing, and many others injured. The cause of the disaster was later determined to be the malfunction of a gasoline engine generator located in the basement which had been used to power incandescent lights in the two saloons. Weeks passed before all the debris and rubble could be removed.

The following morning, Trusty failed to appear in court for the Prosecution's cross-examination. In his absence, Lockhart vigorously attacked both Trusty's character, and his credibility as a witness. Some suggested that he may have been a victim of the prior evening's explosion, since he was known to frequent the Queen City's most popular drinking establishments almost nightly. However, law enforcement officers subsequently discovered that following his testimony, Mr. Trusty had immediately departed from Newport for "parts unknown". Rumors persisted that Trusty's uncle, John Seward, had invented the story that William had recounted on the stand the previous day. It was theorized that the objective of the outrageous lie was to cast doubt on the prosecution's claim that Pearl had been viciously murdered in the orchard near Ft. Thomas. Rather, they wanted the jury to believe that she had succumbed during an illegal abortion, which she presumably had chosen to undergo. What Trusty and Seward hoped to gain by this fabrication was not immediately apparent. However, six months later, the two men were located and arrested. Trusty pleaded guilty to perjury and Seward confessed both to subordination and perjury. The duo was sentenced to the penitentiary for one and two years, respectively.

On May 7, the Commonwealth was ready to conclude its case. It was an unusually warm and humid day, and perspiration dotted Colonel Nelson's upper lip and forehead as he began his summary argument for the prosecution. He began calmly and deliberately, declaring, "I have no personal enmity against the prisoner. I don't even know him. But I have a duty to help bring about the punishment of the perpetrator of this horrible crime." As Nelson continued, he grew more impassioned. "Considering the unimpeachable testimony presented by the prosecution, I don't think the jury will have any difficulty in determining the defendant's guilt. Clearly, there is only one suitable punishment for the perpetrator of this atrocious crime." His voice resonated ardently, "I speak for the entire world: nothing less than hanging by the neck till he is dead will do!"

Nelson followed his emotional declaration with a brief history of the case, beginning with Scott Jackson's initial move to Greencastle, and then proceeded to his initial meeting with Pearl Bryan. From there, he progressed to inform the jury precisely how inaccurate the defense had been in attempting to refute the validity of the Commonwealth's case. As he spoke, he became increasingly cynical and caustic, declaring, "Scott Jackson swears that he did not see Pearl after Wednesday. If that is true, then Druggist Foertmeyer, Mrs. Holmes and John W. Foster, each of whom saw Jackson and Walling together with Pearl on Friday morning in Bellevue, must be lying. And the credible testimony of Mrs. Weeks; apparently she is lying against people she doesn't even know, nor has any interest in whatsoever. What would be her motive in doing so? And then there is David Wallingford, the saloonkeeper, and his porter, Allen Johnson, who saw Pearl Bryan with Scott Jackson on Friday evening. Apparently, they too are committing perjury. Yes, all these witnesses are liars and perjurers, if you believe Scott Jackson.

And the list of liars goes on and on! Will Wood, Dr. Gillespie, and George Jackson are all mistaken, or liars; as is Mr. Pinckard, who saw the defendants with Pearl at the Atlantic Gardens on Friday. If Scott Jackson is telling the truth, one must conclude that all these people have come into court and sworn falsely against a man on trial for his life. Well, I'll say this to you gentlemen of the jury. If I owned a respectable dog and he actually believed Scott Jackson's explanations in this case, I wouldn't let him live until sundown! As for the testimony of William Trusty, it would be an insult and a waste of time to consider that man's words any further.

Regarding Miss McNevin's statement that Scott Jackson was in her boarding house in his room on the night of the murder," Nelson smiled condescendingly, shook his head, and added, "Well, I do believe that this lady is sincere in her testimony and believes it to be true. However, it isn't reasonable to believe that she knew the whereabouts of each of her numerous borders during the entire evening of January 31 and the early morning of February 1. It simply defies logic."

Nelson continued, thundering at Jackson, "Why did you write to Will Wood and ask him to compose the letter home and sign the name of that murdered, mutilated girl to it? Why did you have her clothing in your locker and her handkerchiefs in your pockets?" Nelson turned to the jury, saying, "Jackson and his defense team can't answer any of these questions satisfactorily. What they have presented to you makes no sense. If you believe Colonel Lockhart's explanation for the events of this murder case, Pearl Bryan must have committed suicide and then concealed her own head." He concluded, "We have established in this case by absolute and irresistible proof, that Scott Jackson is guilty of seduction, of murder, of mutilating a dead body, and of killing his unborn child. You must do your duty and find him guilty!"

The following day, Colonel Crawford replied for the defense. He argued that Pearl's death had taken place in Ohio, not in Kentucky as recorded in William Trusty's sworn statement. He insisted that Miss McNevin had provided Scott Jackson with an airtight alibi on the night of the murder, and that Wallingford, Johnson and George H. Jackson, who claimed that they saw Scott that night, were unreliable witnesses. Crawford finished by stating that the no one had actually seen Jackson commit the murder, and that the muddy footprints found at the crime scene were too large to have been Jackson's.

After Judge Helm had presented his instructions to the jury, the 12 men retired to an adjacent room to reach their decision. At this point, the State had called 113 witnesses, and the defense, 83; thus, the jury had much testimony to consider. However, in less than two hours, they filed back into the courtroom to tender their verdict. With each passing moment, the drama continued to build. Two armed policemen were positioned on each side of the prisoner, who now stood facing the judge. Numerous plainclothesmen were distributed among the spectators, and the gallery was warned that regardless of the outcome, order must be maintained. It was apparent that if the verdict was "not guilty," the authorities feared possible violence.

THE PEARL BRYAN MURDER TRIAL JURY 1896
GEORGE PETER STEGNER FOREMAN

The all-male jury which served for Scott Jackson's murder trial.
George Peter Stegner (top row, 4th from left) served as the Foreman.
www.nkyviews.com/campbell/fortt_pearl.htm

The excitement was palpable as the jury foreman was called upon to read the jury's decision. George Stegner's voice was forceful and clear as he uttered the words, "We find the defendant to be guilty of murder in the first degree." Staring straight ahead, Jackson reacted with minimal emotion. However, a ripple of quickly checked approval ran through the audience. Instantly, Scott was hustled back to his cell, and within moments, the courtroom was cleared. A few days later, provoking little surprise to anyone, Judge Helm announced Jackson's capital sentence. For the murder of Pearl Bryan, the 26 year-old ex-dental student was to be hanged by the neck until dead.

CHAPTER THIRTEEN

At the completion of Scott Jackson's trial on May 14, Judge Helm declared a two-week recess before beginning Alonzo Walling's court case. Helm had been so emotionally drained by the prominence and intensity of the first trial, that he felt compelled to take some time off to unwind and recharge. Two days later, he and attorney Leonard Crawford traveled north together to a popular resort of that era, Put-in-Bay, Ohio. This retreat was located on South Bass Island in Lake Erie, and many vacationers visited there to enjoy rest, recreation and rejuvenation. Steamships holding up to 1500 passengers regularly serviced the island, and a wide variety of hotels was available for lodging. The Beebe House, the best known, was the largest resort hotel in America. It could house over 800 guests, and seat nearly a thousand persons in its dining room. Eighty-three years earlier, these islands had been the base of operations for Commodore Oliver Hazard Perry, who defeated the British fleet in the Battle of Lake Erie during the War of 1812. Perry's battle report to Major General William Henry Harrison included the famous words, "We have met the enemy and they are ours." (Not to be confused with the famous words of Pogo, the cartoon character, who stated, "We have met the enemy, and he is us!")

When he returned from his vacation, Helm tentatively established Walling's trial date for Tuesday, May 26. Early on that morning, Scott Jackson was moved a few miles west from Newport to the jail in Covington, Kentucky, a relocation which the authorities believed would provide him greater security. On May 29, after a short delay, the following jury members were secured: John Kirt, foundry man, Bellevue; Frank Griffith, cigar salesman, Dayton; Robert Miles, teamster, Dayton; Charles Fererder, saloon keeper, Newport; Jesse Batson, motorman, Glen Park; Frank Shush, grocer, Dayton; M. R. Moran, grocer, Bellevue;

Fred Dietz, cigar packer, Dayton; J. A. Cello, manufacturer, Dayton; Peter Wern, rope maker, Dayton; E. M. De Rose, machinist, Bellevue; and James Ware, grain merchant, Newport. The two attorneys for the defense were Colonel George Washington and Mr. Shephard. The attorneys for the prosecution were, once again, Colonel M. R. Lockhart, and his assistant Colonel Robert Nelson.

The trial, very similar in substance to Jackson's case, involved many of the same witnesses. One of the additional individuals to testify for the prosecution was W.C. Martin, a waiter at Heider's Hotel restaurant on Fifth street, who testified that Walling booked a room with him at 3 am on Saturday, February 1, just a few hours after the estimated time of Pearl's murder. His testimony showed that Walling had not slept in his boarding house room the night of the killing. William Tegeler, an employee of the John Church Music Company, was also a new prosecution witness who swore that he had seen Alonzo Walling talking with a young lady matching Pearl Bryan's description at the junction of Elm Street and Baker

A rare photograph of Alonzo Walling.

alley on the afternoon of January 31. The fact that this discussion had taken place 48 hours after Walling stated that he had last seen Pearl was clearly damaging to his case.

Detective Cal Crim followed Tegeler on the stand. He informed the court that Walling had admitted to him more than once that he knew of Scott Jackson's intent to kill Pearl Bryan.

The defense put Alonzo Walling on the stand to begin its case, but his testimony failed to impress the attentive listeners. He was not as articulate as Scott Jackson had been, and his admission of being with Pearl on several occasions after her arrival in Cincinnati was incriminating. Nor could Walling provide a reasonable alibi for the time of the murder. He claimed to have slept at Heider's Hotel the night of the murder to avoid contact with Jackson, whom he said was dangerous and plotting a crime that he wanted no part of. Yet when asked if he had believed the murder plans emanating from Jackson were credible, he denied it, saying "Jackson had never shown any signs that he would do anything that drastic."

Lockhart seized upon this contradiction and pressed him hard. "So, if you had believed Jackson was a serious threat to Miss Bryan, you would have warned her?"

Walling quickly replied, "Of course."

At this point, Judge Helm directed several questions to Walling, seeking clarification of the many inconsistencies in his testimony. However, neither the Judge, nor anyone else present, felt that the defendant's responses provided any transparency to his convoluted story.

Walling's trial concluded on June 18. With all the testimony now recorded, and the charges explained to the jury, few in attendance doubted the outcome. As the jury foreman pronounced him guilty, Walling abruptly smirked, snickered sarcastically and waved to the gallery, while his two brothers dropped their heads in sorrow. Like Jackson, Wallling was quickly removed from the courtroom. Within 48 hours, he was also given the identical sentence: "To be hung by the neck until dead." The following day, Alonzo was moved to the Covington jail to join Jackson, in an effort to minimize the risk of violent acts against him. Hence, the fate of the two prisoners remained intertwined in yet another setting.

Two months passed uneventfully, but in the late summer of 1896, a group of fellow prisoners in the Covington lockup engineered a bold jailbreak. Although both condemned men were urged by the seven fleeing fugitives to join in the escape, they wisely chose not to participate. On hearing news of the breakout, a rowdy mob quickly assembled and rushed to the jail, intent on recapturing Jackson and Walling, and likely administering their own brand of vigilante justice. However, when this gang of ruffians learned that Jackson and Walling had remained meekly in their cells, they rapidly dispersed. Later, Scott and Alonzo admitted that they did not try to escape because they knew that they were much safer in jail, locked away from the unruly mob.

Following the jailbreak incident, the two convicted murderers were once again relocated, this time some 10 miles south to the Alexandria, Kentucky jail, where they remained for many months until the final resolution of their cases had been determined. After March 17, when the prisoners had been delivered from Cincinnati to the Kentucky authorities, members of the press were no longer permitted to have contact with them. However, over the next year, while they were incarcerated in Kentucky, the two captives were visited by hundreds of individuals who had no connection to the press. These individuals included family members, friends, former classmates, and an assortment of others, some of whom were merely drawn to the notoriety of the captives. Among this latter group were mawkish females, bearing gifts of clothing, flowers, and baked goods. Emma Roberts was one of these women, and during the autumn of 1896, she became Alonzo's self-professed girl friend, and called on him frequently over the next nine months.

Following the jailbreak in Covington, Jackson and Walling were moved to the Alexandria jail (pictured above), which was considered to be a more secure facility. Here they resided until the morning of Friday, March 20, 1897 when they were returned to Newport.

In an effort to spend more time with her son, Scott's mother temporarily moved to the region in Kentucky where he was jailed. She regularly provided him with his favorite New York City newspapers and magazines, clothing, writing materials, and other personal items. While he enjoyed being given these thoughtful offerings, at times he paid a hefty price for receiving them. Fellow prisoners and guards made thoughtless remarks to both Scott and Alonzo, crudely reminding them of how little time they might have left in this world to enjoy such material benefits.

On one occasion, Mrs. Jackson delivered a new pair of handmade, black oxford shoes to Scott. After she left, one of the jailers slyly grinned at him and said, "Dusty, where'd you get those dang fancy shoes? Just before you keep your date with the hangman, you should make sure to donate them to me. So, in the meantime, don't be wearin' those soles down by walkin' too much."

On another occasion, a new prisoner charged with assault and battery was being escorted past Scott's cell. He paused and glared, growling, "Hey, Jackson! You think you're such a tough guy because you murdered and beheaded a pregnant woman! Why you wouldn't last five seconds in a fight with me! You'd better pray I never get you alone! I'd tear your friggin' head off, you little twit!!"

Although Dusty tried to ignore such taunts and threats whenever they arose, he was constantly wary of possible assaults from other prisoners or even from some of the more hostile jail guards.

Because Jackson and Walling spent many of their waking hours in jail using their imaginations to stave off boredom and to hold 'the blues' at bay, the two cronies' days were not as monotonous as they might have been. Typically, they devoted much of their energy to corresponding with their families and friends, and also to the construction of assorted small trinkets and muslin ornaments. As the two young men completed these decorations, they dispensed them to their mothers, other family members, friends, Jailer Wagner, and to their favorite jail guards: Cottingham, Murray, Sutton, and Truesdell.

In their spare time, Dusty and Lonnie usually smoked their beloved cigars. In the evenings, they took pleasure in singing popular songs and playing their musical instruments. Jackson owned a harmonica, and as he played, two other prisoners in adjoining cells joined in with mandolin and guitar. Although each was imprisoned in an individual cell, the felons managed to at least temporarily escape the confinement of the iron bars by blending together their voices and instruments. Those within hearing distance described their musical offerings as being quite good.

Occasionally, the guards would bring out an old phonograph which had been donated to the jail. Not only did it provide a musical interlude for the guards, but, it seemed to soothe the souls of the prisoners and to lessen their aggressive behavior. Jackson's taste ran toward instrumental music. He particularly enjoyed accompanying a lively banjo duet that would radiate out of the Victrola by playing his harmonica. In contrast, Walling generally requested that vocals be played; his favorite was the popular song, "Au Revoir." Sometimes, the prisoners and guards would sing together. Guard Sutton, was the lead voice, Jackson, the tenor, and Walling and guard Murray, the bases. This quartet crooned a passionate version of "A Mother's Appeal for Her Boy," and no one who heard it could miss the irony of that selection.

Throughout the 1890s, Americans were displaying a fanatical interest in two sporting activities: bicycling and baseball. Before their incarcerations, Scott and Alonzo were devotees of both pursuits. Scott had pedaled a bike all over lower New York City while serving as a teenage messenger boy there; while Alonzo had belonged to a bicycle club in Brookville before he moved to Greenfield. Every summer weekend, he would participate in a lengthy ride through the surrounding countryside with his fellow biking enthusiasts. But currently, neither young man had access to a bicycle, nor the freedom to ride one. Thus, their interest in bicycling waned substantially during the period when they were residing in a succession of Kentucky jails.

In contrast, they managed to closely follow the progress of their favorite baseball teams, for they had access to second-hand newspapers dropped by the jail daily by an assortment of thoughtful citizens. Alonzo, who was born near the Indiana-Ohio border, had become a fan of the Cleveland Spiders as a boy. He idolized their ace pitcher, Denton True (Cy) Young who was from Gilmore, Ohio. Eventually, this sports star was to win more games than any other pitcher in baseball history. He was inducted into baseball's Hall-of-Fame in 1937.

While Scott was living in the New York area, he became a zealous follower of the Giants baseball team, whose star pitcher, (George) Jouett Meekin, was originally from New Albany, Indiana. Now that they lived in continual, close proximity of each other, the two imprisoned men often bantered back and forth, comparing the performances of the two teams and wrangling over which one had the better pitchers. When the Cleveland Spiders and the New York Giants actually played against each other, their arguments reached a crescendo.

In 1896, a year when the Spiders were clearly superior to the Giants,

Lonnie would condescendingly and self-righteously heckle his comrade. In particular, on May 27, the Chicago White Sox took advantage of Jouett Meekin's 13 walks and 3 wild pitches and pounded the New York Giants, 11-5. When he read this news, an elated Lonnie suggested, "Maybe the Giants would be a better team if they demoted that guy, Meekin, down to the minor leagues." Jackson flared back, "Anyone who would make a statement like that doesn't have the brains of a snail! If you can't make an intelligent comment, just keep your trap shut!!"

Not limiting themselves to following sporting events and other daily newspaper reports, the two men also spent a significant amount of time reading books. They particularly doted on the trashy sentiment contained in cheap novels and the cynical humor found in the profound writings of Mark Twain. Late in the year, the first comic strip, "Hogan's Alley" (with "the Yellow Kid" as the main character), appeared in Hearst's New York World. Scott especially enjoyed the ghetto-style language employed in this strip. It brought back memories of his years spent among the rough and tumble element that roamed the streets and alleys of New York City.

To keep their minds diverted from their dire circumstances, Scott and Lonnie would pounce upon any outside form of amusement. They would discuss any conceivable topic ranging from God to sex. With the prodding of Pastor Lee, they had extended conversations about a full range of spiritual issues. These discussions were particularly prevalent as they lay in their beds late in the evening. During the still of the night, their conversations also turned to carnal thoughts: their sexual exploits, real, embellished, imagined and fabricated.

Occasionally, they talked sadly of 'what might have been.' What kind of men could they have possibly become, if events had been different? Neither man had probably read John Greenleaf Whittier's poem, "Maud Miller," but both souls must have resonated with the poet's sorrowful quote, "For of all sad words of tongue or pen, the saddest are these: what might have been." In private moments as each of these men reviewed his life, and its possible meaning, what an assemblage of bittersweet thoughts and deep regrets might have permeated the archives of their troubled minds.

Over time, Scott and Alonzo grew accustomed to the loss of privacy within the confined areas of their cells, and even their need to use the chamber pot, placed conspicuously in an open corner, became routine.

Nevertheless, they never quite adapted to the lingering, chronic malodor that hung heavily over their living space and invaded its every nook and cranny. Even though the janitor removed the covered receptacle every morning for an emptying and a cursory cleaning, a dull excretory odor seemed to permeate their very being.

Jackson frequently complained about cramping and weakness in his legs, which he insisted was related to his ongoing confinement in such tight quarters. He was consistently denied his requests to exit the cell and walk the corridors of the jail. Both men gained weight during their captivity, due to their general state of physical inactivity and their habit of overloading on what food was offered to them. Meals were by no means superb, but the portions provided a more than adequate caloric density, and a request for seconds was usually granted. Their typical fare included beans, potatoes, casseroles, corn, bread, and assorted cheap cuts of meats, including squirrel, rabbit, and wild turkey when this kind of game was available. Also, strong, hot coffee stored in a big pot on the downstairs wood stove, and always available on request, kept them well caffeinated.

As their spiritual advisor, the Reverend J. A. Lee, pastor of the Third Baptist Church of Covington, was permitted unlimited access to Jackson and Walling throughout their imprisonment in Kentucky. This highly conscientious 'man of the cloth' truly believed that the souls of these men could still be saved. In heartfelt empathy, he sensed that a range of conflicted emotions was coursing through each man's being. Pastor Lee devoutly prayed that, now, after the two had been legally found guilty of their crime, they would both acknowledge their wrongdoing, express their deep regret before the Bryan family, repent before God, ask His forgiveness and bravely face their sentence as prescribed by law. As their prison time dragged on inexorably during 1896, and into 1897, they became somewhat more responsive to his Godly petitions.

The daily distractions that filled the two prisoners' waking hours were indeed purposeful. Certainly, their predictable routines minimized the time they might have had available for contemplative regret, the very penitent state of personal conviction that Reverend Lee was praying for them to attain. While Lonnie may have not been much more than a naïve, blindsided accomplice, Scott was undoubtedly 'guilty' of premeditated intent murder. His despicable crime left in its wake the decapitated body of a trusting young woman. In those inescapable moments of isolation, which he could not completely fill with trivia, did Scott ever break through his clumsily constructed wall of self-protective lies and truly acknowledge his ruinous deeds? Did he feel any conventional emotions during the countless hours of imprisonment when he had time to think deeply? If so, was it guilt, distress, shame and remorse? Or was it simply deep dismay from being charged with murder?

While Scott may have regretted the fact that he murdered Pearl, his self-reproach was primarily focused on how he might have done things differently. "Why couldn't I have found a quick, surefire way to terminate Pearl's pregnancy? Should I have just skipped out of the state or country, and resumed my life elsewhere? Would marriage and fatherhood have been that bad?" His second-guessing continued: "Could I have avoided the death penalty by having a better lawyer to defend me? Or would a different jury have decided my fate differently? How could I have avoided this fatal outcome? Everything has gone wrong for me. It isn't fair! Why did Pearl get herself pregnant in the first place? In fact, maybe she was with another man and he had fathered her fetus. And besides, a fetus isn't a baby. I tried to help her out and abort the thing, but nothing I did worked out." A final question tortured Scott: "Why didn't I bring Pearl's shoes with me after I killed her?" When self-incriminations such as these overcame him, he was left with a chronic, nagging headache that simply would not dissipate.

In contrast, Alonzo sometimes ruminated about why he had allowed himself to become such a gullible fool: *"How did I ever get involved in such a sordid mess?"* One of his mother's favorite quotes kept ringing in his ears: "We shape all of our tomorrows by the choices we make today." There had been countless times during Pearl's visit to Cincinnati when he could have just walked away from the whole shameful can of worms. If he had simply stood up for himself, and refused to become involved in Scott's personal problems, he would not be sitting in this jail cell, desperately waiting for a reprieve from the very 'friend' who had so calculatingly used and then betrayed him.

During his frequent visits with the two young prisoners, Pastor Lee continued to appeal to them. "Dusty. Lonnie. Listen to me. There is no doubt about it. You know you are accountable for whatever acts of evil you have committed. But you must remember this --- if you truly repent of your sins, the Lord will forgive you and cleanse your hearts with His forgiveness. Now, let us approach the Lord together. Almighty God. Forgive me my sins and grant me the serenity of a healed life. And when I meet the Lord Jesus on that promised day, may I enter into His kingdom with a pure conscience, and a contrite spirit. In Thy name I pray. Amen."

Following this supplication, Lonnie unexpectedly asked, "How many men's souls do you think you have saved, preacher?" "I haven't saved any souls, Lon. I'm being used by God to bring the message of salvation to as many folks as will listen. Whether or not they accept His gracious gift is between them and God. For many, it is easy to talk about, or perhaps even to die for religion. What's not so easy is to actually repent of their sins and surrender their lives to Him."

Looking kindly at each man, Pastor Lee continued, "You know, boys, Henry Ward Beecher* once said, 'Heaven will be inherited by every man who has heaven in his soul."

Jackson interrupted. "I've heard of Henry Ward Beecher. He was once the minister at the Second Presbyterian Church in Indianapolis. And he had a well-known sister ..... uh, Harriet Beecher Stowe. I composed a report about her back in high school. She was an abolitionist who wrote that famous book. What was the title? Oh, yeah. Uncle Tom's Cabin."

"Yes, Scott. She was a fine Christian lady who will go down in history for her courageous stand against slavery."

Pastor Lee continued, "And as much as you two love baseball, you must know all about Billy Sunday, the professional ballplayer, turned evangelist.** He once declared that 'Conversion is a complete surrender

---

* *Henry Ward Beecher (1813-1887) was America's most famous 19th century preacher. He achieved fame on the lecture circuit, and was an advocate of women's suffrage, temperance, the abolition of slavery, and Darwin's theory of evolution. He served as pastor of the Second Presbyterian Church in Indianapolis from 1839-1847. Later, in 1875, as a Congregationalist pastor of Brooklyn, New York's Plymouth Church, he fell from grace when he was tried on charges of committing adultery with a friend's wife. However, the jury failed to reach a verdict, and Beecher recaptured his reputation and continued to serve as a respected and popular public figure until his death.*

** *William Ashley (Billy) Sunday (1862-1935) was a highly accomplished National League baseball player during the 1880s. However, when he was converted to Christianity at the end of the decade, he left baseball to serve in the Christian ministry. By the early part of the 20th century, he had become the nation's most famous evangelist.*

to Jesus. It's a willingness to do what He wants you to do.' So, I pray that each of you is inclined to do just that. Tell me Scott and Lonnie. Are you?"

Neither Jackson nor Walling responded to the question, but Walling, anxious to fill in the awkward silence that followed exclaimed, "I remember when Billy Sunday left baseball. My friends talked a lot about it, and we all thought it was a waste of his athletic talent to give up his career in sports just to become a preacher man." Quickly realizing his blunder, Lonnie added, "No offense meant, Reverend Lee." "None taken, Lonnie.

But I sincerely pray that both of you boys will seriously consider what I have been saying to you. I don't believe that either of you is inherently evil. However, you have both been found guilty of an atrocious crime and as a result, your lives may soon be taken from you. I implore you, before it is too late. Acknowledge your sins! Ask God for his forgiveness! And accept Jesus Christ as your personal savior. That is the only path left for you to follow."

After Pastor Lee had departed, Lonnie turned to Scott and asked with great hesitancy, "Dusty. Do you believe in God?" Scott paused thoughtfully, and then replied, "Maybe I do. Maybe I don't. I'm just not certain whether to sincerely pray that there is a God, or to fervently hope that there isn't. If God exists, then I'm probably destined for Hell, unless pastor Lee's story is true. If God is just a myth, I'm soon headed for nothingness, which was my state before I was born. So, how bad can that be? Right now, for me, it's a toss up."

Ignoring Scott's evasiveness, Lon continued in the same vein. "But, does God really forgive people for everything bad that they've ever done? They say he's created every human being who has ever lived on this earth, and he knows their every thought and action, good and bad. He reads their hearts and judges them accordingly. It just makes sense to me to fess up to every major sin I commit, and ask for His forgiveness."

Scott rubbed the short stubble of his beard, and retorted, "Well, it's really kind of God's fault, isn't it? If He is in charge of everything, why does He allow us to get into trouble? If He is so darned powerful, then all He has to do is stop people from doing bad things. And if He doesn't do that, then He's to blame for the evil in the world, not us!"

Furrowing his brow, Walling thought for a moment and slowly answered, "That doesn't sound right to me, Dusty. I think I'm ready to pray to God and ask for His forgiveness. If He hears and forgives me, then that's a good thing. If He doesn't, then what have I lost by asking?"

On July 27, 1896, Scott Jackson filed a Certificate of Appeal with the Kentucky Clerk of Appeals regarding the May 29, 1896 judgment rendered against him by the Campbell Circuit Court and his subsequent sentence of death by hanging. Later, on October 13, 1896, Alonzo Walling filed a similar appeal regarding the judgment and sentence delivered against him on July 6, 1896. Both appeals cited irregularities in the trial processes that had found the two men guilty of Pearl Bryan's murder.

ILLUSTRATION 40

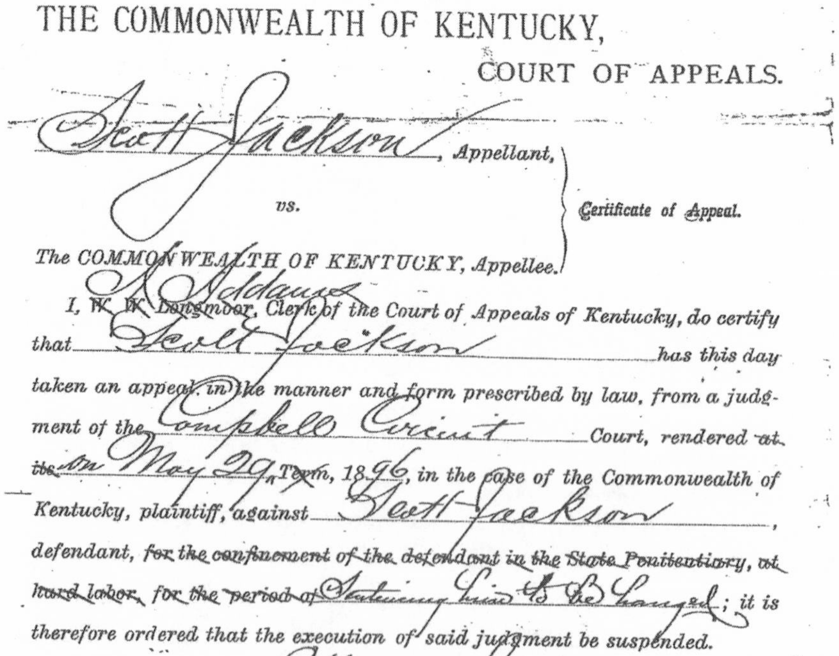
THE COMMONWEALTH OF KENTUCKY,

COURT OF APPEALS.

Scott Jackson, *Appellant,*

vs. — *Certificate of Appeal.*

The COMMONWEALTH OF KENTUCKY, Appellee.

I, ~~*W. W. Longmoor*~~ A. Addams*, Clerk of the Court of Appeals of Kentucky, do certify that* Scott Jackson *has this day taken an appeal, in the manner and form prescribed by law, from a judgment of the* Campbell Circuit *Court, rendered* ~~*at the*~~ on May 29 ~~*Term*~~, *18*96, *in the case of the Commonwealth of Kentucky, plaintiff, against* Scott Jackson, *defendant, for* ~~*the confinement of the defendant in the State Penitentiary, at hard labor, for the period of*~~ Sentencing him to be hanged*; it is therefore ordered that the execution of said judgment be suspended.*

Witness my hand this 27th *day of* July*, 18*96

A. Addams*, Clerk C. A.*

A copy of the Appeal filed in behalf of Scott Jackson with the Commonwealth of Kentucky, Court of Appeals on July 27, 1896.

As each monotonous day inexorably progressed into another predictable evening, a certain abject fear began to embrace both Scott and Lonnie. The two men began to see each morning's dawn as a stealthy thief who was relentlessly stealing their remaining moments on earth. This dogged bandit could not be stopped! As the seasons passed from summer to fall, and winter approached, their worry and gloom proliferated. And then on December 6, 1896, the Kentucky Appeals Court denied both men's petitions of appeal. Their last pillar of hope was quashed!

On February 24, 1897, Alonzo wrote a letter to Pastor Lee, and asked the Reverend to share it with Pearl's family in Greencastle.

It read:

Covington, Feb. 24, 1897
Rev. J. A. Lee

Dear Brother:

I will give to you my belief as to how Miss Pearl Bryan met her death, and kindly asking you to deliver same to the Bryan family, of Greencastle. It is only my belief, but nevertheless I think a true one that be given unless Scott Jackson confesses and makes a statement himself.

On January 9, 1896, Jackson returned from Greencastle after spending his holiday vacation, and said to me on that evening that he had a girl in trouble and did not know what to do with her, and that the only thing he knew to do was to get rid of her. I asked him what he meant by "getting rid of her?" He said, "Why, kill her, of course; that is the surest thing I know to do."

I advised him not to do that, for if he did, he would have to suffer the penalty of the law for it. He then asked me what he should do if he did not do this, and asked me if I knew anything about performing an abortion. I told him no, but rather than have him fulfill his intentions, I would advise him to have that done, and would be willing to assist him in getting a doctor and a room, but that I would not assist him in any other way. This offended him, and he said he guessed he could get along without me. I told him that I wanted nothing to do with it, but rather than have the disgrace come on the parties and their families, it was perhaps best that he adopt the course I have already suggested. He answered and said he would study over the matter.

Afterward, he brought the matter up several times, but I told him I did not want anything to do with it, except as I have stated, and whenever he talked about any other course, I told him that he ought not talk or think of anything of that kind. Although I never really believed that he was in earnest when he talked about the extreme measure, I had never seen anything about him to lead me to think that he would deliberately take anybody's life, and hardly gave the matter a second thought when he talked that way.

As God is my judge, I was not present when Miss Bryan lost her life, nor was I present when anything was done to her for the purpose of taking her life; nor have I any knowledge as to how she lost her life, though I have always had a suspicion that she died in Cincinnati on account of some kind of a drug given to her by Scott Jackson, perhaps without the intention of killing her. But that it did not produce death, and when he found that she was dead, he got badly scared and took her body to Kentucky and cut her head off in the hope that no one would be able to tell whose body it was.

Jackson knows as well as he is living that I was not around when she died, but he won't say so, because he knows that he can't say so without confessing that he was present. Maybe he will do so when he sees that all hope is gone, but not till then. If he can save his own life by sending me to the scaffold, he will do so without hesitation.

I am extremely sorry now, that I did not notify Mr. and Mrs. Bryan of Jackson's talk, and if I had taken any stock in it I think I would have done so; but I had such confidence in him that I did not dream that he would do what I now think he has done, or, at least, what it looks like he has done. This statement I would make if I were on my deathbed, about to face my Maker, and I ask you to consider it.

Yours in sorrow.

ALONZO M. WALLING

CHAPTER FOURTEEN

Friday, March 20, 1897 dawned gray and rainy in Alexandria, Kentucky. Early that morning, Jailer Wagner received a phone call from Sheriff Plummer, informing him of Judge Helm's order to immediately transport Scott Jackson and Alonzo Walling to the Newport jail. As word of the intended move spread throughout the small town, a mass of people gathered around the Alexandria jail. They were awaiting the arrival of a large police carriage, which would transport the two prisoners to the site of their hanging, scheduled for 9 a.m., the following day.

Just one day earlier, Jackson and Walling had made a desperate attempt to save their lives by admitting their roles in Pearl Bryan's murder. In their "confessions," which had been sent to Governor Bradley, they implicated a "Dr. Wagner" as the actual killer. However, because their stories were so inconsistent and contradictory, the governor had refused to grant them clemency. Rather, he issued a formal statement, which concluded:

> **"The law has been defied and the fair name of Kentucky stained with another bloody murder. Twelve men have passed on the guilt of each (Jackson and Walling). The circuit judge and appellate judges have affirmed their action. My oath is that 'I will see that the laws are faithfully executed.' The jury fixed the penalty; I have a plain duty to perform. It is not my province to make laws, but to enforce them; neither is it my province to fix the death penalty, nor is it proper that I should intervene to prevent its infliction when the law and the evidence authorize it. Respite refused**
> **WILLIAM O. BRADLEY,**
> **Governor of Kentucky."**

Promptly at 11:15 am, the driver of the police coach carefully backed his team of six horses to the door of the Alexandria jail. The skies had grown darker, and a steady rain fell on the powerful animals as they waited patiently for their cargo. Each prisoner was handcuffed to a deputy. Alonzo Walling and Deputy Cottingham first exited the jail, followed by Scott Jackson and Deputy Truesdell. The four men took seats on one side of the vehicle, while Sheriff Plummer, Deputy Sheriff Fred Miller, and two guards, Michael Murray and William Sutton, sat opposite them. With a cigar clamped between his teeth and a smile playing on his lips, Walling slid onto his seat. Still exhibiting his typically relaxed and cavalier demeanor, the 21 year old seemed not to have a care in the world. In contrast, a pale and tense Jackson glanced nervously around him as he hesitantly entered the coach.

After the driver climbed to his elevated perch, the 13-mile trip to Newport began. The rain, now into its third day, increased in intensity as the team and coach laboriously plodded on. With the dirt road now completely saturated with water, the horses' rhythmic hoof beats kicked up a steady spray of pasty mud and dark, slimy debris. The police van was a tall vehicle, with tarpaulins attached above the windows. Now rolled down, these heavy shades insured the passengers' privacy and also shielded them from the elements. In contrast, the newspapermen, and the citizenry who closely followed in a long line of open carriages, were subjected to an endless barrage of liquid filth, which plastered them from head to foot.

Curious onlookers, who had braved the weather, lined much of the designated route. After the caravan had pulled onto the Alexandria Pike, it made only a single, brief stop at a roadhouse, where Sheriff Plummer bought cigars for both Jackson and Walling. Further down the pike, at a pool hall on the outskirts of Newport, hundreds of people had congregated. On Fridays, the establishment was always busy with customers waiting to bet on the upcoming weekend horse races. However, on this particular Friday, the crowd was the largest that had ever gathered there. One half mile away, a boy had been positioned on a high spot down the road. From there he could spot the expected vehicle as it approached in the distance and signal to those behind him to "hove in sight." As the entire procession of carriages moved on toward its final destination, additional bystanders began to line the route. As the police carriage approached the edge of town, the many spectators craned their necks to see inside the coach, but, to their disappointment, the heavy, dark tarpaulins were securely attached over the vehicle's windows. When the Newport jail came into view, however, the tarpaulins were raised. Noting the change, hordes of citizens briefly lowered their umbrellas, hoping to catch a glimpse of the two condemned men.

After the primary carriage had reached its destination, others followed in quick succession. When Sheriff Plummer stepped down to the sidewalk, scores of reporters surrounded him. As they pummeled him with questions concerning the executions, one inquiry was repeatedly made: "When will the hangings occur?" The sheriff responded vaguely, stating: "They will take place sometime between sunrise, and sunset tomorrow." Privately, however, he had advised Silas Hayes (a representative of Pearl Bryan's family who had traveled from Greencastle to witness the somber event) to be on hand shortly after sunrise. Meanwhile, Jackson and Walling were being protectively escorted through the surging crowds by their police guards. Upon entering the building, they climbed the wooden stairs to their lockups on the second floor. Each man was held in a 16 x 16 foot room, which contained a cot for the prisoner, a small table, and four chairs for the "deathwatch" team. Officers William Cottingham, William Sutton, Michael Murray, and Ed Truesdale, who all knew Jackson and Walling from their previous incarcerations in the Newport jail, had been assigned to remain in the cells with the two condemned men while they awaited their executions.

Jackson was assigned to the front room and Walling to the one immediately behind it. An oversized door, which separated their quarters, was kept open. In effect, the area of confinement resembled a poor man's version of a two-room suite. Dingy curtains, which hung over the grated window in Scott's compartment, were tied by sashes, and kept open. Alonzo's assigned space had no window. Jackson's cell was also connected to an adjacent chamber, which was occupied by select newspaper reporters. The connecting door to this room was secured by a double bar and lock, which prevented either passage or verbal communication from one side to the other.

Once Jackson and Walling became acquainted with their new surroundings, they removed their jackets and rolled up their shirtsleeves. Walling, seemingly unconcerned about the fate awaiting him the next morning, flopped down on his cot. Nodding off within two minutes, he slept soundly for an hour. While Walling napped, Jackson periodically conversed with his captors, who sat around the table in his room. Eventually, Walling awoke and joined them, since it was less gloomy than were his four walls. With its window facing the jail yard, it provided some daylight and some connection to the outside world. As the hours passed, the guards at the table busied themselves with card playing, while both Jackson and Walling showed increasing interest in the growing crowd assembling below.

Meanwhile, in Frankfort, which was 60 miles west as the crow flies, noteworthy events were unfolding. At 2 pm, a thunderous roll of drumbeats began to emanate from the Armory of the McCreary Guards. The Commonwealth of Kentucky had constructed this two-story, brick arsenal in 1850, in order to house the weapons and equipment of the state militia. The "castle" stood on a cliff, overlooking the Kentucky River as well as downtown Frankfort. Governor Bradley had called for the drumming in order to alert and assemble the area's reserve soldiers. The rat-a-tat-tat cadence continued for a full 10 minutes, summoning the scattered militia to gather on the assembly grounds. As the reverberating rhythm spread from the armory to the surrounding countryside, men stopped whatever they were doing, and hurried toward the beat of the drums. Once organized, the reservists were immediately dispensed by rail to Newport. There, they would be delegated to support the city police in maintaining tight security and crowd control, keeping journalists at bay, and fulfilling any other pressing duties.

Not only were jailer John Bitzer and his deputies, Joseph Frummel, and E. M. Hunt, in charge of the Newport lockup, but also had the task of fulfilling any reasonable needs or requests of the prisoners. This included obtaining desired food items. At 4:30 pm, when Walling awoke from his nap, and Jackson asked him, "Are you hungry?" He replied, "Not yet." Neither Jackson nor Walling had eaten since breakfast. In spite of Lonnie's veneer of bravado, stress and worry had dulled his appetite. In contrast, Jackson was famished, so he proceeded to order both of them an early dinner. The repast had been prepared by a local landlady, and consisted of porterhouse steak, mashed potatoes, peas, bread, butter, and coffee. Walling ate sparingly, but Jackson quickly devoured all of his meal, as well as much of Walling's barely sampled steak.

After 6 pm, a progressively increasing stream of curious people poured into town from Cincinnati and other nearby communities. As the crowds swelled, the entire Newport Police Force of 21 men was ordered to report for duty. It was estimated that several thousand spectators were massed in the area. Hidden among them were numerous pickpockets, aided in their endeavors by the general shoving and jostling which was ongoing. When Jackson and Walling had initially looked out their window, they were amazed by the large number of men, women, and children who had assembled in the jail yard. But now, several hours later, they were absolutely astonished as they observed the expanding sea of people below. Most of these individuals appeared to be curiosity seekers: they merely wanted to catch a quick glance of the two murderers. Jackson and Walling, with little to lose at this point, obliged the crowd by mocking and joking with them through the open, barred window.

At 7 pm, a Cincinnati newspaperman was invited into their cell, and after some preliminary conversation, Walling suggested that they all play cards. The puzzled journalist replied, "I think maybe this is not the time for cards, Alonzo." The latter shook his head and replied, "Oh, all right. As you like." Soon after, the two prisoners were again standing at their window, but now, their mood and demeanor had shifted dramatically. Approximately 5,000 people, now gathered in the general vicinity of the jail, heard the two young men burst forth with these familiar, melodic lyrics:

> **"Say au revoir, but not goodbye**
> **For parting brings a bitter sigh**
> **The past is gone, though mem'ry gives**
> **One clinging thought: the future lives**
> **Our duty first, love must not lead**
> **What might have been, had fate decreed**
> **Twere better far, had we not met**
> **I loved you then, I love you yet"**

At 7 pm, fifty-five Frankfort militiamen and their leader, Captain Noel Gaines of Lexington, had arrived by train in Covington. There, they transferred to streetcars and reached Newport at about 8 pm. Their assignment was to supplement the strength of the local police force and to restrict any inappropriate behavior displayed by onlookers. Officials in Newport were afraid that a potentially unruly crowd might get out of hand. While the streetcars bearing the troops advanced toward the jails, a throng of noisy citizens dashed behind them, shouting and cheering excitedly. As would-be spectators from side streets also poured into the area, the collective horde of people was likened to the masses that had recently gathered in Indianapolis to hear presidential candidate, William Jennings Bryan deliver a campaign speech. By the time that evening had faded into night, the crowd had thinned out considerably. However, a significant remnant continued to mill around, shouting and singing raucously.

Although Alonzo's mother and Scott's mother and sister were now in Newport, staying nearby at the home of an acquaintance, Mrs. Lewis, the three ladies made no effort to see their doomed loved ones. Unable to bear the pain of another wrenching and final separation, they simply stated that their previous parting at the Alexandria jail had served as their final goodbye. As it was, they were still being subjected to heart-jolting agony. Inside the house, they could clearly hear the cruel sing-song voices of the vindictive rabble-rousers, brazenly chanting and calling for the execution of their cherished ones. Clearly, if the hangings were delayed or stayed for any reason, strong worries persisted that unruly citizens might attempt to impose vigilante justice.

After 9 pm, several visitors were allowed to see the prisoners. First to arrive was Chief of Police Pugh, of Covington. He was followed by Jackson's attorney, Col Crawford, who on departing, dejectedly proclaimed "There is no longer any hope for my client. It is all over." Col Washington, who had defended Alonzo Walling at his trial, also came by. He found Alonzo leaning back in a chair, with his legs crossed, smoking a cigar. "Lon, you seem pretty happy under the circumstances," Washington declared. Walling smiled mirthlessly and replied, "Well, I might just as well take it this way. I guess I've got to go, so I may as well take it like a man." The next visitors were three young ladies. Miss Storey spoke softly with Jackson. Miss Emma Roberts, who was Walling's sweetheart, whispered intimately to him, and Mrs. Hughes conversed with everyone present. After their 30- minute time allotment concluded, the three women reluctantly departed. They were all weeping.

Following these sorrowful encounters in the jail yard, Walling spotted a curious onlooker below, clearly delineated by the moonlight. With his head and neck stretched backward, the fellow was straining to look up into the jail cell. As Walling peered down, he cried out contemptuously, "What are you trying to see, Rubber Neck?" Soon, both prisoners were indulging in ribald conversations with several "loose" women who were among the crowd. Minutes later, Walling perched on the window ledge and conducted a prolonged flirtation with a lone prostitute, who stood aside from the others.

The jail keepers shook their heads in disbelief, and must have thought as a renowned poet once so aptly wrote:

> *Alas, regardless of their doom,*
> *The future victims play.*
> *No sense have they of ills to come;*
> *Nor cares beyond today.*

> *Thomas Gray (1716-1771)*
> *English poet*

Finally, tiring of all this banal activity, Jackson stepped away, lit up a cigar and inhaled deeply. Sitting on his cot, he began conversing with the deathwatch team. Pleased to have an audience, he recounted an incident, which had occurred while he was locked up in the Covington jail. Jackson explained how he had offered to give a stubble-faced fellow inmate a shave, but the man emphatically declined the favor, sarcastically replying, "No, I don't want my head cut off!!" After telling this short anecdote, Jackson frowned and indignantly raged, "That SOB! Imagine saying that to me. I will never forgive him for that insult!"

Before long, Alonzo, who had quit sparring with the prostitute minutes earlier, also grew weary of interacting with the contentious crowd below. Exhibiting fatigue, he quietly approached Scott, who was no longer in the company of the guards. The two prisoners stood somberly together, speaking in low tones. Now distanced from all spectators including their keepers, they became thoughtful and subdued. As the hours wore on, a sense of melancholy descended upon the two doomed men. When darkness fell, the gas lamps in both rooms were lit. Beneath the mellow glow emanating from the burners, both cells were bathed in a warm and cozy veneer. However, this external facade belied the dark, icy dread that was seeping into each man's being. Scott and

Alonzo could not help but realize that the clock was inexorably ticking away their remaining few hours on earth.

The rain had now stopped, the night skies had cleared, and the heavens were filled with a myriad of brilliantly shining stars. Looking up from behind the grated window, Walling exclaimed, "Look, Dusty! There are millions of stars out tonight. I wonder what stars really are?" Jackson paused for a moment, contemplated the irony of the question, and then replied, "I don't know, Lon, but I suppose we could both know by this time tomorrow!"

Even at this late hour, the streets of Newport still held the vestiges of an inquisitive crowd. While some people tramped around in the mud and muttered to one another, most folks simply shifted from foot to foot, and looked up toward the light shining from the cell window. Just before midnight, the local police cleared the jail yard and surrounding areas of all spectators. While a work force wired off the four surrounding streets, policemen stood stationed along the wires, enforcing the strict order that no one but the press could pass through.

At 12:30 am, members of the Kentucky state militia relieved the Newport constabulary. The rifles of these freshly summoned citizen soldiers were armed with fixed bayonets, and loaded with cartridge shells. These military personnel, much as their cohorts before them, marched up and down the wire barricade, and halted anyone who came near it. At one point, two men who had wandered too closely to the barriers were told at the point of the bayonet, and in a rich, down-home Kentucky accent, "Y'all can't get in he'ah, gentlemen." The late night show was over. It was time for the spectators to go home.

At midnight, Jackson and Walling were served hamburger sandwiches, pickles, and coffee. Jackson downed three of the sandwiches, while Walling could barely finish one. As they sat at the table eating, they heard the sound of rattling wheels, coming from the direction of Fourth Street. Jackson sprang up from his chair and rushed to the open window. As he peered out, he expected to see a carriage. Instead, he caught sight of a horse-pulled wagon bearing a casket. Undertaker Costigan was driving the vehicle. Scott's curiosity peaked, and he asked the jailers for details concerning this delivery. Grimly, he was told that his family had hired Mr. Costigan to carry his body away from the gallows after the hanging. The plan was to temporarily store the coffin in the workhouse behind the scaffold until it was needed.

On hearing these morbid facts, Scott headed for his cot. Sitting there, he began to turn his thoughts back to his early high school days and more pleasant memories. He recalled that he had rarely studied, but always received reasonably decent grades. When he really liked a course, he did his best work. Public speaking and English were his favorite subjects, and they had served him well up to now. He believed himself to be gifted with the power of persuasion, the ability to convince almost anyone to do his bidding, if he were only given enough time and the right opportunity. But now, his time was running out.

Suddenly, the quiet mood in the room was interrupted by a thunderous racket, which extended upward from the floor beneath them. Uninterrupted shouting, wailing, banging, and crashing sounds assaulted them. Just that morning local officials had declared Mr. Gus Shuster, one of the town's shoemakers, to be insane. For weeks, Gus had been displaying bizarre behavior, both at work and at home. As a result, he had been escorted to the jail that evening to ensure the safety of both himself and of others. At that moment, he was flailing his right arm in the air, and clutching his terrified young daughter with his left arm. His distraught wife, following right behind him, was gesturing wildly, as she repeatedly attempted to retrieve their small daughter from him. The jailers were struggling to physically restrain Gus and he had knocked over several pieces of furniture. As he bellowed out incoherent gibberish, his wife fitfully recounted their tragic story: a month earlier, their older child, a son, had died unexpectedly of appendicitis. Ever since that shocking loss, her husband had not been "right in the head."

After the officers had finally contained Gus's exertions, he agreed to be locked in the jail cell if he could carry his little girl in with him. With permission granted to do so, he entered the cell, and sat on his cot, where he gently and tenderly cradled the small child in his arms. The frightened girl had just calmed down when the jailer told Gus he must now relinquish her to her mother, but he adamantly refused. As a result, the jailers forcefully pried her from Gus's arms as she wailed in terror. Amid this chaos, his wife stepped forward and reached for her child, who in great relief clung to her mother's bosom. Again, Gus began incoherently ranting and raving. His babbling continued unabated until the deputies had forcefully physically subdued him.

From his jail cell one floor above, Walling quipped in a mocking tone, "Sounds like they're having one hell of a good time down there!"

For some minutes, the ruckus downstairs had broken the pervasive spell of doom, which had been suspended like a black cloud over the prisoners upstairs. However, once the uproar had ceased, their sense of foreboding had returned. After midnight, both Jackson and Walling were offered drinks of whiskey, ostensibly to help them cope with their impending fate. Both men took two generous swigs from the half full bottle. At 1 am, Walling fell asleep on his cot, but Jackson stayed awake. With his tongue loosened by liquor, he resumed bragging and joking with the deathwatch squad, but his attempts at humor failed to entertain the men, who themselves were feeling increasingly morose. During the next hour and a half, Jackson penned several letters to family and friends, including one to the Deputy Jailer, Dan Veith, which read:

> **Dear Friend Dan – I will try and say a few words of farewell to you, but they must at this time be few. I want to thank you for all your kindness to me during my stay with you. You have been a good friend to me, and you have my heartfelt thanks. May God bless and keep you. I trust you may ever be true to yourself, and to all mankind.**
>
> **Yours. Scott Jackson**

Sheriff Plummer arrived at the jail about 1:45 am, carrying the black hoods and binding straps that would be used for the hangings. Peering into the prisoners' cell, he observed that Scott Jackson was writing intently as he sat at a corner of the table. Alonzo Walling, however, was curled up on his cot, fast asleep. The sheriff told the deathwatch team and Jackson to be ready to leave the jail by 7 am the following morning, as the executions were scheduled for 9 am.

During this time period, George Blitz, the son of Newport's mayor, was being sworn in as the gatekeeper. He would restrict anyone without a valid ticket from passing through the jail yard entrance. At 2:30 am, Sheriff Plummer was busy in the jail yard, carrying the specially manufactured hangman's ropes up to the scaffold, and affixing them to the gallows. With this task completed, he returned to the men's cells, where Walling was still sleeping, and Jackson was finishing up his correspondence. After he had finished writing his last farewell note,

Jackson fortified himself with additional whiskey and slumped down onto his cot. Within minutes, he was asleep.

Two hours later, Reverend John Lee arrived at the jail to meet with the condemned men. When he saw that they were both lying motionless on their cots, he asked the jailers to let him know when the two were ready to meet with him. Meanwhile, he chose to wait downstairs in the kitchen. The Reverend John Alford Lee, Pastor of the 3rd Baptist Church of Covington, Kentucky, had continued to serve as the two prisoners' spiritual advisor. During their initial incarceration, he had only periodically met with them, but since the conclusion of the trials, he visited them more frequently. Reverend Lee was fond of saying, "In all men, there is good." In fact, on the wall of his family parlor hung a cross-stitched sampler which read: *There's so much good in the worst of us, and so much bad in the best of us, that it little behooves any of us, to talk about the rest of us.* Obviously, the preacher lived every day of his ministry by this old adage. His unassuming manner and non-judgmental attitude had eventually enabled both Scott and Lonnie to trust him unreservedly and to find considerable comfort in his counsel.

CHAPTER FIFTEEN

Jackson awoke with a start at 5:25 am, and Walling twenty minutes later. Almost immediately, Jailer Bitzer asked them what they wanted for breakfast. For Jackson, the simple question created a major contradiction. It seemed totally irrelevant what he chose for breakfast, or even if he consumed any breakfast at all. Unless in the unlikely event that Governor Bradley intervened in his death sentence, he would die before even fully digesting this meal. Yet, curiously, if he could transport himself to a mental state where he lived only in the present moment, then what he chose for breakfast would have meaning. To accomplish this mental trick, he must focus totally on maximally living each remaining minute. He reasoned that he could do this, and that, even now, he still had time to experience life. There was still food to be enjoyed; conversations to be held; a sunrise to be observed from his window; and melodic bird songs to be heard.

Thus, Scott and Lonnie ordered a hearty breakfast of buckwheat cakes, ham, eggs and coffee. By jail standards, the food was quite tasty and they relished every bite. When the meal had ended, they took turns cleaning up in their quarters, where each man had been provided with a washbasin. Afterward, they looked at one another quizzically, as if to say, "Why bother? Is it more seemly to go to your death in pristine condition?" With a flash of cynical humor, Scott commented, "I don't want to die with egg on my face!" Then, with an eerie sense of unreality, they donned their black suits, white shirts, and black silk ties. This "formal" attire had been delivered to the jail the prior evening by family representatives, and this morning, had been brought upstairs by the Sheriff. Though appropriate as funeral garb on a corpse, this dressy attire worn by "the dead men walking" only added a macabre-like aura to the ghastly moments that lay ahead. After they were fully dressed, both men asked, with some urgency, to see Pastor Lee, who was still waiting patiently downstairs.

In these early morning hours, security was becoming extremely tight. The jail yard leading to the scaffold was now completely surrounded by an inner cordon of police and an outer row of National Guard soldiers. Thoroughly soaked from all the previous rainfall, the grounds were three inches deep in mud. In spite of this messy inconvenience, a number of select individuals were waiting, passes in hand, to enter the area. Those who were initially admitted included a number of deputy sheriffs, various government officials, jury members who wished to be present and fifty journalists from throughout the nation. Members of the general public who had managed to secure tickets lined up behind them. This "ticket only" procedure had been initiated to restrict the number and character of the crowd. Although the tickets were free, the local police department had issued only a limited number, and they were withheld from any known, or suspected, disreputable characters requesting them.

Although passes had been offered to the Bryan family, everyone politely declined them except Pearl's brother, Fred. At the last second, however, he, too, had decided not to attend. Instead, he gave his pass to attorney Silas A. Hayes of Greencastle. In spite of the good intentions of the law, a handful of unsavory characters, including prostitutes, pickpockets, and other 'toughs' managed to slip inside the gates.

Taken as a whole, the throng resembled an audience that might have gathered to watch a prizefight. In fact, the outcome of the recent Bob Fitzsimmons-Jim Corbett heavyweight boxing championship match was a major topic of conversation among the crowd in Newport that morning. Hailed as the "fight of the century," the bout had occurred 3 days earlier in Carson City, Nevada, where Fitzsimmons had won by a knockout in the 14th round. This match was also noteworthy because two legendary western heroes, Wyatt Earp and Bat Masterson, were in charge of security for the event.

Because there were no seats in the jail yard, the restless onlookers spent the bulk of their time pacing around in the mud, or clustering in small groups. What were they saying to one another as they each contemplated the thought of viewing an imminent hanging? Contrary to yesterday's frenzied, disjointed outbursts, today's collective demeanor was mostly solemn and foreboding, except for the few ribald and crude ruffians, who were obviously attempting to grow in number. Some people doubted that the execution would even take place, assuming that Jackson, and especially Walling, might still be saved by a last-minute reprieve. It seemed likely that if such an edict should suddenly come down, many tempers would flare, and the consequent mentality of the mob might cause violent rioting, or worse.

Back in the jail, Pastor Lee, having responded to the guard's summons, spent an hour seriously conversing with the prisoners. "Even now, you can still claim eternal life in heaven, simply by asking for God's grace through Christ," he emphasized. Although the two listened respectfully, they made no verbal commitment. After their solemn discussion, at Scott's request, the three men joined together to sing *Home Sweet Home*, one of the most popular melodies of the era. Those who were within earshot recalled that they were touched, as they listened to these sentimental strains:

> *Mid pleasures and palaces though we may roam,*
> *Be it ever so humble, there's no place like home;*
> *Home, home, sweet, sweet home!*
> *There's no place like home, oh, there's no place like home!*

Ironically, John Howard Payne, who had composed this number some 70 years earlier, was once quoted from his diary as saying, "The world has literally sung my song until every heart is familiar with its melody, yet I have been a wanderer from the time of my boyhood."

Temporarily departing, the pastor took Scott's letters and some of the men's other personal effects, all to be dispatched appropriately. Again, in a dramatic switch of mood and focus, Jackson and Walling now lit up cigars and perched on their windowsill, where they brazenly bantered with their expanding audience. Jackson disappeared for a moment, then reappeared "on his stage," clasping his hands together in a vertical motion, as if he were shaking hands with the spectators. At this point, both prisoners were summoned from their perch, but returned shortly, now clean-shaven. The Sheriff had hired a local barber, who had utilized a straight razor, shaving mug, and a leather strop to sharpen the blade. Many in the immediate vicinity who observed the transition, remarked that the two men "now looked much younger ... like teenagers." However, their raucous interaction with the rabble-rousers below continued, as once again, they gestured, sneered, shouted insults, and dared the crowd to reply in kind. In some twisted way, they seemed to relish the hostility directed toward them. Being thoughtfully sentimental one minute and caustically crude, the next, the damned pair was riding on an emotional see saw.

When Pastor Lee returned to the cell, he conducted a brief religious service for the two, beginning with a fervent reading from the Scriptures. The good reverend was heartened to see the men listening intently to his words. Pastor Lee then placed a hand on each prisoner's shoulder, and said, "Boys, I know how you love to sing. Let's sing a few hymns together, and while we do, give some thought to the sweet hereafter that awaits us all."

"I think I'd like that, Reverend," Dusty replied softly.

Pastor Lee sang the melody, with Walling singing bass, and Jackson, tenor. The three voices blended together nicely, as they sang, "In the Sweet Bye and Bye.

> *In the sweet, in the sweet*
> *bye and bye, bye and bye,*
> *we shall meet on that beautiful shore;*
> *In the sweet, in the sweet*
> *bye and bye, bye and bye,*
> *we shall meet on that beautiful shore.*

Because Alonzo and Scott had attended church regularly as youngsters, they quickly recalled other favorite hymns to sing. The trio earnestly performed several additional anthems, but the time for singing was running short. Their crooning of hymns concluded with "God Be With You Till We Meet Again." The prophetic words of the last verse and refrain tumbled effortlessly out of their lips:

> *God be with you till we meet again,*
> *Keep love's banner floating o'er you,*
> *Smite death's threatening wave before you,*
> *God be with you till we meet again.*
>
> *Refrain:*
> *Till we meet, till we meet,*
> *Till we meet at Jesus' feet;*
> *Till we meet, till we meet,*
> *God be with you till we meet again.*

As the cherished strains of the sacred songs drifted out over the courtyard, the hearts of many onlookers were filled with both awe and dread. The more than 500 spectators congregated there had come to observe justice being dispensed by carrying out two executions. They were not prepared to experience any empathetic feelings toward the convicted murderers. Yet, ironically, as a prelude to the ghastly spectacle that was to come shortly, scores of people were witnessing heartfelt grace, as the pastor and two doomed men prayed and sang together. Walling was heard to cry out "Amen! Amen!" during several pleas sent heavenward as the religious service ended about 7:45 am.

Fifteen minutes later, when Sheriff Plummer came to check the status of the two inmates, he asked if they had any final thoughts to share with him. Neither man chose to speak, and Plummer departed to deal with various logistical issues related to the executions. At 8:15 am, Deputy Maurer entered the jail with a letter for Walling from his sweetheart, Emma Roberts. Lonnie hesitated as he grasped the sealed envelope. His relationship with this young woman had been a strange one. He had briefly met her while he attended dental school in Cincinnati, but it was only when he was incarcerated in the northern Kentucky jails, that she began to visit him regularly. Initially, he had been puzzled by her interest in him, and he remained somewhat cool and distant. But as time went on, he began to look forward to her visits, and their conversations became more animated and personal. In the past month, a real friendship had developed, and Emma was now a significant comfort to Lonnie during these trying times.

Alonzo tore open the envelope, and slowly read the single page of cursive writing:

> *Dearest Alonzo,*
> *I will always love you. You are the bravest man I know.*
> *Remain strong and die game!**
> *Yours always, Emma*

Walling looked up at the deputy, feeling buoyed by the contents of her concise note. Smiling at Maurer, the two shook hands and bid one another farewell.

When Pastor Lee returned to their chambers at 8:30 am, Jackson

* *To die game: to maintain a bold, unyielding spirit to the very end. To die with dignity.*

asked Sheriff Plummer to join them, and in a stunning development, he declared to the sheriff and the pastor that he wanted to clear Alonzo Walling of any connection to Pearl Bryan's murder.

He promptly wrote a short message and asked that it be sent to Governor Bradley in Frankfort. His statement read:

"Walling is not guilty of this crime. I am." Signed, Scott Jackson.

His declaration was immediately telegraphed to the Governor, and the orders for enforcing the two capital punishment decrees were temporarily halted. During the subsequent 80-minute delay, ex-Sheriff Edward Fauth of Lexington and Sheriff Plummer mounted the scaffold and checked the ropes, which were already sufficiently well greased. Earlier, the nooses had been meticulously covered with bottled sweet oil, which was thoroughly hand-rubbed into the fibers. Fauth had either supervised or assisted in 17 previous hangings, and had been hired by Sheriff Plummer to be in charge of these two executions. He was now on hand "in order to avoid any bungling of the affair." As another precaution against a possible blunder, the hinges of the traps had been generously oiled, and Plummer sprang them to make certain that they were in good working order. When the lever was tested, the trap doors swung down with a loud, piercing **CLANG** that reverberated, causing the crowd to utter a collective groan, "Ohhhh!" As later reported by many who were present, even this partial rehearsal of the unsettling upcoming event caused them to discern a pronounced sinking feeling, deep in the pits of their stomachs.

At 9:50 am, Governor Bradley telegraphed Sheriff Plummer directing him to stop Walling's execution, but to proceed with Jackson's hanging. An official in the jailer's office bolted upstairs to announce that a respite had been granted for Alonzo Walling.

Lonnie, suddenly jubilant, was heartily congratulated by all who were present. However, just 25 minutes later, Governor Bradley sent another telegram to Sheriff Plummer, canceling his initial response to Jackson's brief admission of guilt. The sheriff was ordered to proceed with both executions! However, Bradley added that should Jackson make a full, detailed confession which also exonerated Walling, then even if it occurred on the scaffold, the latter's execution would be stayed, and his sentence reevaluated. Lonnie, understandably devastated by this quick turn of events, convinced the guards to immediately locate Mayor Rhinock of Alexandria, who was present in Newport, and summon him to the jail. When the mayor entered his cell, Walling begged him to sign a dispatch to the governor, asking for a 30-day reprieve. Alonzo insisted, "Scott can save my life if he will, but he won't. I have tried in every way possible to get him to do it, but he won't help me. He ought to save me!"

Although Walling's desperate plea touched the mayor, he had neither the power, nor the legal right to intervene.

"Now Lonnie," Mayor Rhinock responded, "before I can do anything to save you, you need to tell me where Pearl's head is."

Walling replied, "Sir, before God whom I will soon meet, I do not know!"

Shaking his head slowly and wearing a frown of futility, the mayor declared, "Then I can't help you, Lon."

When Sheriff Plummer notified Scott of the conditions that he must meet for Alonzo's execution to be stayed, Jackson breathed deeply, sighed, and said, "No. I can't say honestly that Wally is innocent in this affair. It just wouldn't be the right thing to do!"

At 11:15 am, Governor Bradley telephoned Sheriff Plummer for another conversation. On hearing that Jackson had refused to absolve Walling of participating in the murder, Bradley stated his final decision regarding the executions. "Proceed. There will be no respite!" At 11:20 am, Executioner Fauth appeared on the gallows and adjusted the nooses, once again. After this testing, Sheriff Plummer addressed the crowd, who listened intently.

"Gentlemen*. I want to ask you while this execution occurs to observe the utmost quiet and make no demonstration of any kind upon such a solemn occasion as this. You may agree with and be assured that the law will be properly complied with, but I ask you to make no expression of any kind. It is a hard duty for me to perform, and it has especially been so during the past two hours. At 11:30 o'clock, we expect to have this execution take place. I will ask you to show the feeling and reverence that ought to be shown in the presence of death." Following his words, Sheriff Plummer withdrew inside the jail to begin the daunting process of walking the prisoners to the gallows.

At 11:27 am, Jailer John Bitzer entered the gate and asked Sheriff

* *Apparently, ladies were either not allowed to attend, or they were simply not acknowledged as being present!*

Maurice Hook* of Bracken County to come forward from the crowd. Several days earlier, Sheriff Hook had also been appointed to assist Sheriff Plummer with the execution. He responded quickly and joined Bitzer in entering the jail. This preliminary activity appeared to convince those present that the execution was imminent, and a sense of anticipation settled upon the spectators.

At 11:30 am, a column of participants formed and slowly made its way toward the scaffold. Painted a stark white and bathed in bright sunlight, the looming structure projected a ghastly image on the boardwalk. The stomping boots of those who solemnly marched forward through the muddy field could be distinctly heard. Tramp! Tramp! Tramp! As the inexorable procession approached, the gate was thrown open and thirteen men were admitted. In order of entry, they were: the Reverend Mr. Lee, with his bare head bowed and his hands behind him firmly grasping his Bible; Scott Jackson, gravely walking in step between deputies Miller and Moore; Alonzo Walling, nervously shuffling between deputies Hindeman and Truesdale; four grim-faced death watch guards; and the stoic-appearing sheriffs, Plummer and Hook. The black hoods that Jackson and Walling were soon to don had been draped on top of their heads as caps might be, spuriously projecting on their owners an almost jaunty appearance.

The group maintained their pre-determined order while climbing the thirteen steps of the scaffold at 11:32 am. Immediately, the two condemned prisoners were positioned on the gallows, facing the crowd. Sheriff Plummer gravely read, "Scott Jackson and Alonzo Walling. I am here for the purpose of carrying out the mandate of the government of this state, as expressed to you in the death warrants I read to you last Tuesday. Scott Jackson. Have you anything to say?" Jackson hesitated. Before he spoke, Walling turned toward him with an expression of earnest expectancy, hoping that Scott might utter the words that could save him. However, Alonzo's expression fell as he heard Jackson's reply: "I have only this to say. I am not guilty of the crime for which I am

---

* On January 9ᵗʰ of that year, Hook had overseen the hanging of Bob Laughlin, a tenant farmer convicted of rape and murder. Ironically, Laughlin had shared a jail cell with Jackson and Walling while they were incarcerated in Covington.

View from the courtyard of the condemned men on the gallows with only minutes to live. The four principal figures from left to right are: Pastor Lee (singing "I've Anchored My Soul in the Haven of Rest"); Jackson and Walling (with black hoods on top of their heads), and (likely) Sheriff Plummer. The nooses are not yet positioned on the prisoners' necks. Courtesy Kentucky Historical Society.

now compelled to pay the penalty with my life." Plummer continued, "Alonzo Walling. Have you anything to say?" The ashen Walling replied, "Nothing ... only that you are taking the life of an innocent man, and I call upon my God to witness the truth of what I say."

Sheriff Plummer then turned to Pastor Lee, saying, "Reverend, please conduct the service." The preacher looked heavenward, and sang the hymn based on Hebrews 6:19 found in the New Testament of the Holy Bible, "I've Anchored My Soul in the Haven of Rest." Although his voice was trembling, it quickly gained strength and momentum. From his sorrowful soul, the lyrics and the melody gushed forth:

> *My soul in sad exile was out on life's sea,*
> *So burdened with sin and distressed,*
> *Till I heard a sweet voice, saying,*
> *"Make Me your choice";*
> *And I entered the "Haven of Rest"!*

> *Refrain ...*
> *I've anchored my soul in the "Haven of Rest,"*
> *I'll sail the wide seas no more;*
> *The tempest may sweep over wild, stormy, deep,*
> *In Jesus I'm safe evermore.*

These tender words seemed to touch Scott and Alonzo deeply. As Pastor Lee sang this poignant declaration of saving faith, Jackson must surely have been thoughtfully reliving his early, carefree days at sea with his father.

Meanwhile, many of the men in the courtyard, who stood in deep mud and sweated profusely under a broiling sun, removed their hats. Continuing the service, Pastor Lee read four selections from the Bible:

> Isaiah 45:22 ("Look upon me and be saved, all the ends of the earth, for I am God, and there is none else.");
> John 3:16 ("For God so loved the world that he gave His only begotten son, that whosoever believeth in Him, should not perish, but have everlasting life.");
> Matthew 11:28 ("Come unto me, all ye that labor, and are heavy laden, and I will give you rest.");
> and Rev 22:11 ("And the spirit and the bride say, come, and let him that is the atheist come, and whosoever will, let him take the water of life freely.")

At this point, Sheriff Plummer called upon Reverend Lee to invoke a Divine blessing. In an emotion-laden voice, the pastor responded, "Our Father, our Savior, our God, we pray to Thee, that Thou shalt receive the souls of Scott Jackson and Alonzo Walling and save them; that they may be worthy of Thee, and in Thee alone for life and salvation. O Lord, O Christ, Thou who didst save the thief who died on the cross, be with them today. Oh, admit these boys in Thy love, to Thy mercy, we ask and rely upon Thee, Jesus Christ, today and forever. Amen."

As he listened to the pastor's words, Jackson stood straight and steady. In contrast, Walling, with his jaw clenched tightly and his legs trembling noticeably, anxiously scanned the distant horizon. At the close of his prayer, Pastor Lee shook hands with each condemned man, and said, "Scott, goodbye; Lonnie, goodbye. I ask in the name of the Lord, right now, that you engage in a secret prayer that your souls may be saved." Scott replied in a faltering voice, "Farewell, Brother Lee." Walling's voice also trembled as he said, "Goodbye, Reverend." With tears in his eyes, Pastor Lee moved to the back of the scaffold. In pairs, the four deputies stepped forward, and adjusted the ropes and straps, tied the prisoners' arms, pinioned their legs, and placed the heavily greased nooses around their necks. As Scott and Lonnie bid each other a final goodbye, the deputies pulled the black caps down over the condemned men's eyes.

Seemingly not trusting his positioning of the rope, Deputy Hindeman repeatedly readjusted the noose around Alonzo's neck. Sheriff Plummer, wishing to finish the grisly task, waited impatiently. In utter panic, Walling moaned in a quivering voice, "Go! Go!" Irritated by the inappropriate delay, Plummer finally waved Hindeman off, paused briefly and gave the lever a quick, strong pull. At 11:41 am, the trap doors sprung open and the two young men plunged downward to meet their fate.

CHAPTER SIXTEEN

Hanging is still the oldest and most widely used method of capital punishment in the world today. Generally, it employs one of three techniques, each distinguished by the distance the body falls (drops) during the process. For example, a hangman may utilize a short drop, exemplified in old western movies. In following this procedure, one end of a relatively short rope is made into a noose and placed around the neck, while the other end is tied to a sturdy tree limb. The condemned man, now tautly connected to the tree, is placed on a horse. As the animal is spooked to bolt, the prisoner is left swinging from the tree.

In contrast, the once popular long drop hanging involved a fall of up to 10 feet. Unfortunately, this distance sometimes generated enough force to produce decapitation, not a suitable outcome. In contrast, the standard drop hanging became the major method used in the United States during the latter part of the 19th century. This technique utilized a fall from a moderate distance, typically 4-6 feet, in which the noosed subject plunged to his death from a gallows trap door. A combination of the prisoner's body weight, the distance of his fall, and the force of gravity collectively caused the spinal cord to sever somewhere between the first five cervical vertebrae, thereby producing an immediate loss of consciousness, and death. The noose typically contained from 5 to 13 coils, which would deliver a fatal jolt to the side of the neck as the coils slid down the rope during the gravity-driven descent. This endeavor was more art than science and quite a challenge for the hangman, since his rope needed to be just tight enough, and positioned very precisely behind the condemned person's ear to obtain the desired result.

Sheriff Jule Plummer was a conscientious and meticulous public servant who conducted his law enforcement responsibilities in an orderly and organized manner. In spite of the onerous nature of his task on that fateful Saturday, he was confident that when he pulled the lever on the gallows, the operation would transpire quickly and efficiently. Since he was a relative novice in conducting public executions, Plummer had sought the advice of several experienced hangmen in order to assure himself that the procedure would be conducted flawlessly.

Regrettably, in spite of Plummer's careful planning and preparation, this did not occur, as the knots were apparently not tied sufficiently tight. This shortcoming allowed the coils to slip to the rear of the men's necks rather than be positioned behind the ear. Thus, when Jackson and Walling plunged downward through the double trap doors, their necks did not break, nor were their deaths instantaneous. Scott remained erect, swinging back and forth like a clock pendulum while still alive, whereas Alonzo died even more slowly and violently. His legs periodically constricted upwards while his shoulders jerked back, giving the impression that his body's weight was lifted and somehow balanced on his tied wrists. At least 20 times, his limbs and shoulders contracted in this bizarre manner, lending a horrifying and repugnant appearance to the entire process. It was in this prolonged manner that the two unfortunates were slowly strangled to death.

Two physicians had been assigned to assess the presence of any detectable heart beat, a feat accomplished by pressing one hand firmly on the suspended men's chest until all contractions were determined to have ceased. Jackson was finally declared dead at 11:55 am, some 14 minutes after the trap door on the gallows had opened. Walling died at 11:58 am, three minutes later.

In spite of the protracted, grotesque spectacle of the two men lurching and convulsing in their death throes, most observers milled around the site for many minutes after the victims were declared dead, but remained suspended in air. Since the scaffold and gallows had been constructed in the open courtyard behind the jail, several thousand people who had gathered in surrounding buildings were able to view the entire proceedings from a distance. A great clamor of satisfaction erupted from the crowd when the traditional black flag was raised in the courtyard, signifying that the capital punishments had been successfully completed. When officials in Covington and Cincinnati were in turn notified that Jackson and Walling had been hung, they, too, hoisted the black flag.

The hanging of Scott Jackson and Alonzo Walling. Scene from the courtyard moments after the execution of the two men, whose bodies are visible below the scaffolding.

Courtesy Kentucky Historical Society.

Before the two bodies could be lowered to the ground, the Sheriff was obliged to move all spectators away from the gallows area. When this task was completed, officials removed the two hoods, but were stunned by the appearances of Jackson and Walling. Their faces and tongues were markedly swollen and intensely discolored! Those spectators standing nearest to the bodies turned away in disgust. Without delay, both corpses were carefully positioned in their coffins, and the lids quickly closed. During this process, a Cincinnati newspaper reporter was heard to quote a line borrowed from Shakespeare's Macbeth, "Nothing in all of his (Scott Jackson's) life so became him as the leaving of it." Those who were within earshot of his remark passionately nodded their assent. They were now finally satisfied that the murder and decapitation of Pearl Bryan had been avenged.

Several days earlier, officials of the Greencastle cemetery association had notified Sheriff Plummer that the burial of executed murderers was forbidden at the Forest Lawn cemetery. Moreover, Scott's survivors were sensitive to the fact that Pearl Bryan's remains were interred there, and acknowledged that it would be inappropriate to bury Scott in the same graveyard as his murder victim. Thus, Mrs. Jackson, with the counsel of Dr. and Mrs. Post, secretly agreed to have Scott's remains cremated. They reasoned that this action would prevent the almost certain vandalism that would occur at his gravesite. The trio decided to maintain his ashes in a small urn until public animosity toward Scott and his family had diminished.

Consequently, Jackson's three relatives employed the Cincinnati Crematory Association to surreptitiously incinerate his remains shortly after the execution. When his body was lowered from the gallows, it was promptly loaded upon Undertaker Costigan's wagon and taken to the funeral home. This diversionary tactic was meant to prevent the public from discovering the actual plans already made by the family. Nevertheless, a residual crowd closely observed the entire process. Meanwhile, the press was falsely informed that Jackson would be embalmed at the funeral home, and then shipped to Wiscassett, Maine, to be buried next to his grandmother. During that afternoon and early evening, callers at the Newport funeral home were shown both an expensive casket, described as Scott's burial coffin, and a decorative shroud, portrayed as his final wearing apparel. Additionally, they were told that there would be no open casket viewing.

Alonzo Walling's body was also quickly removed from the Newport jail yard, and taken to the railroad depot for temporary storage. That evening, it was placed on a train car, sent to Hamilton, Ohio, and subsequently dispatched by horse and wagon to nearby Mt. Carmel, Indiana. As his mother, Sarah, and surviving brothers looked on, Alonzo was lowered into an unmarked grave, and buried next to his father, Samuel, who had died on December 20, 1881. When Sarah Walling died on September 5, 1917, she was laid to rest beside her husband and son. An inscribed poem is still visible on the large headstone overlying the three bodies. It reads:

> *They sleep in grace*
> *They live with God*
> *Their home is far above*
> *They have gone to rest*
> *With Christ, their Lord*
> *In joy, pure with love.*

At 7 pm on Saturday evening, the mortician once again loaded Scott's remains onto his wagon, this time driving to the crematorium, where they were met by two officials, Superintendent Rudolph and Secretary Hoover. Within ten minutes, Mrs. Jackson and Dr. and Mrs. Post also arrived at the site in a carriage and entered the building. Shortly after, the crematory personnel placed the casket on an elevator and lowered it to the room below, which contained the retort (a large furnace designed for incinerating bodies). After the coffin lid was removed, a sheet, saturated with highly flammable alum water, was positioned over the body. The container and its contents were placed on an iron carrier, pushed on tracks directly through two sets of metallic double doors, and fed into the glowing, fiery interior of the incinerator. The doors closed behind the casket with a clang. Four hours later, the body had been reduced to little more than 5 pounds of ashes, which were collected, placed in an urn, and presented to Scott's weeping mother.

That evening, several newsmen visited Reverend Lee and asked him to make a personal statement concerning his involvement in the case. Although still visibly upset by the wrenching ordeal of the day, the 31 year-old minister agreed to answer a few questions. He acknowledged that he had just received a joint letter from Scott and Alonzo less than four hours before their deaths.

8 a.m.
3/20/97

Dear Brother Lee:
We hereby both unite in our sincerest thanks to you who have been so kind to us in these, the last elements of our existence. We will both soon be in the everlasting eternity, and, knowing this, we wish to thank you for your more than kind attention during our entire trouble, and know that we will both meet you again. Souls with souls, we are very sincerely yours.
Alonzo M. Walling and Scott Jackson

In an emotion-laden voice, Pastor Lee wistfully re-read the letter's contents, looked intently at the journalists and unaffectedly added, "Those two (young men) certainly died with stout hearts."

When reporters probed to learn more lurid details concerning the murder case, Pastor Lee shook his head, sighed, and stated "I am no wiser than the world is (in knowing the entire truth concerning Pearl's murder). I pleaded time and again with both Scott and Lonnie to bare their souls about the case, but they would not do so. I begged them to tell (the authorities) where the head is, but even to the last moment, they gave me evasive answers. I would rather say nothing as to the men's guilt or innocence, so please do not press me. I can say that I am the custodian of two letters from Scott Jackson. One of these is (addressed) to his mother, which I will mail to her when she gets back to Greencastle. The other one is directed to Miss Storey. Both letters are extremely brief, and, while I do not want to divulge their contents, I will say that they are farewell letters similar in character to others Scott had been writing to his friends. Walling also requested me to write to Miss Roberts in a day or two, giving her his parting thoughts."

In spite of recognizing the horrendous nature of the crime for which the two young men were sentenced, Pastor Lee had privately developed a certain fondness for both Scott and Lonnie. He had met with them many times during the last year of their lives, and had engaged them in intense spiritual discussions. Above all, he was concerned with the salvation of their souls.

After the executions, Cal Crim was repeatedly badgered by newsmen who sought his views about the outcome of the case. When questioned specifically about Lonnie, Cal would thoughtfully rub his chin and frown, while slowly shaking his head side to side. He would generally respond, "You know, I feel badly about him. Alonzo Walling was a simple country boy who clearly just fell under the ruinous influence of an older and much more sinister man. I shudder to think of the additional evil that Scott Jackson might have done had he lived."

In the weeks that followed the hangings of Jackson and Walling, many newspapers continued to issue graphic descriptions of the prolonged suffering experienced by the two men as they dropped to their deaths on the gallows. They further belabored the ghastly groans of the witnessing crowds, and the grossly botched performance of the executions. Many citizens of Indiana, Ohio and Kentucky became highly incensed when they heard about the degree of pain and suffering experienced by the two condemned men during their agonizing deaths. They believed that capital punishment delivered in this bumbling manner was not only cruel and inhuman, but also socially and morally unconscionable. Nevertheless, any community indignation that arose from these amateurish hangings was not persuasive enough to lead to criminal execution reform. In fact, public hanging as a method of capital punishment continued to be practiced for almost 40 more years.

The last public hanging to take place in the United States also occurred in Kentucky, in Owensboro on August 14, 1936, when Rainey Bethea was hanged before a throng of more than 20,000 spectators. Rainey was a black man who had been convicted of the rape and murder of a 70-year-old white woman. The warrant for his execution had been signed by then Kentucky Governor Albert "Happy" Chandler.* Bethea's execution generated so much national interest that at times the proceedings bordered on pandemonium. Journalists from all over the U.S. swarmed into the small Kentucky town to report on the event. Many of the newspaper stories that were published after the fact depicted Owensboro as a backward, unsophisticated, illiterate community. The resulting flood of negative publicity that engulfed Owensboro may have influenced the viewpoint of other American citizens throughout the country who favored public hangings, and thus contributed to their eventual demise.

During the days immediately after Pearl Bryan had been identified as the murder victim, her family twice visited the spot where her remains had been discovered. Solemnly and painstakingly they examined the soil and vegetation at the site, and questioned Mr. Locke regarding the details of the grisly discovery. Privately, Mr. and Mrs. Bryan acknowledged that in spite of her dreadful circumstances at the time, there was some solace for them in seeing the setting where their daughter had spent her final minutes.

Prior to Jackson's trial, the Cincinnati Enquirer reported that a few male relatives of the Bryan's had met with a number of Greencastle's citizenry to consider forming a lynching party as retribution for Pearl's murder. However, nothing came of these ill-advised plans. Following

---

* *Chandler, who went on to serve as the Commissioner of Baseball between 1945 and 1951, oversaw the initial steps in the racial integration of the sport. He was holding that office when Jackie Robinson debuted with the Brooklyn Dodgers in 1947. At the time that Chandler was forced out of his position in 1951, many people believed that it was in retribution for his stance in racially "redefining" the national pastime.*

the executions of Jackson and Walling, the Bryan family publicly thanked members of the judicial system for the outcomes of the trials, and also expressed their "kindly feelings" toward Governor Bradley for refusing to grant a reprieve to Walling. As a gesture of gratitude for his role in helping to solve the crime, Mr. and Mrs. Bryan also presented shoemaker Poock of Newport with a pair of shoes identical to those worn by Pearl at the time of her death.

Both Pearl's murder and the subsequent hangings of her accused killers fueled a spate of cautionary and judgmental sermons adamantly preached by dedicated ministers throughout the tri-state area. Such harangues continued for years. The recurring theme of these discourses was that poor Pearl, a simple country girl, had been led astray by Jackson, the clever, depraved villain. The clergy typically exhorted their congregations to avoid the evils of the flesh, including fornication, lasciviousness, avarice, deceit, lying, drunkenness, murder, and pride.*

It is difficult to comprehend the depth of humiliation and embarrassment suffered by the Bryan, Jackson, and Wood families, all sustained by the outlandish happenings surrounding Pearl Bryan's murder. The extreme notoriety of such an event occurring within this staid and conservative community led to an undeclared local collusion, which minimized any mention of the subject except among close intimates. In fact, the propriety of the Victorian age in general precluded a broad discussion of any kind of sexually-linked affair.

In spite of the general reticence of Greencastle inhabitants to openly discuss the homicide and its carnally-linked rumors, particularly with the press and strangers, there was no reluctance to speculate behind closed doors about every conceivable aspect of the case. Conjecture of this sort continued to run high for years. As time passed, the actual facts became blurred, and often indistinguishable from fiction, as new outlets

---

* In "The Divine Comedy," Dante Alighieri defined pride as "love of self, perverted to hatred and contempt for one's neighbors." In many ancient writings, it was considered the deadliest of all sins, and it served as the foundation for Jane Austen's most well-known novel, Pride and Prejudice. Preachers often quoted Proverbs 6:16-19 in identifying the behaviors most hateful to God. Especially succinct was verse 17, which warned against "a proud look, a lying tongue, and hands that shed innocent blood." Not surprisingly, the clergy often identified Scott Jackson as the prime example of such unconscionable thoughts, words and deeds.

for this ongoing fascination were born and nurtured in oral tradition, folklore, myths, songs and ballads.

Over the next several decades, countless versions of the Pearl Bryan tragedy flowed from the lips of guitar-strumming folk singers, setting the story to music. The underlying theme of these ballads was precautionary: they dealt with the need to protect the safety and well being of innocent young women, who could so easily be deceived by unscrupulous, silver-tongued young scoundrels trying to steal their virtue.

Vernon Dalhart was a popular singer and songwriter in the U.S. during the early 1900s, and became an important influence in the country music field. In 1927, he released a recorded version of the Pearl Bryan story in which the melody resembled "The Beverly Hillbillies" theme song, with the following lyrics:

Now ladies, if you listen
A story I'll relate
That happened near Fort Thomas
In old Kentucky State

'Twas late in January
This awful deed was done
By Jackson and by Walling
How cold their blood did run

The driver tells the story
Of how Pearl Bryan did moan
From Cincinnati to the place
Where the cruel deed was done

But little did Pearl's parents think
When she left her happy home
That their own darling daughter
Would ne'er return again

We know her dear old parents
Their fortune they would give
If Pearl could just return home
A happy life to live

221

The driver was the only one
Could tell her awful fate
Of poor Pearl far away from home
In the old Kentucky State

A farmer passing by next day
Her lifeless form he found
A-lying on the cold sod
Where her blood had stained the ground

Pearl Bryan left her parents
On a dark and gloomy day
She went to meet the villain
In a spot not far away

She thought it was the lover's hand
That she could trust each day
Alas! It was a lover's hand
That took her life away

Young ladies now take warning
Young men are so unjust
It may be your best lover
But you know not whom to trust

Pearl died away from home and friends
Out in that lonely spot
Take heed, take heed, believe this girls
*Don't let this be your lot**

The tale of Pearl Bryan's murder has also evolved into a long-standing oral tradition, passed down enthusiastically, albeit sometimes inaccurately, from generation to generation. Today's visitors to the Newport and Greencastle communities even now are likely to find local citizens more than willing to share their ancestors' accounts of the murder story which have been passed down.

* *As sung by Vernon Dalhart under the pseudonym Jep Fuller on Vocalion 5015, recorded October 5, 1926, and released one year later.*

Pearl's parents were determined to avoid the public spotlight in the years following their daughter's death, and they succeeded. Alexander died in June, 1901, on the same day that Pablo Picasso's first artwork exhibition opened in Paris, and approximately four years after Jackson and Walling had been hanged. Jane passed away on July 29, 1913.

Following the executions of their sons, the convicted killers' mothers continued to anguish over their misfortunes and tribulations. Both were awarded sympathy by their friends and neighbors, who recognized the emotional trauma and the devastating personal losses they each had endured. Over time, both women gradually faded from public life and lived their remaining years inconspicuously.

Several of the individuals who played prominent roles in the Pearl Bryan case later achieved some degree of distinction.

David Calvin "Cal" Crim had received his primary education in the streets of Cincinnati as a youngster. He joined the newly organized Cincinnati police department serving under Chief of Police Philip Deitsch in 1886, and rose rapidly through the ranks from patrolman to Sergeant of Detectives to Chief of Detectives. At the time of Pearl's murder, Cal was heading up what he called the "Purity Squad (Vice)" attempting to crack down against prostitution in the Cincinnati area. In 1901, he was shot and critically wounded by a pickpocket and sneak thief John Foley (Foley the Goat) who was so-named for his propensity to head butt individuals who had angered him. Cal lay near death for days and it took almost a year for him to recover fully.

Detective Crim was eventually promoted to Chief of Detectives in Cincinnati, but in 1913 after 28 years in law enforcement, he resigned in order to form his own detective agency, establishing his office at 5th and Walnut streets. The enterprise became very successful, and in time established branches in 25 cities throughout the country. Some of these organizations bearing the detective's name are still in existence. In 1919, Crim's Chicago Bureau helped expose professional baseball's infamous "Black Sox" scandal in which selected Chicago players were bribed to throw games during their World Series with the Cincinnati Reds. Crim's private investigators unearthed a cache of incriminating cancelled checks stashed away in a secret safety deposit box which seemed to prove that "Shoeless" Joe Jackson and seven other players were guilty of this grievous offense. Although finally acquitted of criminal charges, all eight players were ultimately banned from professional baseball. It was a shocking revelation for fans to discover that a racketeering syndicate had infiltrated their beloved national sporting event. In recognition of his outstanding investigative work in the Black Sox scandal, Crim received a gold-plated lifetime pass to any major league ballpark – and he made very good use of it at Crosley Field for many years.

In 1937, the Indianapolis Star interviewed Cal Crim concerning his role in the famous murder case of 40 years earlier. The detective recalled that on the evening of the homicide, Jackson and Walling had left Pearl's leather grip with a saloonkeeper in Cincinnati. Crim was confident that it contained her severed head. The next day the duo reclaimed the valise, only to return with it later, apparently now empty and weighing noticeably less. Crim believed that they had taken the bag and its contents to the Ohio Dental College. "I am firmly convinced to this day that Pearl Bryan's head was cremated in that building's furnace," he contended. As an elderly man, he continued to be driven to work in his Cadillac limousine, greatly enjoying his continuing interactions with people in the streets of Cincinnati. Crim's favorite saying was "You've got to keep up with the Big Parade. If you don't, it will pass you by!" Crim died in Cincinnati on December 19, 1953 at the age of 89.

When asked by the *Kentucky Post* about his upcoming role at the hanging, Sheriff Julius (Jule) "Jake" Leonard Plummer responded, "It will be my painful duty to spring the traps. Mine will be the hand to adjust the ropes and open the traps. One must not shrink from his duty, however unpleasant it may be." Jule was appointed as a director of the Woodlawn Home Company in 1905 and helped to develop building lots on the Ft. Thomas car line near Pearl Bryan's murder site. Ultimately, these homes became the community of Woodlawn, Kentucky. On October 27, 1917, while transporting a prisoner from Newport to the Southern Railway station in Ludlow, Kentucky, Sheriff Plummer's vehicle was struck by a streetcar in Covington at the intersection of Fourth and Madison Streets. He died the following day from injuries sustained in the accident. He was survived by his wife, Carrie, and their eight children.

Colonel Philip H Deitsch served as the Superintendent of Police in Cincinnati between 1886 and 1903. In 1897, Deitsch served as the head of the National Chiefs of Police Union which was greatly involved in the evolution of criminal identification methodologies, supporting the evolution from the obviously flawed Bertillon method to the much more reliable use of fingerprinting. At this time, he was in charge of more than 500 police officers in Cincinnati. Deitsch died in 1903 while serving as police department commander.

Night Chief Iron Neck Sam Corbin, who questioned Scott Jackson at the time of his arrest, died in a peculiar fashion in 1911. While helping firefighters battle a blaze at the Cincinnati Chamber of Commerce building at the corner of 4th and Vine streets on January 11, he tripped over a fire hose and fell, seriously injuring himself. Sam died eleven days later at the age of 62.

During the time of Pearl Bryan's murder and the subsequent trials of Jackson and Walling, John Caldwell was serving as the mayor of Cincinnati (1894-1897). Prior to this, he was Prosecuting Attorney ond then Judge of the Cincinnati Police Court. After his mayoral term, he served as the 25th Lt. Governor of Ohio (1899-1901). In 1902, he was elected as judge of the Court of Common Pleas and served as such until his death in 1927.

Perhaps the most influential citizen of Cincinnati in the late 19th and early 20th century was George B (Boss) Cox. In the early 1870s, Cox purchased a tavern in Cincinnati and gradually became a well-known and powerful figure in his community. Twice running successfully for City Council, he never again sought elected office. Rather, he became head of the Hamilton County Republican Committee, and over time gained power and virtually ran the city's government. He used gifts and money to build support among the working classes, and in return, asked them to vote for the candidates he supported. As he once boasted, "The people do the voting. I simply see that the right candidates are elected." Cox served as a delegate to the Republican National Convention in 1900, 1904, and 1908. He was indicted on corruption charges in 1906, but was never convicted.

It is ironic to see Boss Cox pictured among all the police officers presented in the 1901 Cincinnati Police and Municipal Guide. The publication says this about Cox. "In writing of municipal affairs it seems fitting to make some mention of Mr. George B Cox, the well-known leader, to whom the taxpayers are, in a measure, indebted for the present excellent administration. It is well known that Mr. Cox holds no office, but he has a great deal to say about the selection of candidates. It has always been his aim to insist on capable men for public office, and those scrupulously honest. Of course, his confidence has (sometimes) been betrayed, but this is only natural."

Progressive groups in the Queen City were eventually able to attack Cox's credibility (or lack thereof) and over time to chip away at his substantial power. In May, 1916, the then politically impotent Cox suffered a cerebral vascular accident and died.

Toward the end of his ministerial career in 1948, Baptist pastor John Alford Lee, then 82, was interviewed by an Indianapolis News reporter while attending a revival at the Salem Park Tabernacle campground in the city. Reverend Lee estimated that at this point in his ministerial career, he had preached 62,000 sermons, married 2,140 couples, helped build a dozen churches, and composed nearly 1000 religious hymns. Reminiscing over his life experiences, he recalled that his desire to save souls began at the age of 10, when he began to baptize corncobs in a horse trough, pretending that each one was a lost sinner seeking salvation. Smiling mischievously, Pastor Lee confessed, "In my early teens, I sometimes broke up schoolyard baseball games with my sermons

George B (Boss) Cox virtually ran the Cincinnati city government during the time of Pearl Bryan's murder and the trials and executions of Jackson and Walling. From the Police and Municipal Guide, Cincinnati, 1901. Published by the Ohio Book Store, Cincinnati, Ohio.

which lured would-be fans to the makeshift pulpit instead, where I preached and my sister sang."

When asked about his pastoral role in the Pearl Bryan murder case, he recalled that his participation in the death walk with the two young dental students was both the most difficult and the most touching moment of his life. Saying that he neither upheld nor denounced the action of the court, Pastor Lee declined to make any further comments about the infamous case of 50 years earlier. He suggested that we leave the past in the past, and was content to add, "We must consistently remember that in all men there is some good."

Edwin Post, who initiated his academic career at Asbury in 1879 at the age of twenty-seven, was forty-four at the time of Pearl's murder. He served as Professor of Latin for an unbroken period of fifty-three years at this institution, which was renamed DePauw University, (Post's achievement may never be surpassed unless the age of retirement is extended well beyond sixty-five). Volume II of *DePauw Through the Years, 1962*, states, "His (Dr. Post's) valuable services as Librarian, Vice President, and Dean were merely appendages to his consummate interest in the teaching of Latin and in scholarly research in his chosen field. Without disparaging the work of any other faculty member, it can probably be safely said that he best represented the highest ideals of scholarship in the history of Indiana Asbury or DePauw."

One of the most bizarre and sorrowful twists of the Pearl Bryan calamity involved the rift that had developed between Pearl and Ida Hibbitt, her best friend and high school classmate. The two young ladies had been almost inseparable until the summer of 1895, when Scott Jackson began calling on Pearl, while also showing a personal interest in Ida. Although the latter did not encourage Scott's advances, resentment began to develop between the two young women, and progressively, they saw less and less of each other. At the time of Pearl's murder, Ida was a seemingly healthy young lady, who worked as a stenographer and typist for Silas A. Hayes, the Greencastle attorney who subsequently helped to prosecute Jackson and Walling.

Several days after Pearl was identified as the homicide victim on the hillside near Ft. Thomas, Ida, who was stunned by the tragic news, made a sympathy call on Pearl's family in Greencastle. The murder victim's parents implored her to tell them anything that might shed light on their daughter's death, but Ida offered no new information. The Bryans were disappointed by her lack of candidness.

As Ida continued to grieve heavily during the weeks following the murder, she became increasingly obsessed by all the circumstances surrounding Pearl's death. She soon grew ill with a mysterious ailment. Among the local citizenry, rumors concerning Ida's plight were flying. Some people suggested that Pearl may have asked Ida to accompany her to Cincinnati, and that Ida, who had chosen not to go, now remorsefully believed that her lack of supportive action at the time had led to Pearl's death. Others whispered that Ida might have felt guilt and shame for not more adamantly discouraging Scott's attentions toward her. Perhaps Ida had actually enjoyed and even encouraged Scott's playful advances. A clear, direct rejection of Scott might have preserved her long-term bond with Pearl, and permitted her to assist her distressed friend at all costs. These speculations had one common theme: Ida now believed that she might have saved her best friend's life, had she only acted differently.

Regardless, Ida's health inexorably deteriorated. In early May 1896, she was diagnosed by her physician as having a "brain disease," and was confined to bed. Within days, she drifted into a coma, and in her delirium, was said to have repeatedly called out, "Pearl! Pearl! Dear Pearl!" Ida died on May 10, taking with her any additional information she may have possessed regarding Pearl's murder. Local schools were dismissed for her funeral services and burial, and on May 15, a long procession of horse-drawn carriages, composing the funeral procession wound its way through downtown Greencastle. It then traveled north to the Forest Hills Cemetery where she was buried not far from her Pearl's grave. Ironically, this was the same day that Scott Jackson was found guilty of murder by the Newport, Kentucky jury. Ida's death was marked by heartfelt and lingering sadness in Greencastle. It seemed to many that she was yet another victim of Scott Jackson's treachery.

On Friday, May 22, the following note of thanks appeared on page one of the Greencastle Banner:

> "The family of E.A. Hibbitt (Ida's father) desires to thus publicly express their thanks to their friends, who so kindly assisted them in their bereavement; also to the teachers and scholars in the public schools for their attention; and to Professor Ogg for dismissing school during the funeral services."

Pearl Bryan and Ida Hibbitt, like most of their "proper" female counterparts of the late nineteenth century, were relatively ignorant about such delicate topics as sexual intercourse, birth control and abortion. During this time, state laws had been adopted which made terminations of pregnancy "categorically and absolutely prohibited unless to save the life of the mother." The illegality of abortions drove many unmarried, pregnant women underground to hidden back rooms to receive their operations. There, the surgical procedures often were performed under primitive, unsanitary conditions by incompetent, unscrupulous practitioners. It was little wonder that Pearl was so fiercely opposed to having an abortion.* She had heard tragic tales involving girls, such as she, who had taken that risky path and suffered accordingly. And when Scott's effort to perform her abortion resulted in an unmitigated disaster, what fear and dread must have enveloped her!

One may speculate endlessly that: if Scott had agreed to marry Pearl; or if Pearl had found the courage to inform her parents of her dilemma; or if Alonzo had refused to participate in Scott's appalling plot; or if the culture of the land had been more forgiving; or if other factors had played out in favor of the defense in the courtroom; or if... if... if; then the final outcome might have been vastly different. Four unnecessary deaths (and the loss of a viable fetus) might have been prevented; reputations of surviving family members might have been spared; and the shame passed down to the extended families of the accused murderers might have been mitigated.

The three major protagonists in this story were severely flawed individuals, each with specific imperfections. Scott Jackson wanted instant gratification for every impulse he fancied, and was clearly at the mercy of his vast array of self-centered passions. He was narcissistic and egocentric, and in the end, he was a victim of his own lusts. Tragically, it cost him his life, and even more odiously, the lives of innocent others.

History suggests that while Alonzo Walling passed all his courses at the two dental colleges that he attended, in the subject of life, he failed dismally. During his trial, his countenance was sometimes described as "radiating with feeling," but deeper scrutiny suggests he may have been shining with ignorance rather than with cerebral contemplation. Lonnie's fatal flaw seemed to be an abiding lack of awareness of his own circumstances. He failed to recognize that he was being cold heartedly

---

* *During the nineteenth century, women healers and midwives generally provided the abortions needed in the U.S., without any legal prohibitions until after the Civil War. They also trained others to do so. Thereafter, cultural standards began to shift toward a more conservative view. Thus by the 1880's, abortions were illegal in most states in the Union, including Ohio, Kentucky, and Indiana with the exception of those considered 'necessary to save the life' of the woman. This change in philosophy was fueled by both religious concerns, and the antifeminist backlash to growing women's suffrage movements and other women's right crusades. Moreover, physicians considered midwives, who attended births and performed abortions as part of their regular practice, as a threat to their own economic and social power, and joined the more conservative movement.*

used by Scott – that he was becoming an accomplice to a heinous crime. One cannot help but wonder, "What was he thinking?"

By all accounts, Pearl Bryan was brought up to be a respectable young lady. She was active in her church and had a conventional family life. Pearl had always been an obedient child, but as she entered her late teens, she began to chafe under the restrictions of her Victorian upbringing. While her sisters seemed to embrace their rather predictable and mundane lives as rural wives, mothers, and homemakers, Pearl wanted much more: more adventure; more fun; more education; and more freedom. While at times she pushed hard against the behavioral boundaries society had imposed upon her, she always remained unscathed ... that is, until she met Scott Jackson. He was a womanizer and she knew it, but, like many naïve young women, she thought that she could help him change for the better. She was simply too naïve and emotionally immature to insulate and protect herself against a deceitful, untrustworthy sociopath, such as Jackson

If you visit Greencastle's Forest Lawn cemetery today, you will discover that only the base of Pearl's grave remains standing. Over the years, souvenir hunters have progressively chipped away at her headstone. Although the monument is now completely destroyed, a few symbolic remnants of Pearl's tragic end still remain visible. One can even now find Lincoln-head pennies glued to the remaining slab covering her grave. They have been placed there by well-wishers who do not want Pearl Bryan to be headless when she meets Christ in all His glory on Resurrection Day. This tradition, that began more than 100 years ago, is still carried on today.

The senior author points to the pennies glued on Pearl Bryan's tombstone base in Forest Lawn Cemetery, Greencastle, Indiana.

MAJOR REFERENCES
AND RESOURCES

Microfilm copies of articles published between February, 1896 and March, 1897 from the following newspapers were invaluable sources of information:

Cincinnati Enquirer,
Greencastle Daily Banner Times,
Indianapolis Sun,
Indianapolis Star,
Indianapolis News,
Louisville Courier Journal,
The New York Times, and numerous others.

Books, Pamphlets, and Journal Articles:

Anthony W Kuhnheim: *The Pearl Bryan Murder Story.* Published by Campb ell County Historical and Genealogical Society. (Spec Col C.U. 901.K85pe, 1998).

Anne B Cohen: *Poor Pearl, Poor Girl! The Murdered Girl Stereotype in Ballad and Newspaper.* Campbell County Historical and Genealogical Society. (Spec Col C.U. 901. c55po 1973).

Reis, J. *Pearl Bryan.* The Encyclopedia of Northern Kentucky. Paul Tenkotte & Jaames C Claypool (Editors). The University Press of Kentucky, 2009. pp 126-127. Lexington, Kentucky.

Pearl Bryan, or a Fatal Ending. A Complete History of the Lives and Trials of Scott Jackson and Alonzo Walling, Both Being Sentenced to Death. Campbell County Historical and Genealogical Society. (Spec Col RB HV 6783, p 33, 1896).

Police and Municipal Guide, Cincinnati 1901. Published by the Ohio Book Store, 726 Main Street, Cincinnati, Ohio, 1995.

Erik Larson, *The Devil in the White City.* Crown Publishers, New York, 2004.

The Mysterious Murder of Pearl Bryan, or, The Headless Horror: a Full Account of the Mysterious Murder Known as the Fort Thomas Tragedy, from Beginning to End; Full Particulars of All Detective and Police Investigations; Dialogues of the Interviews between Mayor Caldwell, Chief Deitsch and the Prisoners. 364.1523 M998, 1896. The Public Library of Cincinnati and Hamilton County.

The following were extremely supportive in supplying vintage postcards, photographs and/or historical information:

The Public Library of Cincinnati and Hamilton County.

The Kentucky Historical Society, Frankfort, Kentucky.

The Indiana State Library and Historical Bureau, Indianapolis, Indiana

The La Porte County Historical Society, La Porte, Indiana.

The Putnam County Public Library, Greencastle, Indiana.

The Campbell County Historical & Genealogical Society, Alexandria, Kentucky.

The Cincinnati Police Department, Cincinnati, Ohio.

The Court House, Newport, Kentucky.

Julie Schlesselman, Franklin County Public Library, Geneological and Local History Division, Brookville, IN.